EUROPEAN INDUSTRIAL LEADERSHIP

Michael B. Abbott

European Institute for Industrial Leadership, Brussels

Being a précis of the philosophical and theoretical core
of the Master of Industrial Leadership Programme of
the European Institute for Industrial Leadership
(www.eiil.net)

ISBN No. 0-9548989-0-7

Published by Knowledge Engineering BVBA

Copyright © 2004 Michael B Abbott

No part of this work may be reproduced or stored in an information retrieval system (other than for purposes of review), without the express permission of the publisher in writing.

All rights reserved

Printed and bound in Great Britain by Antony Rowe Ltd, Eastbourne

MOTTO

**Ne pouvant faire que ce qui est juste soit fort,
faisons en sorte que ce qui est fort soit juste.**

Pascal

(Being unable to make the righteous strong
let us instead make the strong righteous)

Acknowledgement

Among so many who have been of such help and comfort to me in my own varied career, I should like to thank one person before all others, namely Torben Sørensen, founder and former director of the Danish Hydraulic Institute. For myself, he was for the thirty years that I worked together with DHI as a consultant, the model of a direct leader of industry, building that Institute from a handful of collaborators into the largest of its kind in Europe: it continued to grow after his retirement in 1996 and as of 2002 it employed 92 persons with Ph.D. degrees and 255 with MSc degrees. It provided the feasibility studies and the basic design parameters for a major part of the very large (one to ten billion euro in current values) as well as many smaller projects in the water sector from 1970 onwards. Among so many qualities, I admired his integrity, his solicitude towards those he led - even as he demanded so much from them! – and the good friendly relations that he generated through the whole organisation. But most of all I admired his great personal courage in doing what he saw to be right. It was often 'a damn close-fought thing', but he finally won every time through his shear tenacity and certainty of purpose.
Mange tak, Torben!

CONTENTS

Introduction		7
Chapter 1	The Role of Technology in European History	17
Chapter 2	On Leadership	39
Chapter 3	On Sociotechnology	61
Chapter 4	The European Leader in Industry	91
Notes		121
Book References		147
Appendix 1	The Gender Issue	153
Appendix 2	On Definitions	173

INTRODUCTION

Every work of the present kind has its own time and its own place, reflecting the situation within which it has come to be thought and to be written. Every such work then has its own *occasion*, and the purpose of its introduction is to give expression to this place and this time so as to provide a *sense of occasion*.

The work was completed as a first draft on schedule, at 22.00 on the 30th April 2004, just two hours before the accession to the European Union of its ten new member states. Its completion was thus accompanied by great displays of fireworks over the capitals of the twenty five states of the Union and a monopoly of television time celebrating the event with concerts and other festivities. Auspicious beginnings indeed!

The work that follows was prepared as a précis of the curriculum of the philosophical and theoretical core of the European Institute for Industrial Leadership, an initiative of one man that became an initiative of seven. I accordingly called this group The Seven Samurai, after Kurasawa's great cinematic epic, in which one Samurai is persuaded by a band of simple peasants to take up the cause of protecting their village against marauding bandits, and proceeds to recruit some other Samurai to join him in what would normally have been, for Samurai, the most demeaning of undertakings. Our leader had a long career, starting as an officer in the UK Royal Navy, and going on to the highest positions in European and US industries. All the rest of us except one held leading positions in our own fields, and the one who had not this advantage had those of youth and enthusiasm to more than make up for this lacuna – just as in Kurasawa's masterpiece again.

I recalled to our leader the story – a true one as it happens – that when in 1941 the Japanese Navy air arm sunk the battleship Prince of Wales and the battle cruiser Repulse, two of the most powerful ships in the British navy, off the coast of Malaysia, they allowed the escorting British destroyers to pick up the more than two thousand survivors unmolested. They could easily have sunk the destroyers, and certainly no other navy in the world would have hesitated a moment before doing that, but the Japanese desisted, for they had done what was expected of them - and they behaved honourably, as true descendents of Samurai.[1] Our leader replied: "It takes hundreds of years of tradition to do that!"

What had joined us together was a consciousness of our own tradition, as Europeans, and with this our obligations towards the peoples of Europe. This is then something naïve and primitive, as something in the tradition of the Italian primitives such as Giotto and Pierro della Francesca, or the Flemish primitives like Memling and Jan van Eyck. It is the establishing of a relation with what is most simple and most direct and most essential, no matter with what skill it may be rendered in its material expression. It is something that seeks to express itself with an almost childish simplicity, and it can be no accident when our youngest member loves more than anything else to read H. C. Anderson's tale of 'The Emperors new Clothes' to his children, and how the children and he all laugh heartily together when a little boy is so naïve as to tell the Emperor that he is not in fact wearing any clothes at all!

This naivety and primitivity seems now to have penetrated all our lives, conditioning our every life experience. Visiting one of the great centres of business, such as The City in London, we enter one of the soaring cathedrals of finance, our gaze rising towards the heavens of the executive suites, following the batteries of lifts that propel their occupants upwards to make contact with the higher beings - and then just as surely bring them back down again to their own levels. We experience the subtle connections and demarcations of space that indicate and mark out the route of our own progress through this New Jerusalem, and we absorb the excellence of the fine stones and the perfection of workmanship that exude the qualities of those who occupy this place and whose services are being proffered to all who aspire to a similar status. Against this magnificent backdrop we see the movements of smart-looking people scurrying around with personal digital assistants in their hands and serious expressions on their faces, providing the atmosphere of a bustling hive of activity that will transform the baseness of the world outside into the purest of gold - in our own pockets. And through all these impressions we sense the central message that we are intended to receive, which we recall in the words of that most incorrigible of primitives, Immanuel Kant: "*Ich verstehe unter einer Architektonik die Kunst der Systeme //* By an architecture I understand the art of constructing systems". We are then so primitive as to think that all this show is intended primarily to project the image of *a system*, as something systematic and so governed by rational interrelations and interactions, as something governed by laws as rational and inevitable as those that govern the motions of the sun, the moon and the planets.[2]

But then, feeling like peasants from the fields, we ask among ourselves what vegetables these people are growing in this place, or what kinds of flocks and herds they are raising. Or, feeling like craftsmen from their workshops, we ask among ourselves what houses they are building or what furniture they are making. And when we have the temerity to express these thoughts and we are told, with a look of total disbelief at such ignorance and naivety, that the people in this great centre of commerce are engaged in *much higher things*, and that they are *optimising investment flows* and are generally *creating value*, we are obliged to blink just as quizzically back again, not so much feigning, but actually experiencing a total incomprehension.

If then again, and now with a look of total despair, it is explained to us that this great construction and all the others around it in The City are engaged in *making money* - and then by legal means and not by counterfeiting! - and even a banknote is produced to show such oafs what money *is* - we observe that what is shown us is only a piece of coloured paper bearing a thread and embossed patch of metal, such as would be all but valueless in most parts of the world without the immediate presence of a money-changer.

Clearly there is nothing for the sophisticates of the modern world of business to do with such contrarians: since they are not dangerous they can be left to roam the streets and even to set up an Institute - although preferably on the other side of the Channel - if they so wish. We, who are indeed such contrarians in these matters, have this naïve and primitive idea that people should produce objects that are useful, objects that are beautiful and objects that are, to say it all, truthful, and should provide services correspondingly. We have the apparently totally obsolete idea that the world of finance should serve the world of tangible production and of tangible service, the world of industry, and not the opposite. We are thus the subjects of every kind of hilarity and ribaldry on the part of those who consider themselves so much more sophisticated and advanced. For these, "everything is in the intangibles", and the tangible is merely the residue of "real-business success". Thus, for these acolytes of Mammon, it is unnecessary to concern oneself, or to "waste one's time", with the realities of the production of tangible things or the provision of tangible services – all that can be left to "the techies" – and it is only the manipulation of numbers and of people, it scarcely matters which, that counts. Since it makes everything so much more simple, this attitude has raised itself up into an ideology and has correspondingly become immensely popular.

For the purposes of establishing and maintaining this ideology a new kind of institution has been created and has had just as great a success. This is the so-called 'business school', a name that is often associated with the word 'management'. Now even the most contrarian amongst us believes that many forms of business are beneficial to society and everyone would agree that good management is a good thing. What we observe all the time however is that most of the graduates of these business schools know in fact very little about business and even less about good management. They have been taught a few superficial answers to largely irrelevant problems that have been posed in ways that really do not allow for any proper analysis at all. For example, the problem is posed that "You are leaving for a week on a business trip, leaving your team behind. Should you 1) do nothing, 2) tell them to prepare…." and so on. But in all our naivety we would ask: "business trip to where and for what purpose, with what relation to what kind of team, etc. etc?" But such realities of real-world business operations are of no interest to most of these business schools because everything would then get too complicated and even difficult, and that would be bad for the business….of the business schools! So everything has to be kept very, very simple. At the same time, of course, it becomes correspondingly exceedingly easy to provide the equally superficial answers and so to score high marks in case studies and examinations, so that a wonderful sense of achievement, a veritable euphoria, can be created among the student body. Thus young people come away from such studies feeling that they can better the world tomorrow, even though in fact they can only sustain even this self-confidence so long as they never have to confront this world on its own terms. And even when this does happen as it almost inevitably must, few like to admit even to themselves that their education of this kind has largely been a waste of time and money, so that the image of success can be maintained and developed further. The success is true because most people say that it is so, and most even believe what they say, at least for a time. Henry Mintzberg has recently written an excellent survey of this phenomenon (Mintzberg, 2004).

This process, which is by no means confined to business schools but is more pronounced there than almost anywhere else, is commonly called one of 'dumbing down'. It makes excellent business sense for the business schools themselves, who have profited immensely from it. By their own measures, therefore, it is an unqualified success. For contrarians like ourselves, on the other hand, it is totally unacceptable: it lacks all propriety; it lacks all naivety and primitivity. Our task is always to raise up and never to dumb down. We hold with the one and only Søren Kierkegaard when he wrote:

> Is this the kind of self-deception that the present generation needs? Should it be trained in a virtuosity along that line, or is it not, instead, adequately perfected in the art of deceiving itself? Or, rather, does it not need an honest earnestness that points fearlessly and incorruptibly towards the tasks, an honest earnestness that lovingly maintains the tasks, that does not disquiet people into wanting to attain the highest too hastily but keeps the tasks young and beautiful and lovely to look at, inviting to all and yet difficult and inspiring to the noble-minded; in the understanding that the noble nature only enthuses over that which is difficult?

But quoting Kierkegaard necessarily brings us back again to something 'continental European', as something different to what passes muster in many other parts of the world, and in particular, it would seem, in the USA in the first place and in the UK in the second place. Not being confined only within many business schools, dumbing-down generally is seen by many of us in continental Europe as an 'Anglo-Saxon' phenomenon that has infected and threatens to corrupt Europe's own institutions, and indeed having the potential to endanger the very foundations of European societies. To speak of 'Americanisation' in these societies is to speak at least in a tone of disapprobation, more commonly in denigration and sometimes in downright derogatory terms. There is then an association with junk food, junk beverages and associated problems of obesity on a massive scale; with the most hideous cacophonies that are supposed to be 'music' but which in fact merge with what we commonly call by the name of 'muzak'; with the extreme differences in wealth and social possibilities normally associated with a 'third-world' society; with correspondingly low levels of social services, including education, medical care and pension provisions for large parts of the population; with high levels of insecurity of employment; with extremely high levels of criminality and enormous prison populations; with historically unprecedented levels of endebtment of people and of institutions; of military expenditures that far surpass those of any other country; with the 'rogue–state' image of a nation that currently appears to be hell-bent on world hegemony; and so we can continue with at least twenty more items. Europeans generally fear that many of these same negative influences are spreading in their own societies and this greatly concerns them. Some of these negative influences are taken up within the body of this book, but then only to the extent that they may concern the European leader of industry. It cannot be our business here to analyse, let alone criticise the USA. We are all aware that there is much to admire also in the USA and that the problems that we discern are those that the people of that nation must correct for themselves. There is indeed talk here now of 'Europeanising' the USA, but we Europeans really have no interest in such ventures and in fact we have no interest whatsoever in 'Europeanising' anyone. The only concern of our little group of Samurai is to build an Institute in the European tradition, which is then however markedly different from that of a conventional business school in the US and its offshoots in the UK and elsewhere.

This difference resides in the first and most obvious place in our rejection of what has become an *ideology of management*, as something that corrupts more than it promotes true management. We observe that as a result of the virulent spreading of this ideology, our present-day societies are choking under a surfeit of essentially parasitic persons who are really only masquerading as managers. To use an old English expression, one would say that most of these persons "could not even run a cockle stall". We all recognise them as they circulate long, meandering and entirely pointless 'memoranda', call endless 'meetings' to discuss every kind of nonsense, are constantly engaged in purposeless 'reorganisations' and destructive 'restructurings', not to speak of their interminable 'reschedulings', while more recently spreading their wings geographically to encompass the 'outsourcing' and 'offshoring' of the work of those whom they are supposed to be managing. We recognise them also by their being the only ones in the organisation who try to take at all seriously the pretence that they are doing anything other than wasting everyone else's time and energy - for they must always make themselves 'felt' in the organisation and so they constantly interfere in the work of others, and in particular in the work of those who are truly productive. In the case of the UK we recognise them also as they race out after their so-called 'work' to the nearest wine bar to drink away the dim but still persistent awareness of their own incompetence, ineptitude and general parasitism.[3]

One might think that the answer to this problem, which will surely be familiar to almost everyone, is simply to introduce 'better management', and indeed many business schools are claiming, more or less discreetly, to be doing just that, and we like to believe that some really are doing it. Our own position however is that in most cases these managers are entirely redundant, and that the persons who are actually involved in the directly productive work of the organisation can much better manage their own affairs in their own time, and that this arrangement now becomes ever more effective due to advances in communication technologies and the understanding of the right employment of these technologies. We argue that the introduction of self-managing environments, in which power structures came into proper coincidence with knowledge structures as *endostructures*, whereby these structures emerge from the work processes and market conditions directly, rather than, as in far too many cases, from the whims and impositions of pretending 'managers', can provide far higher efficiencies and flexibilities than can most existing, *exostructured* arrangements. A few but really talented and well educated managers will always be necessary, but the incompetent and inauthentic managers in the numbers that we see today are totally unnecessary for the purposes of true, or *authentic* management. This is not to say that this mass of incompetent and inauthentic managers does not serve a social, or rather antisocial purpose, namely that of allowing persons appointed as leaders who in fact have no leadership qualities to stay in control of organisations. The purpose of incompetent and inauthentic management is to enable persons who have gained leadership positions without themselves being leaders, essentially by 'politicking', to maintain distance control over an organisation through a self-serving power structure, as will be described later in this book. At the present time, reductions in the numbers of persons employed as 'managers' of some eighty percent seem to be in order and indeed have been the norm in those situations where properly communication-technologically-supported and well-organised self-management teams have been introduced and maintained by a sound leadership.[4]

Correspondingly, developments of this positive kind, and of the many other kinds that we introduce in our teachings, all necessitate something that is essentially different even to good management, which is *sound leadership*. Management is concerned with order, while leadership is concerned with direction. Developments in information and communication technologies and the proper means to apply these technologies in society have now come so far that the persons working directly in industry can for a large part best order their working processes between themselves, so that far less 'hands-on' or, even worse, 'proactive' management is required, and indeed this kind of management for the sake of managing something becomes increasingly counterproductive.

At the same time on the other hand, the problems of directing industrial activities thereby become so much more difficult and exigent. Just as the task of management then changes from the preponderant one of 'making it all happen' to one that is more concerned with 'understanding what is actually going on', so the task of leadership transforms from one of *directing events simply by the giving of instructions* to one of *arranging matters primarily by persuasion* so that the organisation proceeds along one path rather than others. Of course, the leader still gives instructions, but the processes that intervene as a result of these instructions are not predictable in the way that they might have been previously, being now so much less foreseeable, and the leader has to take a proper account of this situation. Moreover, this leader is now working increasingly in a *knowledge society*, which is then increasingly a world of *multi-knowledge environments*, where two or more different and even disparate knowledges are in play within one and the same workplace, so that *conjunctive knowledges* have to be introduced in order to maintain the very integrity of this workplace. These problems are compounded within the European Union by the fact – which is a very hard and persistent fact – that these multi-knowledge environments are also and increasingly *multi-language environments*, and as such they raise cultural issues of a depth and of a kind that were not within the range of experience of most leaders of an earlier generation.[5] It was all very well for a bunch of Government Ministers meeting in Lisbon in 2003 to proclaim that *Europe should become a knowledge society*, but the realisation of this requires concrete steps, of which the present is only one, albeit, we believe, an important one.

But above and beyond all this again, today's leader of industry already and tomorrow's leader irrevocably, has to lead in a world where there are fewer and fewer purely technical challenges and fewer and fewer purely social challenges, but where his or her world is full of *sociotechnical* challenges. The ideal world of most business schools where one can make business decisions on the basis of a few human relations alone, and even on the basis of balance sheets alone, within the simplistic environment of a static and non-interactive technical environment, is disappearing for ever. *Sociotechnology* nowadays becomes the first among the conjunctive knowledges that the future leader of industry must acquire. Within this perspective, the notion that has been so widely diffused through so many business schools, that the nature of the business is not of significance to the processes of running the business, becomes an ever more dangerous snare and delusion. The leader of a business today has to know that business in and out, and he has not only to know it, but also to understand it so far as it is understandable at all. He has to understand before all else the relations between the people and the equipment in their closest interaction, and then not only within the environment of the organisation within its own walls, but also, and in fact inseparably, within the environment that extends outside those walls. This is the *conditio sine qua non* for the very *sustainability* of the organisation, for without this knowledge the leader cannot plan and prepare the organisation for its future, even as at the same time he or she is plotting and steering its course through the shifting shoals and currents of its environing market and more general social conditions.

This is however a book describing the central core of a course on a specifically *European* leadership. So what is so special about this 'European' in its name? What it is that is so special can be introduced here through the observation that Europe is a place where most persons of culture always seem to be in some kind of mourning. They are forever, it seems, trying to come to terms with something and this something is intimately associated with their past, and indeed it often appears that they are working to overcome their grief over a great loss. They are thus always *à la recherche du temps perdu // in search of a lost time*, but then it must be added that this is only a lost, because past, time in its most refined and quintessential, Proustian, expression. Despite the vandalism that passed and continues to pass itself off as 'modernity' in architecture, many Europeans still respect, admire and maintain many fine and deeply satisfying buildings of earlier times; among all the mass-produced kitsch, they still go to great lengths to select quality in their furnishings, their apparel, their motor cars and other accessories to a commodious existence; through all the cacophony of commercialised 'muzak', they still attend concerts to experience the treasured heritance of Purcell, Monteverdi, Mozart, Brückner and Boulez. Although acutely aware that they no long live in what might properly be called a civilisation, they strive to continue to survive as Europeans among the fragments of previous European civilisations. A civilisation is in its essence a community of mind and of mindfulness, and it is this that has been so broken and fragmented in our current, so-called 'modern' European condition, almost as though it has been and continues to be torn asunder by some alien force. Thus, to the extent that we Europeans look forward to anything at all, we are always looking backwards wistfully towards lost worlds: we are no longer so much as trying to be happy with things as they are as we are trying to be less unhappy with our present condition, and often it is only our filtered memory of the past that makes this present condition bearable at all. There is in this an all-pervading *sense of failure*, which stems from a failure to prevent the loss of a civilisation when this loss could perhaps have been prevented - and possibly could still be reversed and turned around even today. As will be explained towards the end of this work, failure (and the coming to terms with failure, as the prerequisite of an overcoming of failure) is a very important concept in one of the currents of philosophy that we shall be following here, and even when it mingles as it often does in this case with a touch of nostalgia, but we can better leave these matters for later.

But to what do we owe this general condition? It is because, following the motto of Pascal, the earlier European cultures fashioned what was so strong and so long-lasting into something righteous, and thus true, and we Europeans now, in our own time, continue to experience this that is so strong and long-lasting, as bequeathed from the past, as *quintessentially true*. This past carries, so to say, its own truth values with it, and it is upon these that we now so much depend. Thus we Europeans continue to conserve all that carries this truth, regarding this conservation as among our highest responsibilities. To the extent that Europe remains the site of any civilisation at all, it is one that lives for and by its past civilisations. To some extent of course that is true for all civilisations, but in Europe it is the predominant trait and it is recognised, even though mostly only unconsciously, as such.

It is in this deeper sense, as it was established by Sigmund Freud in a now famous article of 1917 entitled precisely *Mourning and Melancholy*, that we Europeans may be characterised as *melancholic*, so that this is not melancholic in the vulgar sense of being merely depressed in spirit, becoming gloomy and dejected, but in the sense of something that, even as it does indeed plunge us into the nether depths of despair and anguish, has also such a voluptuousness, such a poignancy, in the insights into truths that it provides and the creativity that it induces in us that we would never dream of renouncing it. Aristotle already posed the question in his own time: "Why is it that all the men who shine in philosophy, in politics, in poetry and the other arts are melancholic?" Already then, melancholy was recognised as an *æsthetic-creative condition*, as something that reawakens and reifies truths inherited from the past and so inherited in a state of mourning, and this condition has been perennially identified as such from the era of Aristotle and Petrarch to that of Freud and Lacan, so that we have learnt not only to exist with it, but to live with it and for it, recognising in it the very mainspring of European creativity. This condition has recently been beautifully delineated in a book by Marie-Claude Lambotte (1999).[6]

Despite this common trait, Europe is nonetheless composed of many cultures and it is accepted that their differences are essential - in the manner of a rainbow, which is at its best when its colours are most distinct – but these no longer form a civilisation, such as might have been said to have come to an end in July, 1789, or again in August, 1914, or perhaps for the last time in September 1939. In a recent article in *Le Monde*, the contemporary French philosopher Paul Ricœur spoke of the divisiveness inherent in this cultural situation in terms of a mourning for what was fundamental and absolute in the historical foundation of our societies, whereby allowing others to speak in their own tradition is also to mourn the passing of the absolute character of our own tradition. In Ricœur's view it was then principally among the founding events of a tradition that this mourning found its own proper place. There was in Europe no country that had not had to suffer a loss of territory, of population, of influence, of respectability and of credibility at some time or the other, but the very cruelty of the European twentieth century necessitated that this be accepted: the capacity to mourn had thus to be learnt and learnt again, unceasingly. We Europeans had to accept that in our cultural exchanges there would always remain something undecipherable about our life experiences, something irreconcilable in our differences, and something irreparable in the harm that we have suffered and that we have in turn inflicted.

There is the inevitable exception to this behaviour, and it is an important one: we have what is called 'a younger generation' that in fact does not much mourn this 'passing of the past', and then not so much because it does not wish to but because it is for a large part unable to do so. The psychological consequences of such an *Unfähigkeit zu Trauern //Incapacity to Mourn*, to use the title of a notable book on this subject of A. and M. Mitscherlich, have long been known: this denial of the rights of the past translates into a denial of the rights of the present, to a distortion of the very sense of reality of the person in denial in order only to suit his or her own whims and wishes, such as is exemplified today by the obsessive playing of 'action games' and various means of group-distraction, such as the 'binge drinking', vandalism and hooliganism, such as have become so associated with young people in the UK in particular.[7]

We who have founded the European Institute for Industrial Leadership (EIIL) live actively with this sense of mourning for the past that, although it is often mistakenly called 'history', in fact greatly transcends through the very immediacy of its subject matter all the possibilities of any and every historical method of recalling and experiencing the past, so that it is, so to say, 'the living past'. And as we of the EIIL also live with and by this past, so we are just as intensely aware of our responsibilities towards it and so towards the truth that it proclaims. We are aware that not only do our continuing existences depend upon this past, but that only by drawing upon this past, by way of a tradition, can we and this past survive together into our common future. Thus, just as we also and unavoidably live 'the European condition', so we are bound in obligation to draw upon its underlying tradition in order to assure the continuation of this 'essential Europe'. This tradition, as it becomes expressed in a community of discourse, then provides the basis for a pan-European culture.

Now it must be clear that to the extent that Europe as a whole possesses a tradition at all, this must be a *tradition of translation*. By this we do not simply refer to translations between the some thirty more or less distinct languages used in Europe, but point much more to translations between the thought worlds that are contained within these languages, all of which trace their roots back into the most distant mists of time, so that this is itself a task of translating between very different cultures, each with its own cultural heritage. As Paul Ricœur himself observed in his article, despite its insufficiencies, translation manages to create a resemblance there where there initially appears to be only plurality. The translation thus creates something comparable between the incomparables. It is in this resemblance created by the work of translation that the 'universal project' becomes reconciled with 'the multitude of heritages'". And it is by our working out of this project that we attempt to overcome the loss of our European civilisation.

The EIIL is our own contribution to assuring this continuation, and even possibly the restoration of what we might still call 'European values'. We have been long enough in business and around enough in the world to understand that no company, no state and no continent ever failed by forces emanating from without, but only and always by forces dividing it from within, whereby it provided its own undoing. Europe has to fear nothing so long as it remains true to its traditions, understood in the sense of the truth that these traditions bear. Thus we are intensely aware that we must draw upon all that remains great and good in Europe itself if we are to sustain this Europe that has now grown to encompass 25 nations in its Union but with some more nations again that, although currently outside the Union, are always close to it in spirit through the cultural heritage that they share with us. The present book, then, is about how we draw upon this cultural heritage in order to assure the future of a Europe to which we so much belong and with which we so closely identify.

It is then necessary to say something here about the book itself. The first two chapters follow the title: first Europe and its industry, and then their leadership. The third chapter introduces and illustrates a few basic but essential notions of sociotechnology and the fourth brings the matters of these first three chapters together around the person of the individual future leader of European industry. The notes at the conclusion of these chapters serve to connect the matters treated there to the wider issues through relating the body of the text to its bibliography. The book is concluded with two appendices that illustrate applications of much of the material provided in the main body of the work. These appendices take the form of two papers originally published in the Journal of Hydroinformatics and are reproduced with the permission of the publishers, the International Water Association Press. Both papers have been modified slightly in order to connect better to the main body of the work, but some overlap and repetition has been unavoidable here. The book as a whole is a mere précis of the core course itself, so that very much even of this core has been omitted. In particular, only one case study is developed at any length in the whole work, out of some twenty proposed in the taught course.[8] Moreover, this work concerns only the core around which several other courses are supported, and especially those on sustainability, cultural diversity, business strategy and interpersonal skills. The book is then only a sketch of certain central elements in a much wider-ranging course of study.

As will appear from the bibliography, the present work draws much more heavily upon French and German sources than it does upon any others. It is supposed that those following the courses of the EIIL will be fluent in one language and will have a good working knowledge of one or more others. English translations are indicated to most of the works that are referenced, but the limitations of translation often make some recourse to the originals desirable, and even in a few cases necessary. In all cases other than those otherwise indicated, the translations are my own and I must take full responsibility for their undoubted inadequacies.

It should further be explained that the EIIL course is quite highly customised to the interests, intentions and capabilities of its individual participants, so that what will be highly relevant reading for one may not be so pertinent for another. Certainly, no one can be expected to cover anything like all the works cited in reference, and indeed only a few of these works need be consulted by any particular participant in the course.

This book has been prepared as part of the preparations for the courses of the EIIL in general and as a statement of the underlying doctrine of the EIIL in particular. It is not necessarily a doctrine to which we at the EIIL would all subscribe in all its parts and I personally take full and undivided responsibility for what is said in it. I am myself neither a philosopher nor a theologian, but only an engineer who reads philosophical and theological books and who tries to apply their lessons. I have none the less endeavoured on this basis to encompass the doctrine that holds us together in our mission, the source of which is expressed within the body of the work as "a fascination with technology is a fascination with truth", but then in such a way that this fascination should never degenerate into a one-sided 'idolatry of truth', such as would threaten the most basic spiritual values of benevolence, benignity and compassion, those timeless values which are the only certainties in our lives. In the words of Kierkegaard (1844/1855/1960, p.186 // 1980, p.139): "He who has observed the present generation can hardly deny the discrepancy in it, and the reason for its anxiety and unrest is this, that in one direction truth increases in scope and in quantity, and partly also in abstract clarity, while in the opposite direction certainty constantly declines". Or, to quote again from Pascal (1670/1967, p. 681):

> I do not in the least admire an excess of virtue as a value if I do not at the same time see an excess of an opposite virtue - like [the Greek statesman and military leader] Epaminondas, who had extreme worth and extreme benignity - because otherwise this is no more a raising up but a falling down. One does not show one's worth by being at one extremity, but well by touching both extremities simultaneously, and filling everything between them.
> But perhaps this is only a sudden movement of the soul from the one to the other extreme and it is never an effect at one point - like the flame in the fire. Whatever; but at least this demonstrates the agility of the soul even if it does not demonstrate its range."

As one who understood as well as anyone this doctrine adopted by the EIIL, of this peculiarly European fascination with truth when properly counterbalanced by spiritual awareness, Pascal expressed the expectations of our enterprise in his aphorism that: "The miracles arise from the doctrine, not the doctrine from the miracles". This book then contains a statement of the doctrine, and the EIIL itself is then the first of its miracles. [9]

Chapter 1

THE ROLE OF TECHNOLOGY IN EUROPEAN HISTORY

1.1 Technology as the foundation of all industry

We speak about industry, conventionally, as systematic work or labour, and then in the first place as intelligent and skilful employment necessitating diligence and assiduity in the performance of its tasks. For the purposes of performing this kind of work satisfactorily, those who engage in it are said to *draw upon technology*. The processes through which they do this however are by no means simple and straightforward, and indeed the whole notion of technology itself needs to be carefully examined and thoroughly understood if we are to proceed anywhere in comprehending the essential nature of industrial activity as it 'draws upon technology'. Such a comprehension is of course fundamental for every leader of industry.

As is usually the case in such matters, the first obstacle that has to be overcome in arriving at any deeper understanding is the belief that *we already understand enough*, that is, enough for us to perform the work that we have in hand, so that no further investigation is required. Thus, in the present case, it may at first appear that everyone knows what technology is, such as 'technology is the sum of the means directed to an end through human activity'. It is then understood that technology is not the human activity itself, but the means directed to an end that are drawn upon during the human activity. For example, glass-blowing for the manufacture of vases and other household articles is a craft that draws upon certain elements of glass technology for informing the processes that it employs; just as cabinet-making is another craft that draws upon other and generally very different elements of technology for informing the operations of its craftsmen. For the craftsman such as the glass-blower, such a definition is entirely adequate, for he does not need to *explicate what it is* that is being drawn upon by his mind in conjunction with his face and throat muscles, his breath, his hands and arms and indeed his whole mind and body as he goes about his productive activities. He simply 'knows it intuitively' as he 'does the job'. Accordingly, since technology is not itself the actions of the mind and body of the craftsman that makes the production possible, but the means for guiding all the activities of the mind and body in this productive process, technology is that which prepares and informs the craftsman for and during his work: technology is then not the act itself, *but that which makes the act possible*.

On the one hand, technology then appears as a kind of knowledge, but on the other hand, to the extent that it prepares and guides the coordinated mental and bodily processes of the craftsman so as to produce a craft, it is something that also transcends knowledge in the ordinary sense. Thus, to the extent that it is admitted as a kind of knowledge at all, it is an *extra*ordinary knowledge. It is certainly not intellectual in most cases and it is only existential to the extent that it is inseparable from the existence of the person or persons possessing just this specific knowledge.

The above simple way of defining technology, still widely current, implies that those who engage in any such particular activity can do so by drawing upon some elements of technology in ways chosen by themselves and directed to an end of their own choosing. Accordingly, in this view, technology can serve as a mere instrument, in that those who are using it can *select it, master it and use it within well-established limits*, implying in this view that *it is entirely in the hands and under the control of those who are using it*. In this view, then, technology is entirely subject to their will and their control. This view remains so prevalent and is so widely accepted that it is taken for granted as something eminently realistic and always attainable. It is then for just this reason that when we observe that a particular application of technology threatens to slip out of our control so as no longer to be subject to our will, as is currently exemplified by the case of so-called 'weapons of mass destruction', *our will to be the master over the technology becomes ever more pronounced and urgent, and ever more compulsive*. Thus, to the extent that we can use this characterisation of technology as a definition at all, we must circumscribe its realm of application, and we accordingly refer to such a definition as *an instrumental and anthropological definition of technology*.

In his great seminal work, *The Question Concerning Technology*, which first introduced these and several consequent notions, the great German philosopher Martin Heidegger pointed out that, although such a mode of definition might be adequate for the popular and everyday view of technology, it was not at all adequate for those who have to work and live with technology, who have to understand *technology in its essence,* and so are obliged to define *technology as such*. He thereby posed the question of what technology was *in its essence*. Thus: what is technology, essentially?

For the purposes of his investigation, he began by employing the classical philosophical distinction between *what is correct* and *what is true*. To start with an example, in everyday speech we may well say "I think that is correct", or even just "That is correct", even when we understand that there is the possibility that we might be wrong about it, so that it is not necessarily true. Accordingly philosophy makes a quite sharp distinction between what is correct and what is true. This becomes most evident nowadays when we say ironically that some statement is 'politically correct', where we imply that this is a statement that is just as likely as not to be untrue!

Heidegger accepted that the instrumental and anthropological definition could be regarded as *correct* within certain circumscribed contexts, but he then further demonstrated that *it must be untrue for technology as such*. He showed that technology, in its essence, was certainly no mere means, but had, so to say, 'a way of being of its own', albeit one in which human activity was intimately connected. It is vitally necessary that we understand this, and we shall follow Heidegger's demonstration accordingly, introducing some of his vocabulary that we shall have frequent occasion to use later in this work.

In order to arrive at this deeper understanding of this-that-makes-all-industry-possible that we call technology, we can then best follow *how technology functions*, with a special concern with how it enters into industry. We can then say at once that every industrial activity *changes* as technology enters into it, so that technology is in some way *at the source*, or even is *the cause*, of what changes in industry. Technology is thus in some way *responsible* for what comes to presence in industry. The introduction of technology into industry *starts something moving towards a new way of functioning*, so that something new *comes into being*, is *occasioned*, or *comes to presence*, in industry, and it is in this way that technology is responsible for something in industry to *move forward, to bring something forth.* Observing this, Heidegger was led to refer back to a particularly relevant observation of Plato, from the *Symposium*:

> Every occasion for whatever passes over and goes forward into presencing from that which is not presencing is *poiēsis*, is bringing forth [*Her-vor-bringen* in Heidegger's specially hyphenated German].

It was at this point in Heidegger's analysis that technology begins to appear in a new light, as something that is called in English *poietic*, that is, *as something creative, formative, productive and active*, and then indeed *as such in its own right*.

For his part, Heidegger emphasised further that, for the Greeks, *poiēsis* applied not only to handicraft manufacture, and even not only, continuing further, to visual-artistic and poetical expressions, but it applied just as well to the acts of nature where something new came to presence, such as the bursting into blossom of a flower.

This in turn, however, inevitably recalls Goethe's celebrated aphorism (see Dilthey, 1976, p 60) that "Just as in the sphere of morality we are meant to approach the highest good so, in the intellectual sphere, contemplation of an ever creative nature is intended to make us worthy of participating in its productions". In this exalted view, then, *technology is nothing less than the continuation of the Creation by human means*.

There is, of course, a vital difference between an act of nature, such as the blossoming of a flower, and an act of technology, in that the one proceeds out of itself with no external agency other perhaps than a change of temperature – which is again an act of nature – whereas the manufacture of a new product necessitates an intervention from outside technology itself, as realised by the craftsman or the artist or whatever other human agent. We shall subsequently have cause to return to this distinction between that which drives the ever ongoing creative processes of nature and that which drives the processes of human creativity. As we subsequently come to follow these in several manifestations and in depth, we shall see that this difference is reduced and even in some cases disappears when we extend our technology so as to comprehend its human interventions, making of it a *sociotechnology*. We shall then see that we cannot really understand the poietics of technology without integrating them into the parallel poietics of those social, including institutional, changes that catalyse technology and that are in their turn catalysed by technology again, a process that occurs once more, so to say, 'in its own proper time'.

Thus, echoing Goethe, once we take their interacting social developments into account, the productions of the arts and crafts, like the productions of nature, come to presence 'at their own given time'. As an example that will be considerably amplified later in this work, the development of modern communication technologies, as manifested by the Internet and the radio-networked mobile telephone, occurred precisely as the societies in which these technologies came to presence moved from a modern condition into a post-modern condition, that is, as their populations transformed from predominantly 'knowers' to predominantly 'consumers of knowledge'.

This is to say that if we think in terms of technology exclusively, without taking account of its multiple and recursive interactions with the social, we shall be dealing with an *incomplete system*, usually with negative consequences for our understanding. We say in such a case that we are thinking *technocratically*. Only by thinking within the realm of the sociotechnical can we hope to attain to some measure of completeness in our analyses and thus obtain some reliable results. The already classical example of thinking technocratically was the so-called 'technology bubble' that marked the end of the twentieth century, whereby 'human waves' of hundreds of thousands of persons supported by hundreds of billions of dollars were thrown into technical developments, for the most part in the communication technologies, without regard to their related social interactions and so with scarcely any measurable economic benefit, with a subsequence collapse of the corresponding stock markets and losses to investors of several trillions of dollars and other measures of wealth.

If however we turn aside from these contemporary matters and return to follow, with Heidegger, the thinking, and with this the language of the Greeks, we may arrive at a much deeper understanding again. We have seen that with technology as something poietic, we have to do with a bringing-forth, which can be either something of nature or of the arts and crafts and all other modes of production. However, any bringing-forth involves *something being revealed that was previously concealed*, and we accordingly call the process through which this occurs *revealing*. But then the Greek word for revealing, *alētheia*, was used also with the connotation of *truth*: to say that "it is revealed to me" was the same as saying that "it is true" and it was only the more legalistic Romans who translated this by the word *veritus*, which then in turn translated most directly into our word, 'truth' Even to this day in fact we may still talk of a truth that has struck us with great force by saying that "it was a revelation", and this usage remains firmly grounded in Biblical and in standard literary usage. Similarly, as we shall shortly exemplify, we can still describe something that we experience in technology as an expression of profound truth as "a revelation".

Arriving at this point, we can now do no better than to follows one of Heidegger's most memorable and most quoted passages (ibid, pp. 12 and13):

> Technology is therefore no mere means. Technology is a way of revealing. If we give heed to this, then another whole realm for the essence of technology will open itself up to us. It is the realm of revealing, i.e., of truth.
> This prospect strikes us as strange. Indeed it should do so, should do so as persistently as possible and with so much urgency that we will finally take seriously the simple question of what the name 'technology' means. The word stems from the Greek. *Technikon* means that which belongs to *technē*. We must observe two things with respect to the meaning of this word. One is that *technē* is the name not only for the activities and skills of the craftsman, but also for the arts of the mind and the fine arts. *Technē* belongs to bringing-forth, to *poiēsis*, It is something poietic [i.e. creative, formative, productive, active]
> The other point that we should observe with regard with *technē* is even more important. From the earliest times until Plato the word *technē* is linked with the word *epistemē*. Both words are names for knowing in the wider sense. They mean to be entirely at home in something, to understand and be expert in it. Such knowing provides an opening up. As an opening up it is a revealing....
> Technology is a mode of revealing. Technology comes to presence in the realm where revealing and unconcealment take place, where *alētheia*, truth, happens.

We may now provide a *definition* of 'technology' that will be true for every one of its instances, for every one of its denotations and connotations, applying to all possible forms of the Platonic Form of 'technology':

Chapter 1

> *Technology is the continuation of the Creation by human means as this comes to presence in the realm where revealing and unconcealment takes place and so where* alētheia, *truth, happens.*

It may be useful at this stage to exemplify this very compact and concentrated presentation with a few familiar instances of its application. Clearly a product cannot be expected to be successful if it does not respect the true properties of its materials, if it is not made with the truly necessary and sufficient forms and dimensions, if it is not properly suited to its true purpose and if it is not manufactured by those who express the truth about how it can best be manufactured and subsequently used. (These correspond indeed to the four types of causes, the *causae,* of antiquity: the *causa materialis,* the *causa formalis,* the *causa finalis* and the *causa efficiens.*) Consequently, the engineer waiting at a nineteenth century railway station may while away his time by 'reading' the construction of the wrought-iron roof structure above him, tracing the lines of force passing through the structure and their associated shearing forces and bending moments under the different loading conditions to which the structure may be subject. In the case of a truly great structure, such as that of a Brunel, the engineer reads this with much the same pleasure, and indeed with much the same deep satisfaction, as he would read a poem. Such a structure *exudes the truth.* It is a revelation! We can trace what is essentially the same aesthetic in the efforts of the conservation movement as applied to industrial artefacts, such as in the painstaking work of restoring steam locomotives and their other rolling stock, together with track and signalling arrangements, or even in the modelling movement, in which a certain aesthetic is recreated in miniature as an alternative source of pleasure and satisfaction, as another kind of revelation again.

Taking the opposite case, when confronted with a product that does not satisfy these conditions of truthfulness, the person with passion for technology experiences a deep revulsion, bordering on disgust, as an ethical as well as an aesthetic reaction. For example, the monotonous reproduction of what is structurally the same and totally anonymous apartment block or the same totally anonymous office building, again and again and again, ad nauseam, everywhere on Earth, is deeply repulsive to the creative instincts of the structural engineer who really cares about structural engineering - just as it should be also to the architect who genuinely cares about architecture! As we shall see in more detail later, it is primarily because of these kinds of aesthetical and ethical impulses that the European Institute for Industrial Leadership is concerned to recruit most of the participants on its courses from *engineers,* understood as those who know and apply technology. It is then this property of technology, as the place where truth happens, where a certain revelation occurs, which generates the aesthetic fascination, the ethical passion and even the quasi-religious fervour that so often emanates from the engineer. Of course we have every right to be suspicious of such exhilarations, as mentioned in the introduction and as we shall subsequently discuss again later, but there is no denying their presence in the engineer – and indeed in many other feeling persons besides – when confronted with the products of technological excellence. If we may try to concentrate these experiences into a single aphorism, it is then this:

> *A fascination with technology is a fascination with truth*

1.2 The origins and nature of modern science and its influence on technology

Technology as introduced above is common to all technology, regardless of its origins and the nature of the social environment within which it comes to presence. We have to do here, however, with technology as it first developed in Europe, and in order to understand this we have to understand that which marked out this technology from all other technologies, which was its relation to *modern science*, as a specifically European innovation. If we define a science conventionally, as a totality established through an interconnection of true propositions, then each science can be regarded as the body of knowledge that is expressed by, or encapsulated in, this totality. When we speak about the physics- and biologically-based sciences upon which most of the technology used in industry draws for its sustenance, we speak in *the spirit of modern science*, this being conventionally dated from the *Condemnations* (of Heretical Doctrines, issued on the Seventh of March, 1277), following the historical studies of Duhem (initially from 1913-1917) and most succeeding historians of science (from Gilson, 1938; Copleston, 1953; and Gilson and Böhner, 1954, onwards). These conceptual origins of modern science were however traced back by these historians from way beyond the Condemnations, to a distinction in the nature of knowledge that had been made already by Plato some fifteen hundred years earlier (see, for example, Duhem-Brenner, 1997, p24):

> There are three degrees of understanding.
> The lowest degree is that of the knowledge of the senses ($α\"ισθησις$); it perceives what is born and what dies, that which endlessly changes and passes away; it grasps nothing permanent, nothing that is forever, indeed nothing that can be called true.
> The highest level is that of the pure intelligence ($νόησις$); the pure intelligence contemplates the eternal and, above all the astral bodies, the sovereign Good.
> Through the union of pure intelligence and the knowledge of the senses there arises a sort of mixed, bastard ($λογισμός, νόθος$) reason which occupies an intermediate position; one species of knowledge that is born of this level is geometry. This knowledge attains to propositions that are precise and permanent; indeed that are true....It prepares the way to participate in the $νόησις$, which alone reveals the eternal species.

The ancient Greek science, with astronomical prediction at its head, scarcely progressed beyond Plato's intermediate level, where each and every astral body had its own laws of motion determined by the god with whom it was identified, and which could be emulated by geometrical constructions, such as in the geometry of homocentric spheres and that of excentrics and epicycles. It thus corresponded to a *polytheistic cosmology*. This level of science is again often called *instrumentalism*, since it satisfied itself with providing an instrument – a geometrical construction in this case – for computing the trajectory and instantaneous position of each astral body individually without enquiring into any underlying 'cause' that would apply to all such bodies, let alone to all material bodies whatsoever. Plato's highest level of science, however, was concerned with identifying 'laws of the universe' such as would apply to all processes in all places at all times, and this only came to realisation when the theologians of the late middle ages recognised this level as the only one appropriate to their one and only God, so that it corresponded to a *monotheistic cosmology*. This level of science might then be called *essentialism*. All science that did not satisfy these conditions thus came to be described as 'pre-modern'.

The development of modern science from Buridan's recognition of the law of conservation of momentum – of *impetus* – onwards, has been recorded so extensively that no further commentary on it should be needed here. Clearly any science of this kind must always deal with ideal situations, which rarely if ever correspond at all exactly with the real situations treated by technology. Indeed, it was originally only in the case of planetary and other such celestial motions, where frictional resistance and other effects were so insignificant that the laws of mechanics could apply to them with negligible error, that modern science could convincingly demonstrate the generality, and thence the power, of its doctrine. However, the introduction of empirical, but carefully measured, coefficients into these universal laws in such a way that these coefficients could be constructed from combinations of the variables entering the ideal laws, subsequently made it possible to extend these laws to many other and less idealised processes of specific kinds so as to apply also over wide ranges of processes proceeding at all places and at all times, albeit within certain limits, a process that has been greatly advanced over the last four centuries (See Newton's *Principia* for one of the first clear formulations of this methodology). The ethos of the modern-scientifically-based technologies that follow this tradition can then also be described as 'essentialist', while the regressions to devices that disregard many, if not all, of the productions of the physical, and biological, sciences, such as are still being very actively promoted today in many places, can continue to be described as 'instrumentalist' in that they are only concerned to reproduce some observed results, and even then only for particular combinations of processes occurring in specific places at specific times and often further only under specific anterior conditions. As regressions to an earlier era, preceding that of modern science, they have the same concerns as had the ancient Greek astronomers, of *saving the appearances (σώζειν τά φαινόμενα)* of certain observed phenomena, while disregarding all, or almost all, concern with *understanding*. For example, it has been one of the disappointments of most of the developments in data-mining technologies that much of the excellent pioneering work that has been done in this area over the last two decades has already been widely misused in this way.

There are eight features of modern science and the modern technology that flowed from it that are of particular significance to any leader in industry - and which are essential to every future European leader:

1) Modern science was in the first place the creation of the Christian Church, and even of the Western Church, and, although severe in its judgements, the Condemnations that established its principles were generous in the acknowledgement that they gave to Islamic and Judaic scholars for their scientific insights, even as it pointed clearly to the ways in which these and their derivatives deviated from Christian doctrine. The Condemnations were originally, in the best senses of the words, as *catholic* in their tastes as they were *severe* in their disapprobations.
2) An instrumentalist science was of little or no value to technology since it was impractical to construct special geometrical systems for each and every individual piece of technical equipment. There was thus little relation between science and technology during the period preceding the era of modern science. Such applications as there were, such as those of aids to timekeeping, and hence to navigation, and to surveying, were themselves essentially of a geometric nature rather than a physical one, and indeed in France a surveyor is still called *un géomètre*. Only through modern science, with its emphasis on universal laws as expressed algebraically, could the

physical and biological sciences come to serve technology. Moreover, this kind of development in technology in turn served to provide the scientific apparatus necessary to advance the frontiers of modern science itself still further again. Since, however, modern science came to presence almost exclusively in Europe, and even then in that part of Europe in which the Catholic Church and subsequently its reformed offshoots became dominant, it was just this part of Europe that first developed a major 'competitive advantage' over all other parts of the world through its elaboration of what we may now call 'modern technology' – and this advantage exists to this day. These origins of modern technology in social developments shows us already that technology cannot be understood or explained exclusively on its own terms, but must be understood and explained in terms of an interweaving of social and technical threads of development, the one sometimes reinforcing and at other times weakening the other. We then return once more to the capital role of sociotechnology in all such understandings and explanations.

3) The progress made possible by technologies that were increasingly supported by modern physical science, which together we call 'modern technology', was further accelerated by the socio-religious changes brought on by the Reformation. In the words of the German theologian and educational reformer Friedrich Schleiermacher, "The antithesis between Protestantism and Catholicism may be provisionally conceived thus: the former makes the individual's relation to the Church dependent on his relation to Christ, while the latter contrariwise makes the individual's relation to Christ dependent on his relation to the Church". The resulting 'freedom' from this ethical determinism of institutionalised religion in the form of the Roman church led, in Protestant Europe, through what the German sociologist and political economist Max Weber called 'The Protestant Work Ethic', to new forms and intensities of capital accumulation and thence an ever accelerated industrial development. Weber saw in this the true dawn of industrial capitalism. Alongside its many positive aspects, unfortunately, this also provided the individualistic ethic and, inseparable from this, the industrial potential to prosecute ever greater and ever more destructive wars, so that Europe, and especially its Protestant Western parts, gradually developed new sociotechnical means, primarily those of *sea power*, to extend these wars to any place on Earth. It was at this point that the fascination with truth that drove technology came out of balance with the Christian virtues of benevolence and benignity, even though many individual industrialists did try to redress the balance by their own independent actions.

We should already here state clearly that, although we point to an understanding of these religious and specifically Christian influences as essential to an understanding of European industrial history, it is by no means necessary to be of the Christian faith or indeed of any religious faith at all in order to accept this role of Christianity within European industrial history. As observed later, in Chapter 3, this history remains most relevant today because it is essential to explaining the discrepancies in industrial and mercantile development between Western Europe on the one hand and Central and Eastern Europe on the other, differences which are still with us and with which the 2004 enlargement of the European Union has still to contend.

4) The social-religious-economic developments over the period roughly from 1450 to 1950 had in turn the consequence that one part of Europe came to colonise almost the whole world. Indeed, some parts of the resulting colonial empires, and especially those in South and North America and in Australasia, ultimately became populated predominantly by Europeans and persons of European descent. However, a military

and naval rivalry between France and Great Britain led to a coalition of the British colonies in North America achieving independence, leading to the establishing of the United States of America, as a predominately Protestant nation. Beyond this again, as the sociotechnical capacities of the Protestant Western-Europeans and the United States came to overtake those of their Catholic neighbours, so the former tended to displace the latter, either by direct conquest of their territories, as in the case of the USA, or by aiding and abetting the subversion of the European Catholic powers by their own local colonists, such as occurred in Latin America. Whatever their origins, however, these newly independent colonists then came to play their own part in the continuation of the colonial adventure, and especially through their virtual extermination of most, and in the United States and Australia almost all, the original, indigenous, populations. The colonial activities of the European powers continued also, and the attendant atrocities were sometimes also on the very largest scale.[1]

5) These hitherto, and still to this day, unprecedented acts of genocide were accompanied by what was also the greatest age of slavery in absolute terms in the history of the world, largely enforced and administered by the newly independent European and mixed-European populations in the newly independent states. It was this that provided the first economic foundations for nations like the United States to rise to become major economic competitors to the European powers, even as the European powers had, with certain notable exceptions, outlawed slavery by that time and in some cases were actively suppressing it.

6) The resulting new slave economies, such as that which 'transformed the black gold of slaves into the white gold of cotton', although it led to the accumulation of vast wealth, brought these economies into conflict with the new industry-based economies of European origin and especially within the United States, ultimately and indirectly leading in this last case to the American Civil War and the gradual elimination of the world's slave economies as major influences in economic affairs as a whole. Slavery was found to be incompatible with an industrial economy and, with the slave economies virtually eliminated as major economic competitors, growing economies became ever more predominantly industrial, following the European model. This was a model of an increasing social tolerance and, over time, the rise of an institutionalised respect for 'human rights' and 'social rights', such as entitlements to unemployment payments and retirement and disability pension rights, subsequently extended further to the provision of medical, educational and other social services. Outside of direct government legislation, these rights also became anchored in the power of trade unions, cooperative societies and other such institutions. Although some attempts were subsequently made to combine part-slave and part-industrial economies, and notably in the then Soviet Union between 1930 and 1960 primarily as a means of building an industrial base in Asiatic Russia, and in Germany between 1942 and 1945, following heavy losses of German industrial workers from aerial bombardment and from massive war losses on Germany's Eastern front, slavery could not be reconciled with social structures which were symbiotic with a balanced and sustainable industrial development.

7) The process of 'positive feedback' in weaponry, strategy and tactics from the colonial wars into European conflicts led inexorably to the two great wars and subsequent upheavals that dominated the history of Europe, and thus came to influence the whole world, in the first half of the twentieth century. The first of these wars and its aftermaths exhausted most of Europe, although, outside of Russia, it did not devastate it, while the second both exhausted and devastated almost the whole of Europe, even

Chapter 1

as the neutral nations and others, such as the United States (which played scarcely any military part at all in the first such conflict and only a secondary part militarily in the second - see for example Liddell Hart, 1970, p. 530 - but which obtained all the economic advantages of a neutral country in both conflicts) prospered greatly. By 1945 the United States had some 75 percent of the world's industrial production, while most of Europe was in ruins, with its population reduced for a large part to penury. By the 1950s it started to become clear, despite the continuation by some European powers of colonial wars that attained the largest scales of all times and entailed the suppression of local resistance with unprecedented ferocity, that the European domination of the world was in fact at an end. The continuation of these wars by the United States, with some support from Australia, which unleashed a totally unprecedented paroxysm of destruction, similarly led to such internal tensions that these nations had to admit a de-facto defeat. As the ancient Greeks had long since discovered, "One cannot enslave others without becoming enslaved oneself". Once again, already in the 1950s in the case of Europe, it became clear that one could not suppress and dominate others without damaging the entire social fabric upon which one's own prosperity and development was dependent. The project of European Unity, still only getting under way at that time, had its origin in this experience: in the rejection of all forms of suppression and domination and with this the rejection of all aspirations towards hegemony. It was finally understood that one's own human and social rights, freedom of expression and rule of law were incompatible with the suppression of these rights in the case of others. The resulting understanding of the necessity of European Unity has been a direct consequence of the many dreadful events and experiences that flowed to a large extent from modern technology and the modern science upon which it so much depended and continues to depend. European Union can then be seen as a *turning away* from a path that not only brought unprecedented misery to so many of the peoples of this planet outside Europe, but which finally came to visit these miseries upon the peoples of Europe themselves.

8) All of these social events are then seen to be closely associated with modern technology as this originated in Europe, even as it had such far reaching and ultimately its mostly negative consequences, initially outside of Europe but finally within Europe also. It is then necessary to understand what kind of technology this was, and indeed still is, that could be and can still be turned to such negative as well as positive purposes, and thence to penetrate to some understanding of the forces that drive technology in the one or the other direction. After all, how is it possible that modern technology, founded as it was upon modern science as a gift of the Church, could have forgotten its compensating Christian virtues to such an extent that it could be misused so as to cause such great sufferings? It is essential for every European leader of industry to recognise and understand this Janus-like face of modern technology and the modern science upon which it draws so much of its strength and to understand how modern technology must itself be served by Christian or other religious virtues if it is to show its true face of goodness.

1.3   The characterisation of modern technology

We have already introduced some of the features of modern technology through its relation to modern science. We now, however, have to proceed further, into how modern technology has acquired an own character as a result of its applications, rather than as a result of the way in which it originated under the influence of modern science. This is then to characterise a technology that has lost its balance, having largely divorced itself from the benevolence and benignity of the religious impulse. We have indeed to see how technology has itself used - or many would say misused - modern science essentially 'for its own ends'. We have then to do here with how modern technology has come to be employed within human societies and in particular how this mode of operation is now changing as our current societies move from modern to post-modern conditions.

What we at once observe when we consider modern technology as we ourselves experience it today, and especially how we come to use it nowadays, is that, although it remains a form of revealing, it more usually does not unfold as a bringing-forth in the way of poiesis. It does not arise as though it were a rose bursting spontaneously into bloom. Instead, the form of revealing of modern technology is observed to be that of *a challenging*, as something that is forever *challenging us out*. We less and less do things on our own volition in our own good time, such as a rose that is blossoming according to its readings of its environment and its own inner programme, but instead *we are constantly driven to do them* by the ever mounting pressures exerted by our environing world. Thus our ever growing needs for energy challenge us out to find and exploit ever more, and ever less accessible, sources of energy, our ever growing needs for foods of certain kinds challenge us out to find new ways to increase the yields of crops and fields, even at the expense of a depletion of water resources and the spoliation of lands through the applications of agrochemicals, while our own very physical existences challenge us out to use ever more and ever more potent pharmaceutical products and to undergo ever more complicated surgical and other medical interventions.

A first immediate consequence of this is that we are challenged out further to provide 'reserves', such as in stockpiles, for all our future needs. We are forever challenged out to prospect for energy for future needs, we are forever challenged out to develop new seed varieties, new herbicides and insecticides and new forms of mineral additives for our fields, as well as new pharmaceutical products and growth-promoting substances for our livestock, we are for ever challenged out to develop further surgical and medical interventions, and are today even building up 'banks' of human organs for future transplants. Similarly, humans are no longer real, live individual persons, but they have become increasingly undifferentiated 'human resources'.

This process nowadays becomes extended throughout the whole world of nature. Every river is now seen as a reserve and a source of water for domestic and industrial use and as a reserve and source of electric power; every forest becomes a reserve and a source of timber, wild animals and tourists, every so-far unspoilt area of nature becomes a 'nature reserve' as a future source of 'reserves of genetic material'; and so we can continue indefinitely. All of these 'reserves' are there solely for our future use, whereby we can *set upon them* and *exploit them* whenever we wish. In his work on technology, Heidegger (ibid, p. 17) called all such constructions *standing reserves* and observed that "The fact that now, wherever we try to point to modern technology, the words 'setting upon', 'ordering' and 'standing reserve' obtrude and accumulate in a dry, monotonous and oppressive way, has its basis in what is now coming to utterance". Elsewhere again, in a much earlier work, Heidegger expressed the feeling that we experience when confronted with this situation as one of encountering *a world deprived of its worldhood*.

Of course most of us find this view most uncongenial, even though it all happens in our own names and we are ourselves agents in one way or the other in all its spoliations. One result of this situation is that many individuals oppose the one or the other aspect of this process, even as everyone appears to be ultimately caught up in its operations. In this world of modern technology, we are each and every one of us challenged out to think in this way. Similarly, despite our deep respect for modern science, the dominant processes of this increasingly disturbing and even repulsive modern technology appear to be the same as those that have become so characteristic of modern science, namely those of *ordering, numbering and computing*.

Heidegger called this challenging-out process *Enframing*, since it provides the same experience as that of putting something – a photograph for example – in a frame, as something that gathers that which it encloses into its folds, so as to separate it from its surroundings and so reveal it more clearly in its own right, challenging out our gaze to dwell upon it rather than what is around it. It is by these means that the balancing forces of religious virtues can be uncoupled from the truth values of technology itself. Enframing, it then turns out, is not just one of any number of other features of modern technology, but it is of the essence of modern technology. Thus (ibid, p.23):

> Because the essence of modern technology lies in Enframing, modern technology must employ exact physical science. Through its so doing, the deceptive illusion arises that modern technology *is* applied physical science. This illusion can maintain itself only so long as neither the essential origin of modern science nor indeed the essence of modern technology is adequately identified through questioning.

From the side of modern science, it is clear that Enframing cannot be properly attributed to it, since modern science originated as the search for the highest truths, as those which would hold through all processes in all places at all times. From its very origins, then, we must always speak of the *natural goodness of modern science*. In this case, however, these negative attributes of modern technology that we so clearly identify must arise, not from a use, but from a misuse of modern science. And that which misuses modern science in this way can only be man himself, working through his technology. So what then is it that causes man to behave in this way through his technology and so to abuse the goodness of modern science? In what kind of web of delusions is man so caught up, apparently inextricably, in Enframing?

Since almost all technology proceeds nowadays through our being challenged out, we see at once that, to the extent that we experience that there is something highly irregular in our technology, we must conclude that *we are being challenged-out in 'the wrong way'*. But what is it that causes *us* to be challenged-out 'in the wrong way', this being a way that we otherwise experience, albeit subjectively, as not being a way of truth at all, but a way of deception, of untruth? Since modern technology must still remain technology as 'the place where *alētheia*, truth, happens', what we experience as happening now is that our observations of the present-day applications of technology *are telling us the truth about an untruth* that is not itself attributable to technology as such at all, but must be attributable to something *within our own selves*, something that comes to presence through the frame that *we* set around our worlds, in *our* action of Enframing that serves to negate the balancing forces of religious virtues.

But what is this 'something'? This is a question that has in fact persisted throughout history, but which became increasingly urgent in the Europe of the nineteenth century as the negative influences attributed to modern technology and the changing ways of life that it engendered became increasingly more evident. It became posed with increasing force again during the first half of the twentieth century, where this question demanded increasingly clear answers in response to the rise of the forces of bolshevism, fascism and nazism, almost entirely in Europe, with their glorification and prosecution of modern technology in its most terribly efficient, brutal and barbarous forms. Since that time, this negative force has taken on less obviously ugly forms in that part of the world that likes to call itself The First World, having transferred its nefarious attentions much more to the so-called Third World, but it still remains most active, and ever more dangerously so in Europe, and indeed just as much and perhaps even more so than elsewhere just because it is so much less evident. Thus in the words of Jacques Derrida, responding to the empty-headed 'optimism' of Fukuyama's book entitled *The End of History*:

> Never have violence, inequality, exclusion, famine and thus economic oppression affected so many human beings in the history of the Earth and of humanity.... no degree of progress allows one to ignore that never before, in absolute figures, have so many men, women and children been subjugated, starved or exterminated on the Earth.

If only for these reasons alone, we have no alternative but to outline this response here already if we are to understand the essential features of modern technology in its Enframing, in its divorce from religious virtues, but we must do this for other reasons besides. The leader cannot ignore, and indeed must take into proper account, the existence of this negative force in all that passes around him. Our object here is thus also to arm him properly with an understanding of this force so that he can more quickly identify and subsequently defeat this adversary wherever he encounters it.

But what, everyone will ask, is the name of this adversary? It – for we have here to do with an 'it' - was introduced in Søren Kierkegaard's Danish as *Intet*, which translates literally as 'nothing', and *Intethed*, which we can only translate as 'nothingness'. It correspondingly entered German as *das Nichtige*, and into French as *le néant* and into English, and more awkwardly so than ever, as *nothingness*. In philosophy it was described as a *nihil* and its manifestations were described as *nihilism*. We now have, most unfortunately because it is very unpleasant matter, to introduce this 'it-which-can be-no-thing'. As we shall see, it is this 'nothing', this *nihil*, which touches everything as it strives to destroy all that has been created, whether by God or, by extrapolation, by mankind.

1.4 From nihilism to the kingdom of nothingness

The subject that concerns us here has a long history and must have perplexed every one at some time or the other. Put in Christian terms, the question naturally arises of why, if God is so good, He allows so much suffering in this world of His own creation? We all know at least some of the reasons and rationalisations presented by the Church to explain this discrepancy: 'the fall', 'original sin', 'the devil', to name but three of the many that have been and continue to be so widely employed. Such devices sufficed for the most part so long as only a few 'upper class' persons were literate and sufficiently educated to think further about these matters, but the experiences of 19th century European industrialisation, with all its negative manifestations, became associated with the simultaneous rise of a new, more highly educated, so-called 'middle' class, to make these sophistries untenable. In the incisive words of the foremost among such persons, in the words of Nietzsche, written with his usual biting irony:

> The decline of belief in the Christian God, the victory of scientific atheism – this is a combined European achievement (*ein gesamteuropäisches Ereignis*) for which all races will claim their own share of merit and honour.

And to this he elsewhere added, in deadly seriousness:

> The greatest recent event – that God is dead, that the belief in the Christian God has become unbelievable – is already beginning to cast its first shadows over Europe.

To Nietzsche's rhetorical question that arose immediately from this situation: "Are we not then straying through an infinite nothing?" Heidegger, in his own time, of the mid twentieth century, responded (1977, pp.60-61):

> The pronouncement that 'God is dead' contains the confirmation that this Nothing is spreading out. 'Nothing' means here: absence of a suprasensory, obligatory world. Nihilism, 'the most uncanny of all guests', is standing at the door.
> ...Nihilism is a historical movement, and not just any view or doctrine advocated by someone or other. Nihilism moves history after the manner of a fundamental ongoing event that is scarcely recognised in the destiny of the Western peoples. Hence nihilism is also not simply one historical phenomenon among others – not simply one intellectual current that along with others, with Christendom, with humanism, and with Enlightenment – that comes to the fore within Western history.
> Nihilism, thought in its essence, is, rather, the fundamental movement of history of the West. It shows such great profundity that its unfolding can have nothing but world catastrophes as its consequence. Nihilism is the world-historical movement of the peoples of the Earth who have been drawn into the power realm of the modern age.

This is to say that, for Heidegger, nihilism was not only a product of the nineteenth century, even though it was primarily in that century that its presence became more clearly recognised and its name established, but its origins proceeded much further back, back through all the histories of the Western peoples, which meant, in the first place, that it proceeded back through all the histories of the peoples of Europe.

This view of the mysterious nature but only too manifest influence of 'nihilism' was however essentially a philosophical one, and it was by no means the view of those with a more theological foundation who persisted in speaking of 'nothing' and 'nothingness'. Thus, even though Heidegger, for example, did have a substantial theological education, he was not himself a theologian: his knowledge of theology provided him with a certain theoretical apparatus for his philosophical work, but this work was itself in no way theological. It is then first necessary to explain this difference between the philosophical and the theological in order to follow why it is that nothingness, in its essence, can only be understood from a theological, and indeed from a 'dogmatic-theological', standpoint. We repeat again that it cannot be at all expected nowadays that everyone interested in such matters is Christian, or indeed has any explicit faith at all, but none the less all persons concerned with such matters as the present one can and must learn from theological studies.

We have seen that a fascination with technology is a fascination with truth. Technology is grounded in a seeking after truth in the world of human creativity, and in our present case it seeks and finds its truths in acts of industrial creativity. Industrial technology is only one, but still one, of the many, many ways of seeking after truth and experiencing truth that give us hope, cohesion and guidance as seekers after truth in an otherwise so troubled world. Among all seekers after truth, however, some are more aware of the object of their quest than others and are more directly concerned with arriving at its sources, or its origins. They are therefore concerned not only with knowledge, as that which bears or contains truth, but also with wisdom, which is the arbiter and organiser of knowledge, and so the source of truth. It is this which obliges them to seek beyond the surface of appearances and so, ultimately, as 'believer' or otherwise, to enter into the depths of theological studies. In Christian-theological terms, all such searchings and strivings are borne by a covenant of the spirit that we commonly call 'love', and the most profound of these movements is the love of wisdom itself.

For well over two thousand years now, it has been normal within the so-called Western tradition to distinguish between a love of wisdom translated into works without the explicit supposition of any agent external to mankind itself, and so by reason alone, which is called *philosophy*, and a love of truth as the issue of a wisdom that includes but also necessarily transcends the powers of unaided human reason, which is called *theology*. Thus philosophy requires human understanding, as mediated by reason, while theology requires not only this human understanding but also something more again, which is called *faith*. Thus, within the Christian tradition, as in other religious traditions besides, faith is that which surpasses human understanding, which transcends reason, so that 'faith is a miracle, otherwise it is not faith'.

Every culture appoints some persons as the repositories and the transmitters of wisdom, whether as Shaman, Buddhist monk or Hindu sage, but in the Christian tradition this task is mainly appropriated by a social institution, called in general terms the Church with an upper-case 'C'. By its very act of appropriation this institution cannot form one unity, but must find itself divided into many institutionally separate churches, and so spelt with a lower-case 'c'. It is accepted within most churches that, being human constructions at least in part, they cannot be perfect, and indeed that they can transgress very far from perfection and may even descend into downright corruption. Despite this, the actual survival of the churches is seen by many, and not only among their congregations, as some proof of the power of faith alongside and supporting the power of reason. Thus faith and reason, *Fides et Ratio*, are seen as friends and allies and not as adversaries, and that is our position here when we seek to understand the essential nature of nothingness.

When introducing nothingness in his great *Church Dogmatics*, written during the ascendancy and destruction of fascism and nazism - the second volume being written while he was serving in the Swiss Frontier Guards during the Second World War - and completed during the aftermath of that war, the theologian Karl Barth introduced our present subject as follows (Vol. 3, Part 3. p. 289):

> There is amongst the objects of God's providence an alien factor. It cannot escape God's providence, but is comprehended by it. The manner, however, in which this is done is highly peculiar in accordance with the particular nature of this factor. It is distinct from that in which God's providence rules the creature and creaturely occurrence. The result is that the alien factor can never be considered or mentioned together in the same context as other objects of God's providence. Thus the whole doctrine of God's providence must be investigated afresh. This opposition and resistance, this stubborn element and alien factor, may be provisionally defined as nothingness.

All theology involves a struggle to express in words the many experiences, impressions and feelings for which language was never developed to describe and for the expression of which language remains always inadequate. This is nowhere more evident than in the present case. In theological terms, the relation between God and man becomes broken by this alien element, with the consequence that every attempt to describe nothingness, even theologically, must itself be broken in thought and in utterance. This is to say, however, that *this description cannot form a system.*

Now this first observation concerning any view that we have upon nothingness is already of great significance, for it means that whenever we encounter nothingness *we are always confronted with an absence of system.* Of course, all the manifestations of nothingness try to pass themselves off as systems, as being systematic, but it soon becomes clear to the critical observer that under the surface of their pronouncements and outer appearances there is in fact no system at all, but only unprincipled opportunism, muddle and confusion. This became very clear at the largest scales in the cases of fascism, nazism and bolshevism, but it is characteristic, albeit only as a symptom, of all movements and organisations and even individuals that are beset by the attentions of nothingness. With the present state of our world before our own eyes, and even through the distancing, depersonalising and alienating influence of the written text and television, Barth's generalisation of this characterisation (*loc. cit.* p. 354) must ring as something uncannily familiar:

> Nothingness is absolutely without norm or standard. The explicable conforms to law, nothingness to none. It is simply aberration, transgression, evil. For this reason it is inexplicable, and can be affirmed only as that which is inherently inimical. For this reason it can be apprehended in its aspect of sin only as guilt, and in its aspect of evil and death only as retribution and misery, but never as a natural process or condition, never as a subject of systematic formulation... Being hostile before and against God, and also before and against His creature, it is outside the sphere of systematisation. Its defeat can be envisaged only as the purpose and the end of the history of God's dealings with His creature, and in no other way.

Clearly the leader in industry must be able to identify nothingness, but he must also be able to combat it. For the 'non-believer', Barth's first observation on present-day man's chances in this combat must then appear at first sight as decidedly discouraging: "God alone can summon, empower and arm the creature to resist and even to conquer this adversity...The creature as such would be no match for nothingness and certainly unable to overcome it." From the Christian-theological point of view that is adopted here, however, it is not of much consequence whether the person who is summoned, empowered and armed to combat nothingness is immediately aware at all of the source of his strengths, and he may well be a match for nothingness without the slightest inkling that he is such a match because he is by no means standing alone in this confrontation. From a theological point of view of course, he would be better prepared again if he were aware and alert to this support, but it is not the most immediately essential issue. The essential issue is that the person so 'chosen' is prepared to face his responsibilities in such a combat - and after that it is our present responsibility to prepare him for this combat with such weapons as theology has prepared.[3]

This person confronted with nothingness – which is every one of us – has first to recognise its reality. Thus, written with the demise of Nazi Germany still fresh in the memory (*loc. cit.* p. 524):

> It is, for the Bible, no mere figure of speech or poetic fancy or expression of human concern but the simple truth that nothingness has this dynamic, that it is engaged in invasion and assault; not a kingdom that has to be feared; [in fact] a kingdom of that which is improper; a kingdom which by the fact that God confronts it is characterised from the very outset as weak and futile; a kingdom which is usurped and not legitimate, transitory and not eternal; yet a real kingdom, a nexus of form and power and movement and activity, of real danger within its appointed limits. This is how Holy Scripture sees nothingness... And in this sense it reckons with [its] actuality.
>
> We see at once the similarity of this sphere with that of the kingdom of God, the kingdom of heaven...[But] what is the basis of this similarity? It rests on the fact that *in se* nothingness is falsehood. As such it gives itself similarities with the kingdom of God. It ascribes and arrogates to itself a being which, because it is neither God nor an earthly or heavenly creature, cannot belong to it. In so doing it is falsehood in its very being...It lies by pretending to be glorious and attractive on the one side or terrifying on the other. It lies by assuming form and power for a particular purpose. It lies in its whole movement and activity, in its whole march, in its whole invasion and assault.

With a reference to the successors of fascism and nazism also, however (*loc. cit.* p. 526):

> Nothingness lies also and supremely by trivialising and concealing itself, spreading abroad a carefree optimism, being content only to be present, to be in fact a powerful kingdom subtly controlled, and thus to declare, express and maintain its power. Nothingness rejoices when it notices that humanity thinks that it can tackle its lesser and greater problems with a little morality and medicine and psychology and aesthetics, with progressive politics or occasionally a philosophy of unprecedented novelty – if only its own reality as nothingness remains beautifully undisclosed and intact.

Nothingness is then falsehood that may masquerade as anything, including goodness, so that its very *modus vivendi* is that of imitation and concealment. To the extent that it has any existence at all, it is no more than a mimicry. And even though this is all so immensely successful, still this very success is only really the success of falsehood. It all succeeds only so long as the falsehood is not exposed. Nothingness itself is real enough, but the mimicry that it presents to us as reality is but a pretentious semblance of reality, possessing in itself no reality at all. Thus, returning to Barth (*loc. cit.* p. 528):

> They are powers indeed, and yet they are only the powers of falsehood. Hence we must not regard them as real powers, or the mimicry with which they make fools of us a reality. They work so long and extensively and deeply as they can work as lies, and are not shown to be such, or set over against the truth, and thus dispelled as lies. Anything other or less than the truth is no match for them, whether it takes the form of zealous goodwill, knowledge or techniques. Only the truth is strong enough to meet them. This is so immediately, basically and conclusively. Yet this must be the whole truth, the real truth [corresponding to] the truth of God and His Kingdom ..., the truth which they have attempted to imitate and in the imitation of which they are so powerful. Other truths may be profound and excellent, but they are of no value because they cannot touch, let alone destroy, their power, the power of imitation and falsehood, which makes then so great and powerful.

It follows that the weapons necessary to combat nothingness are those of expressing and communicating and inculcating truth at this most exalted level. Thus (*loc. cit.* p. 529): "That the lie should be exposed is what is most appropriate to the lie itself and most helpful to those who are threatened, oppressed and tormented...And as it is done the lie looses the vital breath which enables it to threaten, oppress and torment. It is vanquished and driven from the field."

Among the many examples of this process, the paradigm case is surely provided by the so-called 'Tét offensive' launched by the Vietnamese resistance to the US domination of their country in 1969 (see Nguyên Khăc Viên, 2004). An unprecedented, highly sophisticated and hugely expensive campaign of propaganda, although directed in the first place towards the people of the USA itself, tried to persuade the whole world that Vietnam had been 'pacified' by the more than half a million US and some seven hundred thousand South Vietnamese troops, including seventy thousand in the special police and other forces exercising extreme repression, including the extensive use of torture. This had the effect that the people of the USA wavered in their opposition to the war, seeing only peace, quiet and the illusion of prosperity in Vietnam on their television screens, and being thus led to believe that the war was essentially won, that the Vietnamese were liberated and happy and that 'the boys' would soon be coming home. The Vietnamese resistance accordingly launched a massive and well-prepared uprising that provided 'great news material' for the television chains – who were not then 'embedded' – and led to the total exposure of the lie that the US government and military had worked so hard to construct. The people of the USA, as elsewhere, were aroused to extreme anger as they witnessed the obvious deception that had been practised on them and insisted on the withdrawal of its armed forces. On the other hand, through the Tét offensive the people of Vietnam suffered the most grievous losses, since for the most part they could only mount their attacks with the light arms of a resistance movement against the armour, helicopter gunships and other heavy and sophisticated equipment deployed by the US. In military terms they could only and in fact did suffer a near-total defeat at the hands of this technically far superior force, *but this was acceptable because all that was necessary was that the lie should be exposed.* The US government was forced by its own public opinion to withdraw almost all its armed forces and to completely 'Vietnamise' the continuation of their political and economic domination, a policy that could only end with the defection of the armed forces of the US-backed puppet government to the side of their own people, joining the forces of the North of the country to drive out all influences of the invader. [4]

Since a fascination with technology is a fascination with the truth, one would expect that engineers, as technologists, should be well suited to this task. However, engineers, like other technologists, are not educated and trained in *how* to tell the truth, or even *how* to recognise it, outside of technology itself, and even there they may have considerable limitations. Even less again are they trained to identify the nature of untruths and how these are functioning within a given environment. For this reason, if for no others, engineers and other technologists who are not forearmed cannot expect to succeed in environments in which nothingness has already taken hold, which is to say in most businesses, governments and other institutions in our present times. The weapons required to defeat nothingness are the means of telling and indeed inculcating the truth without destroying one's own self in the process, and it is these means that we have in our turn to inculcate in this place.

Chapter 1

Lying is an art, and its practitioner is in his own way an artist. Machiavelli, who had a great experience of liars and swindlers at the highest levels of society, wrote the truth about them and was excoriated and damned by polite society for his pains. Thus:

> To those seeing and hearing him, he should appear a man of compassion, a man of good faith, a man of integrity, a kind and religious man...Men in general judge by their eyes rather than by their hands: because everyone is in a position to watch, few are in a position to come in close contact with you. Everyone sees what you appear to be, few experience who you really are....[Pope] Alexander VI was always, and he thought only of, deceiving people, and he always found victims for his deceptions. There never was a man capable of such convincing assertions or so ready to swear to the truth of something, who would honour his word less. Nonetheless his deceptions always had the result he intended because he was a past master in the art.

Exposing the lie is also an art, but it is one that demands another kind of artistry. We shall return to this art later in the present work. In our own times, however, lying has itself resorted to new and in some ways unprecedented means of expression to convey its falsities. These means are what are generally called *simulacra*, as the devices that are used to produce *virtual worlds*. These are the dynamic coloured images of a life-like reality that project the most attractive expectations onto one's computer screen, but which in fact are far removed from any physical reality. These are the television 'commercials' that purport to provide a happiness and even a bliss that can be yours for a small expenditure upon the product or service which they promote, but which in reality can never deliver anything of the kind. These are the political 'documentaries' depicting all manner of unmitigated failures as great successes in the most glowing terms, and so we can continue. From the point of view that will be advanced later in this work, the simulacra are technical devices that are still employed for the most part in order to facilitate the art of lying. As will be emphasised when we arrive at that point, they correspond to the transformation of this art from a social to a sociotechnical discipline, and we shall then show that this discipline corresponds to a socially-extended view of technology that provides what are nowadays often called *The Technologies of Persuasion*. It will then be our objective at that stage to show how these technologies can be turned around against the lie and placed in the service of truth, and how then, as technologies, they can much better serve the interests of truth than they can the interests of the kingdom of nothingness with its panoplies of lies.

Nothingness thus corresponds to the untrue as the *inauthentic*, as that which strives always to subvert, degrade, corrupt and ultimately destroy the *authentic*. In order to do this it must put on the clothes and a mask of authenticity and it must imitate the language of authenticity, but it does this only for the purpose of deception. Nothingness plays at creation but creates nothing; it only destroys what others have created. For this purpose it seduces with false promises, such as those of higher money incomes, of better 'life styles', and in brief with promises of success, fame and fortune – promises which it has no intention whatsoever of keeping.

Nothingness is everywhere, and by no means least in industry. In terms of its false promises, it is most evidently present in the hordes of so-called 'managers' – millions upon millions of them – who for the most part create nothing of any value at all to the organisation that feeds them, but only serve the interests of other 'managers' again and the failed and bogus 'leaders' of what is still supposed to be an 'enterprise'. Taking up again a theme of the introduction, these persons themselves 'manage' nothing, but instead waste the resources of the organisations in endless memoranda writing, in calling and attending all manner of pointless meetings, in launching so-called 'reorganisations' and 'restructurings' and generally consuming not only their own time and energy, but the times and energies of the productive, authentic parts of the organisation, demoralising these also in the process.

Nothingness, however, now plays another game again, of towering above industry in the form of another great army, but now composed of financial advisers, deal-makers, bankers and 'facilitators' of every kind, that is always ready to invade and assault the authentic business enterprise. These are the persons who understand better than anyone else that *the quickest way to make money is to destroy value*, a principle that we shall discuss in the EIIL course in some detail. Putting on again the clothes and the mask of the authentic, they are forever speaking loudly about 'creating value', 'building businesses', 'realising synergies', even '*engineering* management buy-outs' and generally uttering similar fine-sounding phrases, very few of which are reflected in their activities. Of course, within the ranks of this army there are still men of principle, who do provide valuable services, and every leader of industry must locate such persons and value them most highly, if only because such individuals are so exceedingly rare.

Nothingness plays its biggest game of all in what has always been its favourite hunting ground, which is that of politics. As has been so frequently observed, politics condemns, even as it condones, deception; what it cannot condone is the situation that arises when the politician is exposed in his deception, when he is 'found out'. For this constitutes a threat both to the body politic as a whole and, in a parliamentary democracy, to the political party or faction to which the guilty politician belongs. But, apart from that, deception, distortion, lies and 'spin' are the norm throughout all parties and all fractions. Pluralising the description of Machiavelli's pope, "there never were men capable of such convincing assertions or so ready to swear to the truth of something who would honour their word less". It is indeed this feature of politics that is often employed to justify the continuation of monarchy and monarchical systems alongside parliamentary democracy in several countries, and of unelected 'upper houses' in most parliamentary systems.

The powers of nothingness are currently concentrating their efforts on their most daring and audacious adventure of recent times, which is a concerted attack, by an alliance of inauthentic-management-dominated and money-fixated industrial interests on the one side and many governments on the other upon the rights and privileges of the general populations of their respective nations. This is associated in some countries by legislation placing further restrictions on such restraining powers as the unelected and thus less opportunistic part of the legislature still possess. This is a new and concentrated invasion and assault upon the achievements of decades and even centuries of struggle for the human and social rights of the general population: the rights to security of employment, to health and other care, to pensions and other social benefits. Of course, it is understood that these rights also suited certain business and political interests when they were legislated, but they have now become established as rights and, despite their frequent abuse and misappropriation, their benefits to society as a whole have been undeniable. As a consequence, in Europe they have even become a certain source of pride, as another, positive kind of specifically European achievement, and one with a long history in Christian charity, general benevolence and human solidarity. The people of

Europe have, so to say, 'a well-founded right to these rights', and indeed it is these that in fact provide the very foundations of European industrial competitiveness, despite all the propaganda to the contrary. This kind of social development is also, of course, in the tradition of all other religions too.

This new invasion and assault on European, Christian and other religious values is naturally once again conducted in the name of increasing 'efficiency', 'competitiveness', 'flexibility' and other desiderata on the part of the workforce, even though it is obvious to every informed observer that it is in fact driven precisely by the personal greed, the ignorance and the incompetence, with a corresponding uncompetitiveness, of so many European 'leaders'. The loud cries of certain industrial interests (most of them essentially financial interests) that are taken up and emphasised by governments and their dependents, that social services have to be reduced, that life-long security of employment is unsustainable, that present pension expectations cannot be met and so on, are then simply the bankruptcy statements of a failed leadership. All their arguments about aging populations, of the superiority of a so-called 'US and UK business model' over a 'continental European model' and similar deceptions are easily refuted and there is now more than sufficient evidence to expose their falsity. We shall return to this subject of failed leadership later here when we look at the influence of nothingness upon leadership itself, and we shall then make the distinction between a true or *authentic* leadership and its mimicry, as a false or *inauthentic* leadership. We shall at the same time introduce the technologies of persuasion that have been mobilised in order to propagate these self-serving falsehoods – but which can just as well be turned around to combat these forces of darkness.

The true answer to the problems that are raised concerning the sustainability of human and social rights is then to be found in sound, well-educated, well informed, and above all honest and thus *authentic leadership*. The EIIL has then been founded precisely to ensure that such leaders are identified, educated and trained, with their faculties honed to a fine cutting edge so that they can cut through the verbiage of confused thinking, disinformation and deception that is such a feature of our present age of an all-pretentious nothingness.

Chapter 2

ON LEADERSHIP

2.1 On leadership in general

The quality of leadership is widely recognised even though it appears in different individuals, within different contexts and in different forms. This capacity to recognise one and the same essential quality within many different manifestations of the quality marks leadership as a *Form* (and so with an upper-case 'F') in the sense initiated by Plato in his *Theory of Forms*. Such a capacity is then something, inherent to many of our fellow creatures as well as ourselves, being a capacity to map many different things that appear to us separately in our consciousness into just one thing which is common to all of these manifestations even as it is not itself any particular one of them. This general capacity to intuit one immutable and eternal Form behind many mutable and transitory forms might be supposed to be something that is genetically programmed into us. Indeed, as just one example, observing leadership so widely among our fellow creatures, we may suppose that the propensity to develop Forms is more archaic than *Homo sapiens* himself and thus more archaic than language and logical ratiocination. It is accordingly still experienced as much, or even more, at the level of the limbic system than it is experienced at the level of the cerebral system itself: it is experienced as much, or even more, at an emotional level than it is experienced at an intellectual level. There is then always something ineffable, and something of a mystery, about our every individual experience of leadership and this necessarily arises as we relate any one of these experiences back to the underlying Form.

Accordingly, from a more theological standpoint, leadership corresponds to *a natural form of bonding*, where we use the word 'natural' in the sense of 'as given in the Creation'. As such it corresponds to 'a law of nature' and so to a law that cannot be violated so long as it truly is what it claims to be.

Despite the fact that our experience of the Form originates at a level that is more basic than that of language and of logic, it is still possible to explain it and to make it intelligible, so that it is possible to define it, but then only so long as we accommodate the ineffable, or mysterious, element as an indefinable component. This was achieved already by the Scholastics of the Middle Ages, who applied the notion of *intention*, and the more precise concept of *intentionality*, for this purpose: in the present context, it is the intentions of the leader that drive a process of leadership by inducing a more common intention within a social group. This, however, is always realised through a process that is associated with the presence of an ineffable, 'totally other', element that provides, so to say, the binding force of leadership that makes the induction possible. Thus, at a level of generality that itself necessarily verges on the incomprehensible:

The leader is one who imbues a social group with a common intention by linking this social group with an ineffable, totally other element, called leadership, as that which mobilises the Form which makes this process possible.

This element called leadership thus transforms the intentions of the one, the leader, through establishing a relation between the leader and the group, into a something which structures the actions of the others, and so introduces, or even imposes, a *structure of intentionality*, or an *intentional structure*, upon the group. It is because of the ineffability of this 'totally other' that leadership cannot be taught, although it can be identified, encouraged, developed, refined and polished. Thus one cannot 'teach leadership', but one can provide a course in leadership studies: leadership, like mathematics in this respect, "must be caught rather than taught", and that is of the essence of its study.[1]

To every Form there corresponds a specific system of ratiocination, which we call *a logic*, and in the case of leadership this is a *logic of obligation*, that is, it is a *deontic logic*. By this we are not of course saying anything like 'leadership *is* an obligation', which would be incorrect even if it were true in some particular instances, but that:

The logic of leadership is *the logic of* obligation.

By way of simple exemplification suited to the engineer, we may consider the difference between a structure or a mechanism, which in each case is a physical object, and the logic of a structure or the logic of a mechanism, which is a product of the mind that may have a representation, such as in a set of marks on a piece of paper. In the case of the logic of a structure this is a structural analysis that has a central formalism representable through successive differentiations with respect to the distances along the directions of the members of the structure as represented by an algebra of ordinary differential equations, while in the case of the logic of a mechanism it is a logic of geometrical conformity between the links of the mechanism, such as may be represented through a geometry of instantaneous centres.

The serious study of deontic logics goes back at least to the scholastics, but the systematic search for a satisfactory axiom system for deontic logic was initiated only in our own times by the Finnish logician and philosopher Georg Henrik von Wright in 1951, and since that time several systems have been elaborated, and through this effort the understanding of such logics has developed extensively. Thus the possibility of mapping patterns of leadership behaviour into graphical and algebraic representations and thence into computer codes has also been considerably advanced. We shall not enter into such formalisms at all here, only observing that, being deontic, the logic of leadership *is not in itself a logic of preference*, even though it may in its processes of leading appear to proceed through logics of preference – and even though von Wright also wrote a classic on this class of logics too. For example, leadership is almost always transitive, in that if A leads B and B leads C, then A effectively leads C, while preference is commonly not transitive: if A prefers B for a certain position or a certain task and B prefers C for a certain subordinate position or task, it does not follow that A has such a preference for C and indeed he may not accept the preference of B. (Since neither leadership nor preference are symmetric on the other hand, neither satisfies the axioms of an equivalence relation.)

In short: to the extent that the leader is obliged to lead at all, it is in the last analysis through an obligation issuing from his own inner self, and those who are led are obliged by their own inner selves to follow *through the power of leadership in itself*. It is this leadership and nothing else that provides the relation between the self of the leader and the selves of the led: there can be no experience of preference in the case of true leadership. When seen from without, we experience this power as *commitment*.

Thus, to proceed at once to the sublime in exemplification, the historical Jesus of Nazareth, as the archetypal leader, did not take upon himself the obligation of leadership as the Messiah as any kind of preference, and his twelve true disciples did not take on their obligations as a preference for one way over others: there was throughout one and only one way, experienced, essentially gladly, as *an obligation to one's own self* which came to presence in the outer world of name and form as commitment. The thirteenth disciple was the only one subject to a logic of preference, and he chose the pieces of silver, with consequences that are well recorded. It is this property of obligation to one's own self that subsumes the essential mystery of leadership. [2]

We can take this search for the origins of and essential nature of leadership to a greater depth again if we return to the theological, and even more strictly 'spiritual' level of understanding, which necessitates that we read and try to understand those who have used all their faculties in promoting their understanding, which in turn necessitates that we learn how they used certain faculties that are nowadays very little employed, if at all. We have just introduced the natural as 'that given at the Creation', but we have now also to introduce what theologians and other students of the spiritual existence of humans call 'the supernatural'. This has of course nothing whatsoever to do with the common or vulgar use of this term in everyday speech, but with "that which proceeds beyond the Creation, as the intervention of God in the present world". This is obviously open to all manner of misinterpretations and misrepresentations and it requires a very special knowledge, and kind of knowledge, to 'read' such interventions and thus to interpret them correctly. So rare and so uncertain has this 'spiritual knowledge' now become that it is generally discounted in our so-called 'Western' societies - perhaps only Teilhard de Chardin would pass muster in our own time - but it is certain that it did exist even in Europe among some of those whom we still read, so that they become 'the immortals', and that it still persists even today in some societies outside Europe. Accordingly, we can best pass outside our present specifically Christian context if we are to follow this thread of understanding. Thus, from the *Īśā Upaniṣad*, in what still remains its most popular, Purohit and Yeats, English translation:

> Natural knowledge brings one result, supernatural knowledge another. We have heard it from the wise who have clearly explained it.
> They that know and can distinguish between natural knowledge and supernatural knowledge shall, by the first, cross the perishable in safety; shall, by the second, attain immortal life.

At this level then, leadership is *the recognition* in the first place, and thence *the natural acceptance*, in the second place, of the obligation of leadership, as a being-true-to-one's-own-self in one's own situation in one's own time, and the mystery of leadership resides in the leader recognising himself in the places and times - and the places and times recognising themselves, so to say, in the leader. Continuing then, with italics added:

> Then hope for a hundred years doing your duty. No other way can prevent deeds from clinging, proud as you are of your human life.
> They that deny the Self, return after death to a god-less birth, blind, enveloped in darkness...

Chapter 2

> The Self is everywhere, without a body, without a shape, whole, pure, wise, all knowing, far shining, self-depending, transcending; *in the eternal procession assigning to every period its proper duty.*

At this level of understanding then, the mystery of leadership is that which assigns to the leader his proper duty at the appropriate place and time as the natural expression of his most inner self, or 'Self'. It is, again so to say, 'a mystery of integration', and thus belongs to the Form for which the paradigm case is the entire biosphere in all its natural state. Evidently, only someone possessed of supernatural knowledge could ever attain to any kind of understanding of such a mystery. [3]

2.2 The variety in the forms of leadership

One Form commonly provides the one archetype of many different forms, but these forms can in turn be divided into classes in terms of certain similarities that are exhibited within each such class. It is usual to choose one, or at most a few, exemplars from among the class as a way of characterising and even defining the class as a whole. We call these exemplars *paradigm cases* and the class that corresponds to any paradigm case in this way is called a *paradigm*. Since leadership has, or is, a Form, it provides several different paradigms of leadership which in turn characterise the different classes of leadership. We may list some of these in a roughly historical order, as follows:

• The paradigm of the leader who intends (and in this case is intended) to change the behaviour of a social group which is currently governed almost exclusively by ethical norms without true religious faith by himself exemplifying the power of faith over conventional ethical behaviour. The paradigm case here has to be the Biblical and Koranic archetype of Abraham and his 'teleological suspension of the ethical' by his willingness to sacrifice his only and dearly-loved son Isaac at the Word of the Totally Other which was his God.

This Word was not then accepted as one preference over others, but as an obligation to the own self of Abraham. Concerning the mystery of the connection of this exemplar to its archetypal Form, and indeed to their integration, Kierkegaard exclaimed: "Abraham I cannot understand; in a way all that I can learn from him is to be amazed".

• The leader of a people adapted to subjugation in a foreign land who inculcates in this people the intention to revolt against their subjection and leave for a 'Promised Land', and who then leads them to this land. The exemplar is of course the Biblical Moses. The position of Moses as a link between the forms and the Form in this case was expressed by Moses himself when he said that he had attained to *emunach*, which was to say that, following the great Jewish religious existential philosopher and vehement defender of the human rights of Arabs in the State of Israel, Martin Buber, "He was the reliable and consistent messenger for the expression of the commandments and the confirmation of their power. *Emunach* means in this context: reliable signal". To the extent that the people of the biblical Israel experienced this as an obligation, they were assured of leadership, and to the extent that this sense of obligation wavered and preferences appeared within this people this intimation of leadership within them wavered in its turn.

- The messianic leader who imbues his disciples and through them whole peoples with the faith to proceed beyond the accepted interpretation of a prevailing religion and to embrace its total reinterpretation: the figure of the historical Jesus of Nazareth is again the obvious Christian exemplar, but every religion has its own exemplar again of this paradigm. The mystery surrounding the activation of the Form is here most evident.

- The paradigm of a leader who changes the intentions of a wide class of persons in pursuing a particular occupation, as exemplified by the change in attitude towards reading that occurred in the Europe of the XI and XII centuries, from a *monastic reading*, in which the text was sounded either externally by the voice or within the mind internally, to a *scholastic reading*, in which the text was intuited directly without passing through its sounding. An exemplar in this case would be Hugh de St. Victoire, who clearly delineated the mystery that intervened in this process. [4]

- Following closely upon this, in the XIII century, the paradigm of the leader who changed the intentions of persons seeking to understand the world of nature, as exemplified by the individual scholastics who introduced a monotheistic cosmology in place of the polytheistic cosmology that had been bequeathed to European thought by the ancient Greeks, as already introduced in the previous chapter. Henceforth the intention was to find laws that were true of all processes in all places at all times, as revealed by a one and only God, rather than describing the effects of a variety of laws imposed by a variety of gods and goddesses, as again already introduced earlier here. Only such universal laws could be 'natural'. In this case the intrusion of the 'Totally Other' was assured by the predominant influence of the theologians in this process that led to the formation of modern science through the condemnation of the Greek polytheistic cosmology and its Islamic and Judaic ramifications, in 1277.

- The form of the leader who imbues a group to share his intention to describe a particular world of thought in another way: Galileo's development at the beginning of the XVII century of algebraic manipulations in place of geometric constructions in the scientific description and prediction of physical systems provides a paradigm case. Descartes' almost simultaneous publications of his *Discourses*, his *Meditations* and his *Principles* indicated his awareness of the mystery prevailing when reaching back to the Forms behind the forms of modern science, so that he also could be described as a leader in researching the ways of expressing of scientific truth.

- The paradigm of the leader in promoting qualities of leadership in a student body. Franz (von) Brentano shines as an exemplar as he resurrected and refurbished scholastic theories of intentionality within the (Aristotelian) Theory of Forms and introduced other innovations, to develop such students as:

Tomas Masaryk, who designed, implemented and presided over the world's first multi-national democratic republic, in the form of Czechoslovakia;

Sigmund Freud, who established and developed Psychology as an empirical science;

Edmund Husserl, who researched, established and led the philosophical movement of Phenomenology, as one of the two principle branches of philosophy world-wide in the XX century;

Alexius (von) Meinong, who researched, developed and taught the world's first, and still only, unified object-value theory.

And others - great leaders, even if less famous - in several other fields.

- The paradigms of leadership in sociotechnology, with such exemplars as Edison and Bell in the USA. In such cases we have to do with situations in which one and the same Form, of leadership, is in play in two or more environments at one and the same time, providing enabling archetypes for two or more knowledges that have to operate simultaneously and interactively. Thus, from one of the classics on sociotechnology (Law, 1991, p. 9):

> Edison was a 'heterogeneous engineer'. He worked not [only] on physical materials, but [also] on and through people, texts, devices, city councils, architects, economics and the rest. Each of these materials had to be moulded to his design if the system as a whole was to work. And, as a consequence, he travelled between these different domains, weaving an emergent web which constituted and reconstituted the bits and pieces that it brought together.

- A leadership in artistic production that predicts, and even prophesises, the ethos of a future epoch, leading us to the deepest of insights into the future consequences of our continuing human, and in this case all too dehumanised, modes of existence, for which the painter Francis Bacon provided the paradigm case. His cold and pitiless depictions of the extremities of human agony, of the mutilation of the soul expressed through the mortification of the body, of the depths of an utter and complete despair, always of isolated individuals tortured without the presence of any torturer, always enclosed within walls and in some connotations also within cages: all this together burns a searing shaft of awareness through our collective consciousness and into our individual souls. And way beyond and above even all this, albeit proceeding through it, there is the sensation of the terrible generality of its prophetic import. The writer and painter John Berger (*Le Monde Diplomatique*, June 2004) saw the world without pity that Bacon evoked and tried to exorcise as prophetic revelation, whereby the personal drama of the artist could reflect within half a century the crisis of a complete civilisation. "And how? Mysteriously".

This is then *a leadership in understanding*, which in this case is *a comprehending of a future condition of humanity*. The less that compassion is expressed in Bacon's work, the more the consequences of its absence are impressed upon us, so that we come to comprehend those consequences. The great Sir Isaac Newton, one of the most outstanding alchemists of his age, predicted the end of human existence in 2060, and when we view Bacon we comprehend how this now becomes possible, and we may even regard this time estimate as optimistic.

It will then be clear already that there are many forms (with a lower-case 'f') of leadership.

2.3 Leadership and management

Leadership is about providing direction and management is about providing order. 'Direction' and 'order' are clearly two very different things and should never be confused. Nature provides plentiful examples of both, in some of which leadership predominates strongly over management, as occurs in some packs of predators when hunting, and others where management predominates over leadership, as is the case most of the time in ant nests. However leadership and management differ at another level again, in that one cannot have 'self leadership' – which would be a *contradictio in adjecto* - but one can have self management, and most cases of management in nature involve self-management processes which are processes of cooperative action. As has been observed in ant nests, for example, most cooperative activity arises from individuals carrying out simple, repetitive tasks that are genetically programmed, and what we call 'natural selection' has ensured that these combine spontaneously to provide ordered relations and structures of activity. Such relations and structures are then said to be *emergent*. Nature has singularly few managers in the way that human society has, and certainly not in the way that our so-called 'first world' societies appear to be developing, into 'societies composed mainly of (pseudo-) managers'.

Relations and structures are among the most basic Forms of order. In everyday speech, we regard relations in natural and human societies as for the most part pregiven, inherent and even spontaneous arrangements that are as a consequence usually only hierarchised by custom and usage. The paradigm case is the relation of hereditary, of family, as we normally experience this in our so-called 'Western' societies today. In this particular case it is clear that, in more technical terms, the relations are reflexive, symmetric and transitive: A is related to A; if A is related to B then B is related to A; and if A is related to B and B is related to C then A is related to C. This then constitutes what we have mentioned earlier here as an equivalence relation. On the other hand, other forms of relation do not constitute equivalence relations: for example in the case of ancestry, A cannot be an ancestor of A, if A is an ancestor of B then B cannot be an ancestor of A, but still if A is an ancestor of B and B an ancestor of C then A is an ancestor of C. Social structures, on the other hand, are commonly regarded as more codified, more socially organised and more directed arrangements which are often strongly hierarchised. Thus, for example, in a company hierarchy, it is common that A reports to B and B reports to C, but A does not report to C, C does not report to A or B and B does not report to A: to the extent that we can apply these more technical terms at all, structures are normally irreflexive, asymmetric and intransitive.

Among the most important of the forms of these two Forms from the present point of view are those of power relations and power structures on the one hand, and knowledge relations and knowledge structures on the other hand. In many situations power and knowledge are so intertwined that it is usual to speak only of knowledge/power relations and knowledge/power structures. The forms of power are however often still further divided into a power derived from an established authority (where we might perhaps better speak of 'power/knowledge') and a power derived from influence based upon superior knowledge (where 'knowledge/power' appears to be more appropriate). Most, and indeed nearly all, social organisations possess all of these forms to a greater or lesser degree, functioning simultaneously. However, the predominance of a power derived from authority over a power derived from influence based upon superior knowledge is then associated with an organisational structure that can be described as an *exostructure*, while a power derived more from an influence based upon superior knowledge provides what can then be described as an *endostructure*. Exostructures are then defined by an authority, such as a board of directors and its executive officers, while endostructures are scarcely 'defined' at all, but emerge spontaneously from the work processes proceeding within the organisation. Then not only do almost all organisations have both structures functioning simultaneously, but also functioning interactively. If, however, the exostructure comes to dominate over the endostructure to such a degree as to inhibit the operations of this endostructure, *the organisation will demands the constant attention of a larger number of managers that will in turn feed the exostructure further*. If, on the other hand, the endostructure dominates over the exostructure, *the organisation will become more autonomously managed, or 'self-managed', requiring an even smaller exostructure and ever fewer managers.*

Organisations that are predominantly exostructured are ordered by the *fiat* of their management, usually with relatively rigid organisational structures. The reactions to a changing environment of such organisations must be planned, transmitted, codified and organised by their management and, to the extent that these often involve changes in the management structure through reorganisations and restructurings, these changes must again be implemented by their managers. Organisations that are predominantly endostructured, on the other hand, are constantly reordering and reforming themselves so as to adapt to the changing environment of the organisation. They are constantly *evolving* new working relations that can better react to the exigencies of the organisation's environment. In predominantly exostructured organisations, working arrangements are *imposed* by management, while in more endostructured organisations working arrangements *emerge* from the interactions of the persons who are actually carrying out the work. Endostructures are essentially emergent structures, and it is in this sense that they are, in a traditional-technical sense to be defined shortly, *anarchistic*, and even, but in a very different and specifically modern-scientific sense, *chaotic*. We have only introduced predominately exostructured and predominately endostructured organisations here and we shall return to discuss the manner in which most organisations contain both in the next section.

Endostructured organisations necessitate the constant attention of good leadership, while exostructures, once established, can continue to exist for some time even in the absence of any real leadership at all. It is indeed very common that organisations fall into the hands of persons who, although occupying the positions and titles of leaders, have little or no real leadership capabilities, and organisations most commonly fail through this process. The process itself usually occurs through what is colloquially called 'politicking', which may proceeds in many ways, such as through ingratiation, flattery, obsequiousness and other such means on the one hand and through the withholding of vital information, the encouragement of incorrect decision-making on the part of 'competitors' and subsequent behind-the-back denigration on the other hand, all directed towards those deciding upon the succession. In order avoid an exposure of the resulting ongoing process of failure, the resulting pseudo-leaders are obliged to establish exostructures even where there were previously none, and for this purpose they need to introduce persons who are entirely under their control within all decision-making parts of the organisation. For this purpose, competent managers would be a nuisance, since they would rail against the incompetence, indifference, dishonesty and generally destructive behaviour of such pseudo-leaders, while true leaders would certainly subvert whatever the pseudo-leaders decided in order to save what could still be saved of the productions and good name of the organisation - just so long as they had any power to do so. Thus the only possibility is to 'parachute-in' incompetent managers *above* the potential leaders and to displace or otherwise remove competent managers, most of whom will anyway usually leave of their own accord in such situations. Being so patently incompetent, the pseudo-managers are totally dependent on the pseudo-leaders for their jobs and will therefore do whatever is required of them unquestioningly.

(It should be observed at this point, although it is a sidetrack, that there is in fact a vital difference between incompetent managers and inauthentic managers even though both are pseudo-managers, in that the first is a mere pawn in the hands of the pseudo-leader while the second is just as much a menace to the pseudo-leader as he is to the organisation as a whole. The inauthentic manager, and in this respect like the inauthentic leader that we shall introduce later here, is one who is in the hands of nothingness, with all the resources of nothingness as well as its self-destructive capacities. Such a person, and once again whether as manager or as leader, often has the psychological profile of a psychopath, but it cannot be our purpose here to discuss pathologies.)

We can better return to the point that what has changed so decisively over the last decade is the possibility to strengthen self-organising relations that constantly adapt themselves to changing market and other conditions by using greatly improved computational and communication facilities. Without these new facilities, the possibilities inherent in endostructured organisations would not be realisable, since their 'anarchistic' and even in a certain restricted sense 'chaotic' behaviour would make their behaviour unpredictable and inherently unstable. The task of developing and installing the *sociotechnical arrangements* necessary to instantiate these facilities, however, remains for the most part as a challenge that has still to be faced. This task will then call in the very first place for a much improved leadership, being one that leads the organisation in ways to provide higher levels of *self-management* of productive, distributive and other functions, that is, a management *by* the persons who are actually carrying out these functions. In the limit – a limit scarcely to be attained in practice today however - such an organisation would come to employ no full-time 'professional' managers at all. Several writers on management practice have presaged this development, such as Warren Bennis (as with Bert Nanus, 1985, and separately, 1989) while there have been some outstanding works decrying the excesses of pseudo-management, but all of these appear to look at leadership, and management also, 'from the outside in', while the purpose here is more directed to looking 'from the inside out'. Thus Bennis defines leadership as "the capacity to create a compelling vision and to translate this into action and sustain it", which is often the way that leadership presents itself *to us when we observe it*, while here we are concerned with the sources of leadership; its 'why' and its 'how', *as it comes to presence within the person of the leader himself* and, inseparably from this, *within the persons he leads*. As Husserl long since demonstrated, such an investigation cannot be treated psychologically, but necessitates the application of a phenomenology and, as became increasingly clear over the last century, this must

Chapter 2

proceed through a study of the nature of human existence itself, as an existentialism, whether of the philosophical or the theological variety.[4]

The exploitation of advances in information and communication technologies, and of the developments in sociotechnology necessary to realise endostructured organisations, constitutes the greatest business opportunity and the greatest leadership challenge of our present age. The possibilities have already been adumbrated by a variety of partly endostructured companies, such as certain low-cost operators in the air travel market and even Harley Davidson, the motor-cycle manufacturer, recently described in the FT (13.05.04) as a unique partnership where dialogue and disclosure have replaced command and control whereby significant decisions are taken by committees controlled by shop-floor employees, but these initiatives constitute for the most part only the first, faltering, pragmatic steps. None the less, most exostructured organisations in business today are now becoming every bit as vulnerable to this kind of challenge, as exemplified by the problems experienced by the to-date established air travel market operators, and indeed these kinds of organisations are becoming ever more vulnerable by the day. This oncoming 'sea change' in the nature of business operations is then just as well one of the great business opportunities of our times, and indeed from a narrow business point of view it could even be seen as a *raison d'être* for the European Institute for Industrial Leadership itself.

2.4 The concepts of direct and indirect leadership and their regular and irregular forms

Direct leadership proceeds primarily through *direct person-to-person(s) communication of intentions* (through orders, persuasion, actions, etc) while indirect leadership proceeds primarily through the leader *creating situations* whereby other persons are led in a direction desired by the leader. Direct leadership and indirect leadership can well be, and even in many cases should be, provided by one and the same person. Thus, for example, Ingvar Kamprad, the founder and sole owner of IKEA, by far the world's largest furniture supplier, has long provided both kinds of leadership. On the one side he has provided direct leadership through his decisions, his point-of-sale visits, his inspiring contact with staff on all levels, his personal simple life and his obvious total commitment to the organisation and all who work with it and for it. This direct form of leadership extends further to IKEA's many subcontractors. At the same time, however, and inseparably from his exercise of direct leadership within the organisation, Ingvar Kamprad has provided, and continues to provide, a powerful indirect leadership to IKEA's customers, who thereby themselves provide the delivery and assembly systems for IKEA's do-it-yourself kits. He has achieved this by creating an undifferentiated wholesale/retail trading operation which leads tens of millions of people to acquire their furniture in a new way. The technical innovations that IKEA has introduced – its design of easily assembled kits, its vast showrooms with on-line (intranetted) ordering and sales facilities, the range of trolleys that it provides to customers to transport their various sizes of purchases, its customer-orientated warehousing arrangements, its specially designed payment facilities, its large parking areas and ready sales of suitable roof racks, its restaurant and child-play facilities, its after-sales service centres, etc – are inseparable from the social innovations which these provide and with which they interact. Indeed, it is these facilities that catalyse the new social-organisational arrangement, and it is in this sense that IKEA is *a quintessentially socio-technical system*. The social-organisational innovations that IKEA has realised together constitute a new attitude towards home furnishing in general, being one in which the public joins with IKEA in *a new social contract*: IKEA will supply the means to furnish the home, and its customers, the home owners themselves, will take over the delivery and assembly functions. It is at this point that preference passes over into obligation – the customers take upon themselves the obligation, expressed as a commitment, to transport and assemble the furniture packs – so that it is at this point that leadership is exercised. The savings in costs as compared with commercial delivery and assembly operations are then passed over to a large extent to the customers, which provides a preference which again strengthens the commitment that is the expression of obligation. This obviously also provides substantial reductions in the tax payments that would be otherwise levied on these services, such as would otherwise be passed on to the customers, which provides another preference that transforms into commitment as the outer form of obligation. This social side of Ingvar Kamprad's leadership is thus realised by his *creating a situation* – the technical infrastructure that is the physical IKEA – that catalyses a change in attitude, initiated through a change in preferences, towards home furnishing, but this transforms into a new social contract between IKEA and the home-owning public, and so into a new kind of obligation/commitment. We observe that whereas the direct leadership extends over the some 120,000 persons employed by or through IKEA, the indirect leadership extends over some tens of millions of people. We observe also that alongside its internal, intranetted, communications systems, IKEA operates the largest external marketing-communication system in the world, in the form of printing and distributing 140,000,000 copies of its annual brochures in some 40 languages – another world record again. This *simply-connected* or *broadcast mode* of communication is one of the defining manifestations of regular indirect leadership.

This first example, of IKEA, may now be used to introduce the following principles of direct and indirect leadership and their further subdivisions:

1. Direct leadership is most immediately associated with organisational structures that are defined and regulated from within the organisation itself. They are often hierarchical and have already been introduced as *exostructures*. We now further observe however that, functioning rather like exoskeletons in natural organisms, it is these that give form to the body of the organisation. Like exoskeletons in this analogy, once established they provide genetically-defined and thus totally-ordered biological forms. Exostructures then, like exoskeletons, can only be changed, or 'reengineered', by more or less painful destructive/creative processes of 'restructuring'. We sometimes describe them as 'brittle', being hard but easily fractured by shocks from their environment.

2. The kind of leadership that functions most obviously in exostructured organisations, being one that is regulated by fiat from within these organisations and proceeds through direct communication, may now be introduced as a *regular direct leadership*. As introduced already, it commonly proceeds on the basis of an authority conferred upon the leader by the organisation's hierarchy and it proceeds through the giving of orders whereby anyone disobeying these orders will be disciplined through the

actions of the hierarchy. As constantly recalled here, however, alongside this kind of leadership there is quite commonly another kind of leadership again which is at work within even the outwardly most exostructured of organisations, this being one that is established more by influence than by authority, which we may now introduce as an *irregular direct leadership* which, if suppressed, may become an *irregular indirect leadership*. This is, again, associated with a structure of influence within the organisation that is based more upon knowledge than upon administrative power, so that it is usually less hierarchical, less well defined and less ordered. This is then, of course, also an endostructure.

3. The greatest exostructures of all time were those of the former Soviet Union and its fellow 'command economies' in Central and Eastern Europe. These were so tightly organised in most places and among one another that their endostructures came to work primarily against the economical interests espoused by these same exostructures. Some parts of the regular direct 'leadership' of these exostructured organisations often at one and the same time came together in endostructures to form 'cliques' and worked to subvert the declared objectives of the exostructure, thereby becoming simultaneously something more in the nature of irregular indirect leaders. Under the stress of exploiting rapidly developing technologies and the resulting need for rapid sociotechnical transformation, these exostructures could not restructure with sufficient rapidity and consequently fractured through whole economies and across these economies, leading to what is called in complex-system theory 'a common-mode failure'. This was a failure of regular direct leadership on the largest scale ever, even as some of the individual leaders had also become irregular indirect leaders at the time of failure, and it was a failure that was inherent in the system itself. From a point of view that we shall develop later here, this failure can be associated with an active suppression of entrepreneurial initiatives, whereby when the common-mode failure did finally occur, the entrepreneurial forces that were latent within the societies, and had self-organised themselves into endostructures that had simultaneously penetrated into the exostructures, were capable of taking over almost all the industries of the societies concerned as their own private property. Their leaders then transformed back from irregular indirect leaders to regular direct leaders again.

4. Then, to return to the biological analogy, very much as organisms with endoskeletons are more flexible and nimble, both in their everyday existence and in their adaptation to changing environmental conditions, endostructures are generally more adaptable, and thus more resilient, to their changing sociotechnical environments. Endostructures are forever restructuring themselves. In the same vein, much as organisms with endoskeletons depend upon more complex and highly interactive nervous systems for their survival, so endostructures depend for their sustainability upon highly developed internal and external communications systems. Their basic mode of communication is then that of *broadband*, that is, that which provides *multiply connected* communication. No one necessarily 'reports to' anyone in this kind of structure: there is a natural interdependency between all the parts. Leadership here is regular and indirect, and this naturally places a greatly increased emphasis on

human understanding, on empathy and compassion, on solicitude and on other values that are of a spiritual nature. We repeat: endostructures are self-organising structures that emerge spontaneously within almost every organisation but which demand very different qualities of leadership than do exostructured organisations.

As a first example of a specific irregular indirect leader in the field of military sociotechnology, we may take the case of (the later Sir) Basil Liddell Hart, who became the principle British military historian and contemporary critic of military affairs over several decades. Although not actually 'in' the organisation – as one British general acerbically remarked, "Captain Hart does not occupy a room in the War Office" – he led most thinking in military matters, even though his books and articles had the greatest influence in Germany despite his every effort to influence military opinion in Britain. He saw the effect that a combination of technical advances in armoured vehicles, aviation, radio and other fields would have on the prosecution of war and proposed new organisational forms, tactics and strategies correspondingly. As adopted in Germany, his ideas led to the rapid disintegration of the enemies of Germany in 1939 and 1940 in Continental Europe, leaving Britain alone and isolated after the collapse of her last ally, Greece, in May, 1941 – until the 'Great Coalition' led by Germany attacked the then Soviet Union on 22 June 1941 and the outcome of the war was effectively decided elsewhere. In fact, a major part of British preparations for war in the 1930s proceeded through irregular indirect leadership, such as in the development of much more advanced aircraft, new kinds of aircraft engines, new kinds of propellers, entirely new radar equipment and other advances, and without these Britain would have almost certainly succumbed.

Laurence of Arabia was another and more colourful example, being distinctly irregular in the eyes of most of his British military contemporaries and having scarcely any leadership role at all. For the Arabs, on the other hand, his leadership was regular and direct. Both Hart and Laurence were capable of great compassion and human understanding - and spoke their minds correspondingly – so that they could never become regular in the British army.

We can now make a clearer distinction between *regular and irregular indirect leadership*. The first is that which originates within the exostructure of the organisation, even though it generates an endostructure outside the organisation. The example of Ingvar Kamprad's leadership of IKEA's *'customers = transporters = assemblers'* has already provided an obvious example of regular indirect leadership. This form of leadership also has the property that *it can lead the competition into ruinous courses of action*, and then not at all by deceit, but by exploiting weaknesses in the competitor's own leadership. The best examples and case studies are those of the self-destruction of the indigenous electronics, motor and shipbuilding industries in the UK as induced by the strategies of their competitors - and the subsequent appropriation of the best UK staff by these competitors.

(Another, rather more amusing example, from my own personal experience, arose when it became clear that our company's bids for a string of studies in a particular country were being passed back to the local competitor: his bids were consistently just a shade below our own. We accordingly put in lower and lower bids for each contract, hoping more and more of course that our bids would not be accepted, which indeed they never were because our competitor continued to undercut us as a matter of prestige in protecting his home market. The local competitor must have lost an awful lot of money and been weakened substantially in this way! Such 'tricks' are not recommended of course, being deleterious for the industry as a whole, as will be explained in the concluding section of the present work.)

We are left with irregular indirect leadership: the stuff of spontaneous mass movements, of mass protests, of revolts and revolutions - and the very apotheosis of endostructure. Leadership is always an emergent phenomenon – it is in some sense genetic but only comes to presence in certain life situations - but in the case of irregular indirect leadership this coming to presence is often spontaneous, and even quite unexpected by those who become leaders. Although unexpected, it is always accepted. Abraham provides the archetype of the irregular indirect leader in his own time and place, just as Moses provided the archetype of the regular direct leader. The true disciples of Jesus who subsequently became apostles and thus the prototypes of the regular direct leaders of the Christian Church, provide a range of twelve very different examples of irregular indirect leaders when seen within the context of the time of their 'apprenticeship' as disciples. As introduced above, irregular indirect leadership in such an exalted sphere is never sought, but it is still always accepted, essentially gladly, as an obligation and as an article of faith indivisibly. This is something that we cannot hope to comprehend, and neither to understand, but only to accept.

Irregular indirect leadership is observed at the Kierkegaardian 'level of the aesthetic' also: many poets, painters, musicians, novelists and others may serve as examples. The example of the painter Francis Bacon has been presented as a paradigm case earlier here. More generally speaking, the 'leading of taste' commonly proceeds from persons who are in some sense 'outsiders' to the artistic and general cultural establishment of their times and 'only' influence their environment through their works, and even then quite commonly posthumously. Kierkegaard, Schopenhauer and Nietzsche provide specific paradigms of irregular indirect leadership in philosophy and theology that developed its endostructure, of phenomenologist and existentialist philosophical and theological movements, long after their deaths. Industrial development also has had its share of 'unsung heroes' who were irregular within their own time and only had their say much later. Some subsequently became regular, such as Whittle in the case of the jet engine and Watson Watt in the case of radar, but most remain forgotten outside of a few small circles of industrial historians. [5]

2.5 Anarchistic systems and chaotic systems

The very word 'anarchy' has had all manner of pejorative connotations from the seventeenth century onwards, but any treatment of leadership today must treat anarchistic systems seriously and dispassionately in their own right. This is because these systems have become particularly relevant over the last decade as a result of the current and still ongoing rapid developments in information and communication technologies and, even more significant, their sociotechnologies. It is these developments that are again making anarchistic arrangements, as sociotechnical constructs, viable and increasingly attractive, and not least in industry. The so-called 'open source' movement in software production, such as has produced the Linux Kernel (that in turn drives the most powerful challenge to the Microsoft quasi-monopoly of operating systems) provides a paradigm case to which we shall subsequently return. Clearly, such anarchistic systems pose their own opportunities as well as their own problems for future leaders.

Derived from a Greek word signifying 'without a rule', the word 'anarchy' was first applied within and to Stoic philosophy at the time of the ancient Greeks. From its origins it then also had the connotation of 'without a ruler', so that the essence of anarchism has always been that it is *antiauthoritarian*. Now although authority is usually regarded as something inseparable from leadership in the context of military affairs, it is remarkable that in his highly influential *On the Psychology of Military Incompetence*, Dixon (1976) has shown, following well established precedents in psychology generally, that it is precisely the character trait of *the authoritarian personality* that has been mostly associated with *incompetent* leadership. Possibly more surprisingly still to those uninitiated in such psychological studies, Dixon showed that authoritarianism was at variance not only with humanitarian, but also with disciplinarian traits. Thus (ibid. p. 275):

> Certainly such great leaders as Wolfe, Wellington, Shaka, Lawrence, Monash and Montgomery not only displayed a general absence of authoritarian traits but also showed a lively regard for the prime responsibility of a commander: conservation of his forces and the psychological and physical welfare of his troops. As Trevelyan wrote of Wellington, 'It is fortunate for Britain that Wellington was at once a great humanitarian and a great disciplinarian'.

In order to view anarchism more clearly, we may follow the excellent *Encyclopaedia Britannica* entry on this subject in identifying its basic tenets as being those of *mutualism* between participants (i.e. the recognition of mutual interests and the provision of mutual support), of *federalism* (i.e. the formation of a federal structure between the participants, such as may be provided by a syndicate) and of *direct action* (i.e. the direct involvement of this federation/syndicate in processes occurring in society and the world of nature). Civil rights movements, human rights movements, environmental movements, peace movements and most non-governmental organisations then fall under this category, and indeed the European Institute for Industrial Leadership can itself be regarded as anarchistic in this broader sense. The traditional university, which endured in Europe from the twelfth into the second half of the twentieth century and still survives in a few places even today, provides another example.[6]

One of the most determining features of any anarchistic organisation, as a self-organising and self-managing system, is that *it is held together by a shared ethic*. Now, among most so-called 'higher' animals – those with endoskeletons and highly developed nervous systems – codes of social behaviour which approximate ethics are inculcated for a large part by the playing of games, and of course this applies to human societies as well. Current research into means to inculcate ethical norms into sociotechnical systems accordingly attach great importance to inducing habits of secondary reflection and other promoters of intersubjectivity by introducing Internet-based games (e.g. Jonoski, 2003). Now the essential point about such present-day anarchistic movements as that of open source software development, as exemplified by the GNU/Linux system development, is that *such a development is itself a game, with all of its participants functioning as players*.

Thus, *the ethics necessary to support such a mode of development are self-generating and self-sustaining.*

Another, but already well established feature of anarchistic systems, and particularly of anarchosyndicalist systems, is that they are abhorrent of bureaucracy. The most cited example is that of the Spanish *Confederacion Nacional del Trabajo*, which had some 2,000,000 members in 1936 while employing only one paid secretary!

If they are to be at all sustainable, anarchistic systems necessitate what the poet and critic Herbert Read (1968) described as "a process of individuation, accomplished by general education and personal discipline". However, whatever their general education and personal discipline, such systems have been regularly destroyed by authoritarian regimes and their ideologies: bolshevism was at one with fascism and nazism in its uncompromising and thoroughly brutal suppression of anarchistic movements. An analysis of the success of these suppressions shows however that they only succeeded because the authoritarian regimes had definite socio*technical* advantages over the anarchistic organisations. What is changing in our own time is that the technical means to maintain anarchistic organisations is strengthening by the day through the development of communication technologies, so that, to the extent that the sociotechnology can keep pace with this development, this suppression must meet with an ever stronger and more tenacious resistance - and this resistance to repression must increasingly prevail.

Writers on the subject of anarchism and anarchistic movements have strongly emphasised that anarchism is the antithesis of chaos, and in this they draw upon the wellspring of anarchism, which is the understanding that creativity is always driven by that covenant of the spirit that we call *love*. This theme runs through all the great writers on anarchism: Winstanley, Godwin, Proudhon, Bakunin, Krapotkin, Tolstoy, Ghandi, and so many others. All religions are at one in declaring that it is only with love that anything of any lasting value can be created: "Unless the Lord buildeth the house, its builders work in vain". Thus, what we call 'anarchism' is an essential component in any creative endeavour, and it is surely for that reason that works on anarchism have appealed so strongly to artists of all kinds. To return to the *Encyclopaedia* article:

> [The principles of anarchism] lingered on in the traditions of English Protestant sects and reached their ultimate flowering in the masterpiece of...William Godwin, who in 1793 published his *Social Justice*...
> Goodwin enjoyed great celebrity in the 1790s and influenced such writers as Percy Bysshe Shelley (whose Queen Mab and Prometheus Unbound are virtually anarchistic poems). William Wordsworth, William Hazlitt, and Robert Owen....
> During the 1890s, especially in France, Anarchism was adopted as a philosophy by avant-garde painters and writers. Gustave Courbet had already been a disciple of Proudhon; among those who in the 1890s accepted an Anarchistic philosophy were Camille, Pissaro, Georges Surat, Paul Signat, Paul Adam, Octave Mirabeau, Laurant Tailhade, and, at least as a strong sympathiser, Stéphane Mallarmé. At the same time in England, Oscar Wilde declared himself an Anarchist and, under Kropotkin's inspiration, wrote a libertarian essay: 'The Soul of Man under Socialism' in 1891.

Thus the most misused and abused of all words, *love*, was recognised in anarchism as the source of all creation and thereby the antithesis of all chaos, but this was essentially also a rediscovery of a profound truth of the kind that is always of the essence of the ancient Greek myths, which in this case tells us that Eros, the god of love and fertility, was the son of the god Chaos, as his compensating progeny. Such forms of language as the myths are archetypal and recur incessantly. In the words of Carey (2002):

> We are the children of transience: our imaginations cannot grasp eternity. That is why myths – those events which, in the words of the philosopher Sallustius, 'never were, and always are' - are said to have happened 'once upon a time', when in truth they exist beyond all time. The error of [Western] fundamentalism lies in its attempt to crush the symbol, to freeze and flatten the archetypal deeds of myth into the schematic chronology of history books. It is idolatry.

We cannot enter further into such depths here, although we shall discuss these matters in the EIIL Courses where we shall analyse the reification of this myth and some others in modern science. We shall then see, for example, that in a biology founded upon information theory and thermodynamics, natural creation itself is regarded as the formation of 'entropy-bending structures' providing ever longer 'detours to death', where entropy is itself employed as a universal measure of disorder, including that associated with chaotic phenomena. Creation, as the struggle between Eros and Thanatos in the Greek myths, then becomes resurrected in and through the language of quantum chemistry (e.g. Monod, 1970).

It must then appear that although anarchistic organisations appear as antithetical to chaos, they must also have a close, and indeed the closest of relations to chaos, as the overcoming of chaos, and certain more recent developments within chaos theory also support this view, suggesting that this theory is able to provide the means to study how organisational structures may be expected to emerge and dissolve in self-managing, anarchistic systems within certain sociotechnical environments and at what rates these processes of coalescence and dissolution may occur, or may already be occurring. Chaos itself is then understood in the modern-scientific sense as covering situations in which, although we cannot ourselves discern any order in these situations directly, we may process measurements to arrive at meaningful descriptions of underlying orders that have emerged through interactions occurring within the processes. Thus the possibility arises to identify organisational structures as they are emerging and transforming and passing away again within anarchistic systems. This possibility opens other perspectives again for analysing, designing, constructing and leading self-managed working environments. Of course, the techniques of chaos theory so far provide no more than an instrumentalism – they contain no knowledge-discovery environments - but even with this restricted functionality, chaos theory still has its own utility (e.g. Ababarnel, 1996).

2.6 An existential-philosophical view of the prehistoric origins of leadership

From an existentialist-philosophical point of view, leadership is a calling, and this is a calling from within and a calling from without, so that it is only when there is a conjunction between these callings, including their synchronisation, that true leadership becomes possible. The objective of the EIIL is then to develop a capacity to recognise and analyse situations where leadership is required and to evolve the modes of leadership best suited to each situation. Clearly, it is then necessary to provide an education in leadership suited to a wide variety of kinds of leadership, and then within each kind to promote the innate capacity of each individual for independent thought and action in the exercise of that particular kind of leadership. The theoretical and philosophical core of the Institute's courses of study and exercise is thus intended to excite the interest, strengthen the will and deepen the understanding of situations and events occurring in the world when determining the forms of leadership that are most appropriate to these situations and events. For this purpose it is necessary to provide a raft of theory and a rudder of philosophy whereby the leader can navigate the rapids of industrial business activity more effectively. The central theoretical and philosophical core then also provides the backbone to the course provided by the Institute as a whole, linking with and holding together all its other activities. [7]

We have earlier here identified the origins of leadership in the observed existing behaviour of animals, and especially in the behaviour of our fellow primates, but it then follows from this that leadership must predate the very existence of *Homo sapiens*; it is older than human Being so that, in respect to humanity, it is in its essence *pre-ontological*. These 'primitive' forms of leadership already serve to link categories of leadership with types of social structures, including hierarchies. Salient features are those of divisions between tactical and strategic leadership of both territorial and migrating populations, between leadership by virtue of strength and agility and leadership by virtue of experience, knowledge and wisdom, and between leadership in tactics of phenotype survival and strategies of genotype survival, including sacrificial strategies. Such characteristics of leadership as its circumspective concern (the Heideggerian *umsichtig Besorgen*), its empathy (*Einfühlung*) and its solicitude (*Führsorge*) also appear clearly here. In this sense we might even speak of a *palaeontology of leadership*.

There is then further to this an *archaeology of leadership* which, among other findings, emphasises how authoritarian leadership has always been associated with, and indeed legitimised by 'superhuman' accomplishments, often associated with magical practices that were increasingly subsumed under religious practices which imitated the magical in order to transcend it (e.g. Moses' staff-cum-snake that ate up all the staff-cum-snakes of Pharaoh's magicians).

The *myths* of ancient times were not intended to project the *realities* of leadership, but their *idealities*: we repeat, "They never were, but always are". These myths probed the depths of the collective unconscious of the times of the ancient Greeks in their search for essences, including the essences of leadership in a world whose religious forces were faltering, and which was therefore seeking new, but still necessarily divine, inspiration. Prometheus, as he stole fire from the gods for the benefit of man, provided the tragic-heroic ideal of such a leader, providing the ancient Greek prototype of what has already been introduced as irregular indirect leadership. This is also, as already adumbrated through Shelley's great poem, the prototype of the anarchic leader. Since the collective unconscious of the times of the ancient Greeks was not so very different to that of our own times in Europe, these myths maintain their relevance to this day: "They always are".

From our current standpoint of leadership, Homer stands supreme in his delineations of leadership in the form of *legends* and *sagas*, and especially in *The Trojan Wars*, and then, within that work again, in *The Odyssey*. The leaders in Homer, and especially Ulysses, become steadily more real and less ideal: in the legends and sagas the story takes increasingly the form of the *epic*, as the celebration of the adventures of some heroic personage of contemporary history or tradition. The increasing relevance and refinement of astrology later in this period provided new insights into the forces guiding the 'destiny' of the heroic leader, whereby this leader became increasingly a *tragic-heroic leader*. This model of leadership has never been entirely supplanted by the modern scientific point of view, as demonstrated by the histories of such *inauthentic leaders* as Napoleon and Hitler, where the nature of this inauthenticity will be introduced later here.

Histories of leaders are legion, covering all possible fields of human endeavour and all manner of forms of leadership. Although, unlike the myths, legends and sagas, histories ostensibly proceed exclusively in chronological time, histories of leadership still necessarily contain the residues of myth, legend and saga written, so to say, 'between the lines' of the historical text, and so out of chronological time. Some histories, regarded as 'Grand Narratives', will be used in the EIIL course in order to illustrate the limited historicity of leadership alongside these historiographical aspects.

3 The taxonomies of leadership and their association with the taxonomies of power structures and knowledge relations

Let us start here with some recapitulation. We have earlier distinguished between *direct* and *indirect* leadership. We saw that direct leadership proceeds primarily through *direct person-to-person(s) communication* (orders, persuasions, actions, etc.) while indirect leadership proceeds primarily through the leader *creating situations* whereby other persons, usually outside the organisation itself, are led in a leader-desired direction. We took as paradigm case the person of Ingvar Kamprad and we saw how, through his very obviously *direct leadership* of his employees and the technical infrastructure which they install and operate, he has *created a situation* whereby he *indirectly leads* tens of millions of people outside the company to take over the furniture transport and assembly functions of his business within what is, essentially, a new kind of social contract experienced as an obligation.

Just to recapitulate further, we saw that direct leadership is most immediately associated with organisational structures that are defined and regulated from within the company itself and we called such an *organisationally empowered* leadership *regular direct leadership*. We saw also how indirect leadership can also originate from within the organisational structure, as just indicated, and in this case we speak of *regular indirect leadership*. Even in the most strictly organised and hierarchical of organisations, however, we observed how knowledge relations develop between groups of individuals within the organisation such that some individuals come to exercise influence within these groups:

they thus come to exercise *regular indirect leadership* if they are tolerated by the hierarchy and *irregular indirect leadership* otherwise within the organisation as a whole. In other cases again, however, we exemplified how a leader who does not originate from within the organisation itself, but from outside it, may have a major and even decisive *influence* on an organisation - such as by writing about it and so 'creating a situation' - while being himself no part of that organisation, thereby providing *irregular indirect leadership*. As we saw, however, this form of leadership may well transform into a *regular direct leadership* as this leader's theories and prophetic utterances transform into realities.

As also already introduced, specific categories of leadership are associated with specific kinds of organisational structures. We have seen how regular direct leadership is almost invariably associated with what we have called *exostructures*. By using an analogy with exoskeletons in natural organisms, we saw how these define the form of the organisation and its internal workings through establishing what are essentially *power structures* that commonly take the forms of hierarchies. Thus, exostructures, once established, provide institutionally defined and totally-ordered organisational arrangements. Exostructured organisations then, like creatures with exoskeletons, can only be changed to meet new environmental conditions by more or less painful destructive/creative processes of 'restructuring'.

By way of contrast we have indicated how irregular leadership, and especially the irregular indirect form of leadership, are associated much more with what are called *endostructures*, these being less hierarchical, less well defined and less ordered. Very much as organisms with endoskeletons are more flexible and nimble, both in their everyday existence and in their adaptation to changing environmental conditions as we saw earlier, endostructures are more adaptable, and thus more resilient, to their changing sociotechnical environments. Endostructures are for ever restructuring themselves in response to the changing demands placed upon them. Rather as creatures with endoskeletons usually depend upon highly developed nervous systems for their survival, so endostructures depend upon highly developed internal and external *communication systems* for their sustainability. Having emergent structures defined by their own interactions subject to their external environment, they are for the most part *self-management systems*. As we also intimated, even the most highly exostructured, hierarchical, organisations also have endostructures, so that an irregular, and usually indirect, leadership based upon knowledge/influence coexists with the 'official' regular direct leadership of the organisation.

On this basis, we can proceed to introduce orderings that can be spatialised so as to introduce a *leadership space* as a place where we can trace the changing nature of forms of leadership as trajectories within the space, and in this way also we can construct a *taxonomy*. Proceeding through its legendary and Biblical-historical development, the space of leadership mapped within this taxonomy is *spanned* between Abraham, situated in the one corner in both legendary and Biblical-historical terms, as the archetypal irregular indirect leader, and Moses, situated in the other corner, and again in both legendary and Biblical-historical terms, as the archetypal regular direct leader.

The space defined by this simplest of taxonomies of leadership can be conveniently represented in the form of a table with two rows, corresponding to the regular and irregular forms of leadership, and two columns, corresponding to the direct and indirect forms. All the above features, and more, can be assigned places in a table of this kind and the focus of a particular leader can be traced in time by points associated with particular times and by arrows joining these points (Figure 1). The corresponding power structures of exostructures and knowledge relations of endostructures can be introduced similarly.

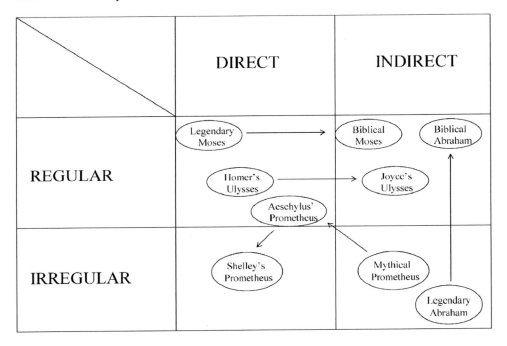

Figure 1

Clearly other and much more extended taxonomies can be generated by introducing further divisions in categories of leadership. Basic differences between tactical and strategic leadership and oppositions between authentic and inauthentic leadership can be introduced into another or an extended leadership space. In particular, the role of *ideology* in the formation of inauthentic leadership, whereby it is the ideology that really does the leading and *the nominal 'leader' is merely a cipher possessed by this ideology*, may be introduced. The 'great dictators' of the first part of the twentieth century provide paradigm cases, but much more cogent today are the still ongoing subversions of *modern science* and of *management* into ideologies, and a particular attention needs to be given to these inauthentic forms. Once again, however, it is the exceptional business opportunities presented by such subversions for well-led organisations that need to be emphasised, discouraging any morbid interest in the pathologies of the processes of subversion themselves.

There remains one further subdivision however which we have not so far so much as mentioned, which is that between *male leadership* and *female leadership*. This division cuts, so to say, orthogonally across every other coordinate in the space of leadership. It is for this reason that we could so far use only the masculine form, ubiquitously, so that while referring to 'he' and 'his' explicitly, we were always simultaneously referring to 'she' and 'her' implicitly: there is little difference between men and women in the forms so far considered. However, although it may be impolitic to say so, we shall argue that there is a major and deeply-founded difference between the tasks of leadership best suited to men and those best suited to women, and that this difference is of an essentially genetic nature. This is the subject of the first of the two appendices that conclude this work and we shall here only outline its conclusions. These have to do with the different ways in which men and women regard two kinds of psychic operations, the one kind of operation being that which carries the mind from an object to its intrinsic or personal value and the other kind of operation being that which carries the mind from this same object to its extrinsic or social value. Thus the first kind of operation may carry the mind of a parent from a photograph of his or her new-born child to the strength of the emotion of love that this experience engenders as an intrinsic or personal value, while accepting that the second kind of operation, that takes the mind from the same photograph to its extrinsic or social value – such as might be measured by what anyone else would pay for such a photograph – might well be accepted as being little or nothing. In a very different situation, the first kind of operation might take the experience of holding a finely machined piece of highly refined steel into a negligible feeling of intrinsic or personal value while accepting that the second kind of operation may transform the experience of this object into an intimation of a quite substantial extrinsic or social value. We all of us have such value measures of all objects. What is demonstrated in the first appendix is that women experience the *balance* between the intrinsic values of objects and their extrinsic values in quite another way than do men, and this suits women much better than men as leaders in certain occupations and even in certain industries, even as men are more privileged, *qua* men, in other occupations and even other industries again. Thus, as more publicised examples, women are often better suited to industrial activities involving highly refined social-aesthetic values, such as in several branches of architecture, clothing, furnishing and publishing, as well as to social-ethical modes of leadership, such as may be concerned with the provision of many public services.

Simply by reading this summary it will be clear that the conception and the employment of this construction is greatly aided by some degree of formalisation, and in Appendix 1 this is realised by drawing upon a few elements of a unified object-value theory (as originated by the Alexius (von) Meinong that we have earlier introduced here as a student of Franz (von) Brentano) together with a few fragments of Category Theory, as one of the more popular of the current 'mathematics of non-mathematical objects'.

Chapter 3

ON SOCIOTECHNOLOGY

3.1 Leadership as a sociotechnical activity

The theory and philosophy of leadership, as introduced above, is essential to the understanding of the nature of the individual leader, but beyond this again the leader needs a theoretical apparatus that will facilitate and enhance his understanding of critical events and situations and promote the transformation of this understanding into well-formed judgements and decisions. In many cases the leader will have to construct the relevant theories personally, or at best with the help of others, and for this purpose some 'theory of theorising', which is a pragmatic description of philosophy, will be required. This third chapter will then be given over to the development of theory through philosophical understanding and its application within the context of *industrial* leadership. It will be demonstrated that *this is a sociotechnical endeavour through and through*: that very few leadership problems in industry are any more purely social or purely technical, but they are for much the greater part sociotechnical. Sociotechnology constitutes a particular species of *conjunctive* knowledge, which is one that joins together two different and otherwise separate knowledges, thereby providing a new field of knowledge with qualitatively different properties than those of its constituent parts. The study and practice of sociotechnology is essential if one wishes to understand how technical innovations have social consequences and how the resulting social changes react back again on the technical developments, and so on and on, again and again, in what become sequences of 'positive feedback' cycles. It will be shown that many subjects which are rarely if ever regarded sociotechnically, take on another aspect when they are so considered, and indeed that within a modernistic ideology 'progress' itself is often defined in a specific sociotechnical way.

3.2 Characterisations of sociotechnology

Sociotechnology is concerned with the study of processes in which social aspects cannot be separated in thought from technical aspects: the social and the technical are so related to one another in the process that the presence of the one makes no sense without the presence of the other. A common metaphor is that of a weaving together of two different kinds of thread, each of which is an essentially a one-dimensional object, so as to form a piece of cloth, which is an essentially two-dimensional object. This object formed by the weaving process is then a quite different kind of object to the threads from which it is materially constituted and it has quite other applications from these. In particular, one cannot very well cloth oneself with pieces of thread, but one can do so with pieces if cloth. A new value is then added through the weaving process. As introduced earlier, in the sociotechnical terms of a unified object-value theory, the two composing objects are then said in such a case to be *implected* or *implexively contained* the one in the other.

Another metaphor is that of the beam of the sociotechnical supported on the columns of the social and the technical: the beam is a quite different kind of structure to the columns upon which it is supported and has to be analysed and designed quite differently accordingly. Another analogy again is with the bridge of sociotechnology joining together the one river bank of the social and the other river bank of the technical.

The sociotechnical knowledge that is involved is in all such cases of that kind that we have introduced earlier as a *conjunctive knowledge*. Thus in the first metaphor the conjunctive knowledge that is used in the process of weaving together the two kinds of threads is a knowledge of weaving processes, in the second metaphor the conjunctive knowledge is a more extended knowledge of structural analysis, and in the third metaphor it is simply the bridge. Sociotechnologies are always conjunctive knowledges and sociotechnology is the study of processes in which the social and the technical are indivisibly combined.

Since it is observed that in our present-day societies there are fewer and fewer purely social problems and even fewer purely technical problems, today most problems are of a sociotechnical nature that necessitate the deployment of conjunctive knowledges. With this observation goes the increasing realisation that many historical developments that have long been regarded either as essentially social or as essentially technical were in fact interacting and interdependent sociotechnical developments and have now to be studied as such if they are to be properly understood. We shall proceed through the institutions that are of the most vital importance to the decision making of the leader in our own times by tracing the principle developments that have occurred in these institutions historically from a sociotechnical point of view.

3.3 Early political and organised-religious developments seen as sociotechnologies

It is clearly essential in our present day and age that the leader of industry has a good understanding of politics in order that he can accommodate himself to its vagaries, its opportunities and its constraints, as he navigates through the muddied currents and eddies of his political environment. Now Aristotle, who was certainly one of the most acute observers of the human condition, actually *defined* man as "a political animal", while, on the other hand, anthropologists and many other students of human behaviour and thought have long *defined* man as "a tool-using animal". Our first purpose here will be to conflate these two definitions into one so that we can get a first glimpse of some of the sociotechnical relations that exist between politics and technology and which are most relevant to the leader of industry.

Humans, as we have observed earlier here, are not the only creatures to avail themselves of the Form of leadership, but humans employ one particular form of this general Form that is almost entirely special to their own kind, and it is this form that is called 'politics'. What we shall show here is that this special form that is so peculiar to man is so special *precisely because* man is "a tool-using animal", and then in the sense that, by using his tools, man has the capacity to continue the work of the creation, as technology. In order to demonstrate this we are then obliged to treat the study of politics in a sociotechnological way, so that we can then equally well say that man develops as "tool-using animal" *just to the extent* that he succeeds as "a political animal". We shall then show that without specific developments in technology, the most significant political developments would have been stillborn, while without specific developments in politics, the most significant technological development would have been suffocated at birth.

As a human activity, politics is automatically afflicted by the invasions and assaults of nothingness, but in the case of politics this affliction becomes particularly virulent, for it is here before all else, at the point of the very leadership of mankind, that nothingness must necessarily concentrate its greatest and most destructive forces. One consequence of this is that politics is commonly described derogatively as 'the second-oldest profession', suggesting that it is more concerned with misleading than it is with leading, but we must refuse to be discouraged by these attentions of nothingness and are obliged to study politics seriously, in the spirit of truth, and it is precisely for this reason and in this spirit that we are nowadays obliged to study it as a sociotechnology.

It is because of the particular attention of nothingness to politics that throughout most of its history, and so far as we can ascertain throughout its prehistory too, politics has been closely and even intimately associated with organised religion. Indeed, we observe as we read from history that, insofar as politics has separated and distanced itself from organised religion, so it has become an ever easier prey to nothingness - and in that case we find ourselves in our reading back again in the presence of a failed leadership. As Augustine and many others after him have observed, man is also "a religious creature" and once again this must clearly be inseparable from his tool-making proclivities through which he continues the *Great Work* of the creation which then appears, in these Christian terms, as a work of redemption.

As must be inevitable in such a symbiosis as that between politics and organised religion, the invasions and assaults of nothingness upon politics must transfer to invasions and assaults of nothingness upon the organised religion, working through the organisers as adherents of the religion, and indeed if there is any kind of prey that is more favoured by nothingness above the men of politics, it is that of the men of religion, whether organisers or otherwise. We shall subsequently here come to talk in this case about the *politicisation* of institutions through the subversion to political ends of those who work within them, and in the case of the organised religions we shall have to do, within the specifically European context, with *the politicisation of the churches*. Since this process is now rather thoroughly completed, and especially in the USA and the UK, it is normally nowadays no longer considered as worthy of much further comment, and certainly not in these so-called 'Anglo-Saxon' societies. It still however continues to excite some interest in what in this distinction is called 'continental Europe'. Thus, as the most immediate example, the emphasis given here upon the role of Christianity in the making of present-day Europe must appear rather esoteric for most 'Anglo-Saxon' readers, but its relevance will still be quite widely accepted in 'continental Europe'. This difference became abundantly clear during the debate around the Constitution of the European Union, even though the division that occurred around this issue did not run along the line of the geographical and cultural difference.

We first need a definition of the Form that will apply to all the possible forms of 'politics', so that it will apply not only to 'party politics', but also to 'company politics', 'academic politics', 'family politics' and to every other denotation and connotation of the word *politics* itself. It is then against our Eurocentric background that we shall here make the following theological, and indeed downright dogmatic, *definition:*

Politics is the immediate manifestation of the struggle between
God and nothingness in the conduct of human affairs.

We may thereby also speak, but hopefully somewhat less controversially, of politics as *the struggle between the authentic and the inauthentic in the affairs of men*. It is in this struggle that the *politician* may be an authentic leader, an inauthentic leader or something of both in the sense introduced in the previous chapter. It is necessary to say however that the politician will always be something of both in practice: there will never be any politician who is 'wholly authentic', any more than there will be one who is 'wholly inauthentic'. This must be so in the first place because we are none of us – not a single one of us! – untouched by nothingness; and indeed one can argue that it is just as well that we are all so afflicted to some extent so that we can come to recognise nothingness for what it is precisely by recognising it in our own selves. This must also be so in a second sense, but to an exponentiated degree, in political life, where the truly authentic individual, as one seeking truth at its highest level, as 'absolute truth', could not possibly survive for long at all as a 'political animal'.

One unmistakable symptom of this unavoidably more pronounced presence of the inauthentic, of nothingness, in the individual politician is that those persons participating in political processes, whether as leader/politician or in the position of the led as the adherents of the politic espoused by the leader, are all commonly called *actors*. This is so appropriate because all such persons are, consciously or (mostly) unconsciously, 'acting a part', or indeed 'acting out a part' in society. Such persons are 'playing roles', often imitating 'role models' in their attempts to play their parts. For example, drawing its vocabulary from psychology and sociology, political science, as the attempt to study politics as a scientific discipline, comes to speak of a "role-theory model of a legislative actor". The play in which they are all acting is then an ideology. [1]

This use of the word 'actor' indicates that the person so involved has renounced a part of his own self, at least for the duration of his political performance, and so suffers a loss of selfhood. There are, of course, many ways to lose one's own self, and antiquity commonly depicted the man so possessed as being one who loses his own shadow, this then being commonly taken into possession by another person. However, to the extent that this person looses his self in this way, but then not to a person, but to an *idea*, then he is said to be *possessed by an ideology*. Ideologies are the very stuff of inauthentic leadership, only surpassed in this respects by idolatries, as already introduced in the previous chapters.

The expressed antithesis of the ideology is, properly speaking, the *doctrine*, originally understood as a coordinated collection of explanations of a body of religious teachings. One may or may not embrace a doctrine, whereas one is oneself caught in the embrace of an ideology. The construction of a doctrine is itself a quest for authenticity and all authentic leadership necessitates the elaboration of a doctrine as the point of reference of all acts of leadership. In the words of Pascal introduced already in the introduction to this work, but slightly otherwise translated: "It is not the miracles that provides the doctrine, but the doctrine that provides the miracles".

The most obvious indications of the sociotechnological nature of politics are so closely associated with the sociotechnical nature of organised religion in earlier civilisations that these indications apply to politics and organised religion indivisibly: they are the great temples and other politico-religious constructions of these earlier civilisations, reaching their apogee in the Egyptian pyramids of the Pharaohs. These constructions probably absorbed one half of all investments in construction within the societies in which they were integrated. This proportion seems to have remained little changed, despite great variation between times, until the end of the European Middle Ages: the investment in every cathedral, in particular, was roughly the same as the investment in all other constructions in the town or city around it combined. We hardly need to explain the tremendous visual and tactile impact of these structures and the awe and respect that they induced, as theatres of intuitive understanding, of numinosity – divineness or sacredness - for the politico-religious actors who played out their roles within them, and even in many cases continued playing these roles even after their very deaths. We shall shortly return to this form of sociotechnology when we discuss the so-called 'technologies of persuasion'.

The definition of politics has been posed in terms of a struggle over the conduct of human affairs and as such it is a struggle over how these affairs should proceed and so over which man or group of men should prevail over others in directing these affairs. We have earlier here introduced this form of influence generally as *power*, but now we specialise this to *political power*. Up until the 1970s and in some cases even later, it became increasingly popular to differentiate political power from other forms of power by the property that it is concerned with 'power over power', and so 'power over power over power', and so on recursively. This view was challenged and in principle reversed by the work of Michel Foucault through his great studies of the developments of such social institutions as hospitals, prisons and lunatic asylums, wherein, as one of his editors observed, "Failure becomes the norm". Thus in a justly celebrated lecture given in 1976 he emphasised (Foucault, 1980, p.99):

> The important thing is not to attempt some kind of deduction of power starting from the centre and aiming at the discovery of the extent to which it permeates into the base....One must rather conduct an ascending analysis of power, starting from its [lowest-level] mechanisms, which all have their own histories, their own trajectories, their own techniques and tactics, and then see how these mechanisms of power have been – and continue to be – invested, utilised, involuted, transformed, displaced, extended, etc., by ever more general mechanisms.

Thus, to revert to the first example just given above, and to anticipate already something of 'the technologies of persuasion', we may consider how the ancient Egyptian farmer working in his field cast his gaze in the direction of a great pyramid around noon so as to catch the piercing flash of light reflected by the brilliant white facing stone of this pyramid, as a structure that was angled and orientated to provide exactly this reflection at exactly this time. The feeling that suffused this farmer, that all was as it should be on Earth as in the Universe thanks to the works of the departed Pharaoh, must have been powerful indeed. This power was greatly augmented by the synchronicity that was built into this sociotechnical construct, an aspect that cannot be discussed here but which is of great importance again in 'the technologies of persuasion', as must be evident from the obvious presence of high levels of synchronisation of activities in all forms of religious rituals.

In much the same vein in the case of the second example, the cathedral of the Middle Ages ascended through its soaring spire to hitherto unprecedented heights, towering above the town or city around it and thereby overawing all its citizenry - while also being visible from equally unprecedented distances to every passing traveller as a further source of wonder. It is by starting from the Egyptian farmer in his field that one arrives at the power that is projected by the pyramid and it is by starting from the mediaeval citizen and traveller that one arrives at the power that is projected by the spire of the cathedral. We see that this form of exercising of power through communication is always *indirect*, in that no direct coercion is involved.

Contrasting this symbolism of its own power of the Western Church to that of the Eastern or Orthodox churches, Hart (2003, p.37) observed:

> Gothic cathedrals are typified by verticality and an upward thrust. Their verticality and pointed arches point outside of themselves. By contrast, most Orthodox churches are typified by the rounded arch, the dome, the cube and undulating surfaces covered in images of saints. They thus point to their interior. They are incarnational rather than ecstatic. Even a church as vast as Agia Sophia does not crush you; you want to take a deep breath and inhale its glory, for this glory is in the space, and you are within this glory. You feel at home. If there is a sense of going out of oneself, it is through an instasy rather than an ecstasy.

Let us look a little deeper again into the sociotechnology of this last example, of the cathedral, but now rather more from its technical and mathematical-scientific aspects. As introduced at the beginning of this work, it has become usual since the works of Duhem (1913-1959//see, for example, Duhem and Brenner, 1997) to start the clock of the era of modern science on March 7, 1277, with the Condemnations at the University of Paris of doctrines that conflicted with the doctrine of the Church. As explained earlier, it was this condemnation that allowed scientific thinking to follow new, more heavenly paths, and these paths were initially traced through the use of geometry in a new way, just as the geometrical methods were themselves used increasingly to trace the actual paths of the heavenly bodies. From the point of view that asks *how* knowledge is and was recorded and transmitted, which as we shall see is essential to all sociotechnical studies, this new realm of application of geometry is of central importance. Knowledge is always transmitted between humans through *tokens* and the principal kinds of tokens are *signs* and *symbols*. A change in paradigm, whether in science or in technology or in whatever other field of human endeavour, is always marked by a change in the way in which signs and symbols are employed. Thus, that which Michel Foucault (*e.g.* 1966//1970) has characterised as *an archaeology of knowledge* always proceeds through a study of the functioning of signs and symbols in knowledge transmission processes. From the point of view of the theory of the ways of functioning of signs, which is the *theory of semiotics* (*e.g.*, Eco, 1967; Klinkenberg, 1996) the most significant of the changes that mark paradigm shifts are recorded by the choice of the *sign vehicles* that are employed. Sign vehicles are, roughly speaking, the physical means that are employed in order to effect the signification process. Thus the application of existing geometrical methods as new and preferred means of signification marked a paradigm shift and one that can be traced in mathematical-science as well as in technology. Thus, for Addis, speaking from the technological side (1990, p. 126):

> Although we may never know how the people of the time perceived what was happening, nor why it happened, there is absolutely no doubt that something extra ordinary occurred in the art of building design and construction in the 12th century. The nature of the 'Gothic design revolution' is apparent from the buildings themselves. After several hundred years of gradual development since the end of the Roman empire, the design of large buildings took a sudden and sharp change of direction."

Addis's studies left no doubt whatsoever about the mathematical-scientific impetus for this design revolution: the translation of Euclid's *Elements* in 1120, just seven years before the construction of the trend-setting basilica of St. Denis was begun. For want of a better name, the Abbot of St. Denis called this 'new look' an *opus modernum*, and this was subsequently called *Gothic* as something synonymous with 'barbaric', and thereby intended originally as a term of abuse. Addis explained:

> Geometry had, of course, survived as a practical art throughout the Middle Ages, but the appearance of Euclid did improve the level of geometrical knowledge that could be learnt. Improved geometry facilitated the more accurate 'description' of proposed building designs and was of great practical use in the construction process, in setting out the building and enabling the finished parts and their relative dispositions to be checked within better tolerances. Such an improvement alone would have enabled builders to contemplate larger and taller buildings.
> However, it was in its capacity to provide 'justifications' of designs that geometry probably had the more profound effect. Euclid introduced a crucial new ingredient — the notion of the geometrical proof. ..... Just as occurred 600 years later, philosophers put the new theoretical tool to use in every conceivable way and created, quite literally, a new type of geometry — '*geometria theorica*'.

Since we have to do here with the means to continue the creation in the domain of mankind, this was a quintessential technological development, but then one that we cannot comprehend without situating it within the social environment that fostered a *geometria theorica* as the precondition for the creative act. Thus, so far as the influence of the theoretical proof upon the practical analysis, design and construction processes was concerned, it was in fact emphasised already by Victor (1979, p.53: see Addis, 1990) that:

> The use of theoretical methods in practical geometry seems to have increased between the twelfth and the fourteenth centuries. At first their role was ancillary to the purposes of practical geometry. Once proofs had found a place in practical geometry, their role increased and changed. Theoretical proof became the goal even of practical geometry.

Thereby however, as Addis himself emphasised (*loc. cit.*, p. 132), "simultaneously not only was a new type of architecture born, but also a new world view." As we have just seen, these constructions greatly increased the 'visibility' and thence the prestige of the Western Church, symbolising the new power of this Church, whereby the claim that salvation itself could proceed only through the intercession of the Church, *extra ecclesiam nulla salus*, could be pressed so much more strongly against the already mounting forces that were pressing for a reformation within the Church itself. The invention of 'purgatory' and the sale of indulgences from the plenary downwards as means of escaping from it, together with incomes accruing from landholdings, the sale of dubious relics and many other sources besides, made of the church more of a secular business than a sacred body in the eyes of the reformers. In the words of Michelet (in Boulier, 1958, p 40): "The finances encompassed everything; they were the alpha and omega of the Roman administration. In its totality this is a story, less of the pontificate and its sovereignty, than of a house of commerce". The reforming elements within the Church were railing against this situation and finding lay-political supporters, and their influence had to be contained. It was then just as much this political exigency that drove the Church to such extremities of technology even as it was through the influence that it gained by communicating its power in this way that the Church could raise the means to finance such vast undertakings. Thus, in the eyes of the reformers, who later came to their full expression in The Reformation, this Western and essentially Roman Church could prevail against the forces opposing its ever greater politicisation and spiritual degeneration by resorting to means that could only be sustained by an ever greater politicisation and spiritual degeneration.

This view can of course in no way detract from the glorious gifts that this past time has bequeathed us and for which we must be forever grateful. Moreover, we should never forget the immense service that the Church continued to provide even during its times of greatest depravation in assuaging the anguish and exorcising the demons that tormented its congregations. Further to this again, account should be taken of the rivalry between towns and cities for the prestige of a bishopric and for reasons of civic pride generally, but the essentially sociotechnical nature of this process is clearly supported from all these several sides.

(We should mention in passing that there is a technical aspect also in play here that is still more subtle. We have always been taught that the great cathedrals were so extraordinary in the sense that, being built entirely in stone, their design had to be such as to introduce no tensile stresses, and it was the Gothic design, as characterised by its flying buttresses, which made this possible in the case of such tall structures. We have been taught that it was only when such constructions reached their zenith, and then over-reached it, that some wrought iron was introduced to stabilise these structures. It is only in quite recent times that it has been discovered that very considerable quantities of wrought iron were in fact worked into the stonework so as to remain invisible, and recent metal-detecting surveys and computer-aided structural analyses of these buildings have shown that this iron was introduced into the stone structure very precisely in order to accommodate the tensile stresses, such as must arise under heavy wind loadings. This could only have been possible through a thorough mastery of geometry. We thereby have also here an excellent example of the application of the Kierkegaardian 'aesthetic deception', as explained in the next Chapter.)

From a sociotechnical point of view, the construction of the great cathedrals then also serves to illustrate how a change in the technical means of expression – the *sign vehicles* of the theory of semiotics – became necessary in order to realise their construction and thus attain to the required social objective. Sociotechnical developments commonly exhibit this feature, that they proceed at several different levels simultaneously, with elements situated at one level interacting with elements at other levels so as to weave these different levels of development together into one, totally integrated development.

We may observe in passing that this birth of a new paradigm in technology predated the Condemnations at the University of Paris by some 150 years, so that we may well suppose - as Duhem also suggests - that the Condemnations were in some respects 'pronouncements after the fact' - with the usual academic lag time! In any event it can be established that a new paradigm was initiated in technology a considerable time before the announcement of the beginning of the era of modern science, but that this technological process was so closely interwoven with social developments that it can only be understood at all within the realm of an overarching sociotechnology.

Before leaving this instructive diversion, let us look, with Jean Baudrillard, at its most recent and most symbolic manifestation, in the form of the twin-towered building of the World Trade Centre and its equally symbolic, and spectacular, destruction:

> In the first place, why the Twin Towers? Why two towers that were twins at the World Trade Centre?
> All the large buildings in Manhattan had confronted one another until then in that competition in verticality which provided the famous architectural panorama of the city. This image had changed in 1973 with the construction of the World Trade Centre. The effigy of the system passed from that of the obelisk and the pyramid to the punched card and the statistical graph. This architectural graphic incarnated something that was no longer competitive, but still numerical and computable, where the competitiveness disappeared to the advantage of the network and the monopoly.
> The fact that they were two signifies the loss of all original reference. If there had been one, the monopoly would not have been perfectly incarnated. Only the doubling of the sign could truly put an end to that which it designated. No matter how high they were, the two towers signified nevertheless a stop to verticality. They did not belong to the same race as the other buildings. The buildings of the Rockefeller Centre mirror their facades of glass and steel in the spectacular infinity of the town. The towers, for their part, no longer had a façade; they no longer had a face. The rhetoric of verticality disappeared together with the rhetoric of the mirror. With these perfectly equilibrated and blind monoliths, there remained only a kind of black box, closed in upon itself as if, as the image of 'the system', it proceeded only through cloning and an immutable genetic code.
> New York is the only city in the world that has traced throughout its history the form of the system and its major events in this way, and then with a prodigious fidelity. One must then suppose that the collapse of the towers – an event unique in the history of modern cities - prefigured the dramatic end of that form of architecture and the system that it incarnated. By striking there, the terrorists thus touched the neuralgic centre of the system.
> …The collapse of the towers was a major symbolic event. Imagine if they had not collapsed, or only one had collapsed: the effect would not have been at all the same. The shattering proof of the fragility of the world power would not have been the same. The towers which were the emblems of that power also incarnated through their dramatic end another form of suicide. When watching them collapse of themselves, as though by an implosion, one received the impression that they were committing suicide in response to the suicide of the suicide-aircraft.

Lyotard (see Lyotard et. al. 2002) had earlier developed the Kantian notion of *the sublime* and this recurs in Baudrillard's study of the semiotics and the related 'psychoanalysis of things' in his piece on the Twin Towers. The aspect of the 'two-ness or even 'duality' of the structure should be read alongside the analyses of the role of the individual natural numbers in alchemical practises as described by the great Swiss psychologist Carl Jung (1944//1952).

The consequences of this particular action are so well known and so much with us at this time of writing, and likely to continue for so much longer again, that they need no further elucidation. As an exercise in sociotechnical leadership, however, this action remains as a paradigm case. [2, 3]

3.4 The sociotechnology of political development in the transformation from feudalism to capitalism in Europe: the rise of representative democracy

As already explained in the first chapter of this work, the entire social development of Europe after the end of feudalism cannot be understood without taking account of the technological development – together with the increasingly modern-scientific basis for this development - that occurred simultaneously in Europe. At the same time, and as was also adumbrated in the first chapter, this technical and increasingly supportive scientific development would, in its turn, have been nullified if the social developments that supported and nurtured it had been frustrated. The fact that these social developments were in fact supportive of the technical developments can be seen as a consequence of a particular deployment of political power, just as this particular deployment of political power was mightily supported by the technical developments. There then occurred in certain places a synergy between the exercise of political power and the development of industry through the application of an increasingly science-based technology, and it was this synergy that provided the motor that drove Europe to its 'pinnacle' of world domination - and then just as surely sent it down to self-destruction and penury.

As the influence of technological advances upon politics increased, so the influence of organised religion declined. Feudalism, as sanctioned by the Church, slowly became ever more incompatible with the advance of technology and this had in turn its effects on organised religion, whereby technological advance became increasingly associated, largely through the Reformation, with what Max Weber called the *Protestant Work Ethic*. In politics, the cliques formed around princes, dukes, counts, or marquesses - who were kept to some extent in check by the princes of the church and their underlings who were responsible for actually administering the state - were joined by other cliques, composed of merchants, industrialists, businessmen and bankers. As the latter grew to challenge the dominance of the former through the strongly interactive development of commerce and industry, so these two kinds of cliques or 'power brokers' came to form what are commonly called *cadre* or *brokerage parties*. Thereby two kinds of cadre or brokerage parties arose, the one composed for the most part of landowners who drew their wealth from the labour of an illiterate peasantry who were in turn held in check by a traditionalist clergy, and the other composed of industrialists, merchants, tradesmen, bankers, financiers and professional people who increasingly needed more literate and enterprising workers to staff their ever more extensive and sophisticated offices, factories, ships, warehouses and all manner of other organisational and technical constructs. The rise of this second political caste was in fact associated in many Catholic European societies with the rise to prominence of Freemasonry, and especially in Belgium and in

France, as an almost anticlerical movement - but this aspect cannot possibly be taken up here.

The leading of people is an exercise of power and within the consolidating nation states of much of Europe a contention arose in civil society between the cadre or brokerage parties over who was to articulate and exercise leadership and thus who was to articulate and exercise power. The process of consolidation into nation states was itself a sociotechnical process of course, since it depended not only upon military and financial means, but just as well upon the development of means to improve communications within the territories of the consolidating state faster than communications were improving in neighbouring states that had pretensions to this same territory. Since the industry-based cadre parties had an advantage not only in providing, but also in utilising these improvements in military might, finance and communications, they tended to gain the upper hand during these processes of national consolidation. The development of inland communication associated in a large part with the development of canals was important in many European nation states and led, in particular, to the rise of the Netherlands as a major player in European geopolitics, but then through this technical strand of development being interwoven with a Protestant mercantile and processing-industrial ethic to form a sociotechnical system.

The sociotechnical nature of politics becomes much more apparent when we trace the transition from political cliques and factions into political parties, such as occurred in Britain in the eighteenth century and in France after the post-Napoleonic restoration. This necessitated a more active intervention in the affairs of state on the part of the citizenry, which then took on the form of an *electorate*. Of course the suffrage was restricted to men of sufficient means to be worth counting as taxpayers, and also landowners even if they did not pay tax, it being argued that these were the only persons with any real stake in the political process: others in society would have no interest in 'the common good' and would simply sell their votes to real stakeholders even if given them.

It was against this background that Burke, in Britain, which was the first nation state to enter the industrial revolution, argued for a new justification for *party*, which he defined as "a body of men united on public principle which could act as a constitutional link between king and Parliament, providing consistency and strength in administration, or principled criticism in opposition". The means to link the electorates of the contending parties to their representatives over the territory of the nation state were however technical, comprising on the one hand the improvements in road-building and road transport technologies generally that proceeded through the eighteenth century and accelerated rapidly at the turn of the eighteenth and nineteenth centuries and, on the other hand, the almost simultaneous industrialisation of printing processes. Both of these developments were aspects of a more general industrial revolution that was occurring in *communication technologies* at that time. Without these technical advances in communication, which culminated in the relatively cheap production and widespread distribution of news through newspapers that could influence the opinions of the electorate so as to suit the interests of 'their' representatives, the constitutional-representative political structure could not have been maintained. At the same time, without this representative-democratic political structure, the industrial revolution itself would have faltered and been endangered. For example, the legislation of copyright and patent laws that protected intellectual property was a necessary condition for a sustainable technological development. As with all sociotechnical systems, the social and technical 'aspects' were interdependent: the one without the other would have been unsustainable. In such situations, the social and the technical are then commonly said to be 'in system'.

As is well known, the level of representation of the citizenry in Britain, which pioneered this development, was initially highly uneven, with some boroughs being open constituencies and others being mere 'pocket boroughs', which could be bought by money or otherwise acquired through patronage. The extention of a more representative democracy in Britain, unlike for example in France and Germany, had to await the widespread introduction of the railway and the electric telegraph. We then say that the technical development 'catalysed' the social development, but then always in such a way that the social reacted in its turn to promote the technical again so as to constitute a sociotechnical system.

Among the most common of sociotechnical constructs – which may or may not constitute systems in the strict (Kantian) sense - are *networks*. These then collectively provide a specific type of sociotechnical development that has been particularly extensively studied. Thus we may trace fresh water supply and waste water disposal networks from the earliest historical times as the *conditio sine qua non* of every sustainable urban development, while it has been and continues to this day to be just these urban developments that in turn made and continue to make such constructions technically and financially feasible. Irrigation networks have similarly provided the technical foundations of many, and even most, of the earliest of those great civilisations that were in their turn the only kinds of societies that could mobilise the labour, organisation and financial resources to construct and maintain such systems. We may similarly identify sea-trading networks as providing some of the first sociotechnical foundations of trading and banking organisations and other social activities that in turn provided the distribution and financial systems that serviced the trading infrastructure. Road networks, postal networks, canal networks, gas supply networks, rail networks, telegraph networks, steamship networks with their networks of coal-bunkering stations, electricity supply networks, telephone networks, radio and television transmission networks and many others can be identified, all of which were of course sociotechnical constructs in themselves, but all of which had this further property in common: that all had their individual influences on political processes, leading generally to an ever wider extention of the suffrage as they made possible an ever more intensive influence and control over the opinions of the electorate that could be employed to promote these same networks.

To the 'material' or 'outer-world' technological developments were thus added the so-called 'technologies of persuasion' to which we must now turn, and which provided 'inner world' changes, or the formation of 'opinions' within the minds of the electorate, without which representative democracy could not have extended its sway so extensively, even as this extention was in its turn essential to the promotion of the technological advances that, once again in their turn, made political process itself sustainable. In order to grasp the nature of this new class of technologies we need first however to introduce a few more notions and definitions.

The first notion that we have to introduce is that of a distinction between our 'outer world' and our 'inner world'. Put very simply, our outer world is that which we experience more or less directly through the functioning of our senses while our inner world comprehends all our memory-related, thinking and emotional processes that proceed even when we deprive ourselves of our sense experiences. Thus our inner world is that which persists even in the absence of our outer world. Roughly paraphrasing Augustine in a contemporary idiom, we may now define *reality* and *truth*, but then following the later scholastics by doing so in one and the same sentence:

> *Reality is the name that we give to the interface between our inner and our outer worlds and a truth is an intimation of the oneness of these two worlds.*

We shall later return to consider the more obvious objections to this, at first sight simplistic, definition. [4]

So far we have only considered technology as a process of bringing something new to presence in our outer world, but clearly we can also consider another process again, which is that of bringing something new to presence in our inner world. This something new may be a new thought or way of thinking, a new opinion, a new knowledge, a new understanding, a new attitude, a new belief system, a new ideology, a new doctrine and even a new faith - and any number of other such mental and more general psychic constructs.

Reviewing the previous examples we see that sociotechnological constructs arise when two processes, the one proceeding in the inner world and the other proceeding in the outer world, occur not only interactively but also in synergy and so synchronously.

Clearly the technologies of persuasion are the principle tools of the trade of the politician. Since they are always directed by the persuader to *influence the behaviour* of another person, so that this other person becomes the persuaded and behaves accordingly, *the technologies of persuasion are devices for mobilising power through communication*. Since we are again dealing with power we are again led, following Foucault, to start any investigation of these technologies by investigating how they function at their 'lowest' level, at the level of those who are to be persuaded.

There is now a very large and extensive literature on this subject which does indeed start at this level, dealing for example with the inculcation of 'consumerist attitudes' in advertising, 'feel-good factors' and 'promoters of upward social mobility' in party-political election campaigns and within many other contexts, and not least in most 'Business Schools'. Common to nearly all of this is its play upon apparently irrational impulses, so that it is said to function primarily at the level of the *paralogical*, while at the same time playing upon the doubts and uncertainties of those to whom it is directed, so as to induce states of total perplexity, such as by simultaneously supporting incommensurable beliefs, as states of *aporia*, to which it in turn 'opposes' its own states, of *euphoria*. Much of this is obviously manipulative, such as by way of advertisement for this or that product or service, but much is not so obviously manipulative and much too much is not so obviously so at all. Thus, for example, almost all the contents of newspapers and television programmes that purport to report on events, developments, personalities and so on are in fact not only or even so much directed to informing their readers or viewers, but also and even principally concerned to influence the opinions and attitudes of these readers and viewers. Their reports are not primarily *constative*, directed to informing their audience about facts, but much more *performative*, and so directed to persuading their audience about something and so gaining power over them. Thus a performative statement refers to a reality that it intends to create itself, because it is stated under circumstances which are intended to make it into an act (See Manin, 1971, p.81). It is one consequence of this that nowadays one often only asks in the second place *what* the newspaper or journal article or radio or television programme is saying, while asking *why* they are saying this in the first place. In the same vein, before reading an article nowadays one almost automatically looks for the name and affiliation of its author – and then, as often as not, one no longer needs to read the article itself, for the thrust of its presentation and its arguments are already completely predictable. All of this is of course eminently political and in particular it points to the close symbiosis between the party-political machinations of 'government' and 'opposition' and the productions of the 'mass media' with their own oligarchies of 'press barons'.

Writing in 1847 on this same phenomenon but within the context of his own time, Søren Kierkegaard observed that, in so far as we are led to reflect upon real objects, so we have to do with a *communication of knowledge*, while when, as for the most part nowadays, we are led to reflect upon unreal, or more strictly nonexistent objects, we always have to do with the *communication of power*. He saw how, in the limit, there would finally be no communication of knowledge at all, but only a communication of power, and that the absurd situation would then arise that everything that should be communicated directly as power would instead be communicated indirectly, masquerading as knowledge. We should then exist in a *totally manipulated society*, such as George Orwell came to delineate in his '1984'. The result could only be a total confusion and an inability to make any sound decisions at all. Kierkegaard described the behaviour of the communicators in this case as one of *impropriety*, and so as something improper, unseemly and morally reprehensible. The Kierkegaardian "purveyors of opinions" and "merchants of drivel" remain among the greatest menaces of our age, even as this age has become, and now on the largest possible scale, the age of gold for such miscreants.

What the technologies of persuasion are aiming to influence are our *judgements*, and what we have to protect ourselves best from their enticements is our *experience*. Through the 1930s, as Europe advanced towards its last grand military denouement, its final throw of the dice with its destiny, Edmund Husserl prepared the last of his great works, which he entitled *Erfahrung und Urteil // Experience and Judgement*. Husserl emphasised that 'experience' is itself something active and indeed poietic. Thus (p.52):

> Our life-world in its originality…is also the world of experience in the wholly concrete sense which is commonly tied in with the word 'experience'…Thus this commonplace, familiar and concrete sense of the word 'experience' points much more to a mode of behaviour which is practically active and evaluative than to one that is cognitive and judicative.

This is to say that the deconstructions of the communications of the politicians and the mass media that are forever forced upon the critical mind must be based upon an experience of the reality of the world, that is to say upon the oneness of the written and screen-projected world with the inner world of accumulated personal experience.

Some further explanation is still in order. We may first regard the simplest form of a predicative judgement as being a component in a string of inferences, as follows:

(belief system, facts(data))→attitude→position→judgement→decision→action   (3.1)

where in the usual way of things it is only the set of data that constitute an observable and so is underlined accordingly. Experience is that which alters the belief system, as the basis of the inner world of an individual, whereby the same facts as drawn from the same data may lead to the individual taking a different attitude and thence a different position and correspondingly making a different judgement. On this basis a different decision will be made as a result of the experience and this will lead to a different action. If now we reverse the direction of the arrows in this inference string, so that the string of inferences proceeds in the opposite direction, and we take the action also as an observable, we may work our way back to an elicitation of the belief system of the judging individual:

action→decision→judgement→position→attitude→ (facts (data, belief system))   (3.2)

In the event that both (3.1) and (3.2) are known, we say that the judgemental process is *transparent*. What we are then seeking when we are evaluating the pronouncements of politicians and others who are in such compromised and compromising positions is *transparency*.

With this minimum of conceptual machinery in place and up and running, we can move on to consider sociotechnology and sociotechnical arrangements outside of the immediate sphere of the political.

3.5   The sociotechnology of networks as the hallmarks of modernity and the rise of participative democracy

The development of representative democracy was associated with the development of networks that provided new and much enhanced channels of communication. This development is closely associated with the rise to dominance of what has already been introduced as *modernity*. However, modernity has led in its turn to new sociotechnical constructs again, and these may be conveniently introduced quite generally here as *superpositions of networks*. The paradigm case here is the superposition of the Internet on a telephone system which is in its turn superimposed upon both a postal network and an electricity supply network which is in its turn again superimposed upon a coal, oil and gas transport network. Among the feedback loops that are superimposed on this simple superposition, we immediately identify railway, road and pipeline transport systems that depend upon electricity that may in its turn be dispatched through the uses of electronic communication networks, including the Internet. This process of superimposing ever more layers of new networks with ever more complex feedback loops between the earlier superposed layers and their networks is often regarded nowadays as *the culmination of modernism* as has been intimated earlier, where it was seen to be closely related to, or to be 'in system with', the drive towards producing ever more persons as 'knowers'. Now, however, under the influence of the new kinds of networks associated with the Internet (reinforced by intranets and extranets) and mobile telephony, we have to do more with the *post-modern* project of turning ever more persons into 'consumers of knowledge', and this development is more 'in system' with forms of participative democracy - which in turn support the claims to autonomy of these new communication media. Similarly, the move from the *broadcast modes* of communication at fixed times, which have reached their apogee in real-time-transmission colour television, to *broadband modes* of communication operating at all times indifferently of the kind that advanced communication networks and mobile telephony now provide, are already changing social relations markedly, increasingly challenging the decisions and even the legitimacy of representative government, and increasingly successfully. As adumbrated earlier, these last sociotechnical developments open up the possibility of stabilising otherwise unstable self-managing, 'anarchistic' or 'endostructured' organisations by the provision of appropriate technical equipment – which is once again equipment that would have no purpose outside of the evolution of these new self-organising or 'emergent' social structures. It is then often said that in such systems the social and the technical components are 'mutually reinforcing'.

The kinds of networks that are of the greatest interest to the leader of industry today are those composed of closely-interacting technical equipment and people working both as individuals and in teams, such as are exemplified by Internet-connected working environments. Within the increasingly unified European context, these networks often cannot function using natural languages because there are several teams working closely together, interactively and so concurrently, with each team having its own natural language as well as its own technically-specialised expressions. For example, a Finnish team may be installing the communication and signalling system together with a German team installing the electrical system together with a Polish team installing the surface finishing panels inside one and the same tunnel element deep under water at one and the same time. This concurrent mode of working is necessitated by the contract conditions that are directed to completing the tunnel and other works six months before schedule in order to claim the generous bonuses that have been offered for early completion of the project and thus the most rapid return on investment for the owner. Clearly such an operation necessitates the use of an extensively analysed, well designed and competently installed communication system that necessitates in its turn an expertise in graphics and semiotics generally in order to communicate with means, such as portable computers and advanced mobile telephony, that are simple, relatively cheap and reliable. This system in turn however necessitates not only a knowledge of its immediately enabling technologies, such as may include several Java and Java-based technologies, but also an intimate knowledge of all the work processes of all the teams who are employing the system - and then of course the system will need to accommodate many more than just the three teams that happen to be working in this particular tunnel element if it is itself to be cost-effective. In this case there are several different human networks associated with several different languages describing several different technologies that have to be conjoined and synchronised through networks of technical equipment. This is then a typical sociotechnical construct of our present-day Europe.

This development is however connected to, and in fact inseparable from another, which is that of a legislated right to public access to all relevant information, backed by appropriate knowledge-promoting activities allowing this public to interpret the information provided, and a corresponding legislated right of this now well-informed public to intervene in actions that could have deleterious effects upon their living and working environments. In the case of the Denmark-Sweden traffic link from which the previous example was taken, this again required both extranets and intranets supplying information and knowledge services to the general population in such a way that presentations were customised to the specific areas of concern and the specific intentions of each of the interested parties. This flow of knowledge and information was usually mediated by specific non-governmental organisations representing the main interest groups. This so-called 'mass-customisation of knowledge' emanating from a 'knowledge provider' provides a typical example of a system providing the resources to support a movement towards *participative democracy*, as both a complement and a supplement to, and even a replacement of, representative democracy.

3.6 The atrophication of representative democracy as a sociotechnical phenomenon

As remarked earlier, we are currently the witnesses of a quite extraordinary attack and assault on the welfare of the peoples of Europe and one that cannot but continue to create problems for the authentic leader. This takes the form of an ideology that uses any excuse it can find to call for lower incomes, longer working hours, less security of employment, later retirement, reduced social services of every kind and indeed for every other sacrifice on the part of the great majority of the population, even as the 'top echelons' of so-called 'management' give themselves unprecedented financial rewards and other benefits. This is often called *the Anglo-Saxon model of capitalism*, a name which seems manifestly unfair insofar as many British employers and not a few US employers too, have always abjured such an ideology, and in many cases they continue to do so to this day. At the same time, this ideology has been spreading across continental Europe also and poses a major threat to the long term sustainability of European industry through destroying the very foundations of its longer-term competitiveness. Since this ideology is the most actively propagated in the US and the UK and less accepted in continental Europe however, we shall keep to this common, even if unfortunate, nomenclature.

This phenomenon is intimately connected with a parallel development, or rather absence of development, in representative politics in the US and the UK. This is one in which the party political system becomes atrophied by the acceptance of this ideology by both governing and opposition parties. We may then speak in an English idiom, following Lewis Carroll's *Through the Looking Glass*, of *Tweedledum-and-Tweedledee politics*. It is a rather exact description for the US situation, while in the UK it can be extended to include a third, '*Tweedledumdee*' party. In a more Continental European idiom we should refer, following Hergé's twin detectives in his *Tintin* sagas, to *Dupond and Dupont politics*. In these atrophied forms there is no substantive difference at all between the parties, but only wrangling and 'politicking' over procedural details. The basic ideology is shared by all the parties concerned. The reason for this congruence between industrial interests and politics is clear enough and is very adequately described by the frequent observation in the USA that all parties have the same paymasters: the legislative body has steadily retreated from its nominal role of lawmaking in the interests of society as a whole, which is anyway difficult and even tedious, and instead has increasingly directed its attentions to legislating in the interests of businesses and industrial and other special interest groups which will in return contribute to the campaign funds that will ensure the re-election of these same 'people's representatives'. So far has this now gone in the USA that there is no longer any pretence of serving the interests of the nation as a whole. Tax reductions, tax exemptions and tax avoidance arrangements, tariff barriers, subsidies dressed up in any number of ways, contracts for specially favoured corporations, and rule-changes of all shapes and sizes proliferate by the day: the inventiveness of the legislature seems to know no bounds.

And of course in all this there is no difference at all between Democrats and Republicans: both are pursuing the same policy of personal self-interest. The results of this are serious in the extreme however, in that US industry as a whole becomes less and less competitive internationally as it relies increasingly on subsidies, the Federal budget deficit soars out of control and the legislation necessary to restore some balance in incomes across US society remains in limbo: the inequality in incomes in the USA today has now reached a level last seen at the onset of the Great Depression in 1929.

Clearly all of this makes a mockery of all the fine words about democracy that these 'representatives' propound. However, from our present sociotechnological position this situation follows immediately from that introduced in the previous section, whereby power is now for much the greater part transmitted indirectly, through communication, and in the cases of the USA this communication, proceeding through the mass media, is almost entirely in the hands of those who see a clear self-interest in promoting these arrangements and their underlying ideology. Only those with alternative means of communication such as are realised through such devices as the Internet, and who are able to organise quickly and at a distance using mobile telephony, can circumvent to some extent at least the imposition of power through the 'communications' of this mass media. It is only through this technological development that the atrophication of representative politics can be bypassed by participative democratic arrangements that are political in quite other ways. We shall return briefly in the next chapter to these strategies and counterstrategies as they concern the leader in European industry.

3.7 The politicisation of science and technology and the scientification of politics

Nowadays almost everyone is in one way or the other a consumer of knowledge. It is in this sense that we often speak today of a 'knowledge society'. In particular, however, ministers and other politicians like to emphasise that their decisions are based upon scientific knowledge, and that they are founded upon the latest research. In this way they often succeed in giving their decisions an augmented legitimacy, because these decisions are apparently supported by independent, truthful, scientific investigations. Ministers today can no longer justify their decisions by appealing to religion or godly intervention, but they can justify them by referring to and appearing to draw upon accumulated results of research. This respect for the results of research is based upon a reasonable expectation on the part of the general population that researchers will do their best to provide a truthful and adequate picture of reality, even though this may conflict with certain passing political interests. The use, or more commonly misuse, of science and technology by politicians in order to make politics more acceptable by making it appear more scientific, is characterised in some disciplines, such as in Policy Analysis, as the *scientification of politics*. Its other side – the use of political means to influence the workings of scientific investigations – is then characterised in terms of a *politicisation of science*.

It will be useful to take an example that, being well removed from politics and research in the major European nations, may be employed without creating too many political problems. Although we are aiming at the rule of avoiding detailed case studies in this greatly abbreviated *précis*, we shall make this the one and only exception to this rule, and since this is the only such exception, we shall treat it in the considerable detail that it requires.

This example concerns the Danish Aquatic Environment Plan 1 (*Vandmiljøplan 1*) the legislation for which finally passed into law, after much preparation, in 1987. Its aim was to reduce pollution of fresh and brackish coastal waters, principally by reducing releases of nitrogen by 50% and 80% for phosphates. The total cost of the plan over its originally expected 5-year duration was initially estimated at about 12 billion Danish Crowns, or 1.6 billion euro, which was still a lot of money for a little country with only 5 million inhabitants. However, it was clear to many politicians, including several in Government, that the full implementation of this plan at this level of expenditure would place heavy financial burdens upon agriculture, and would thus cause dissatisfaction among persons in many agricultural areas upon whom these politicians depended for votes. Moreover, it would upset several large agrochemical and food producing and processing organisations with considerable political influence. Accordingly, even as the legislation was being debated before being finally passed into law, agriculture was duly mentioned but the way was left open to excuse agriculture from making the contribution to the required investments and other contributions that reflected its true significance. Thus, although agriculture accounted for some 90 percent of nitrogen emissions, it contributed with only 4 billion of the 12 billion Crowns.

Most of the effort and expenditure involved therefore fell upon municipal waste authorities and other industrial sectors. The task of 'policing' this diversion of effort and expenditure to less politically sensitive sectors then devolved in turn upon the respective ministries and their civil servants, many of whom were scientifically qualified and could not but be aware that this exclusion of the agricultural sector made the objectives of the plan as a whole largely unrealisable.

The *Vandmiljøplan 1* had naturally been discussed intensively among professionals in hydraulics, chemistry, biology, ecology, agronomy and other relevant specialisations, and in fact from 1982 onwards. It was clear to most of the scientifically and technically qualified persons involved that, although this would provide a tremendous boost to research and practise in Denmark, the effective exclusion of agriculture from participation would make the plan unrealisable even in 30 years, let alone in 5 years. Hans Schrøder, of the Danish Water Quality Institute (*VKI*, after its Danish orthography), a 'Self-owned Foundation' under the umbrella of the Danish Academy of Technical Sciences (*ATV*), described the result of his own intervention in this debate, through his participation in a radio interview given to Danish State Radio on the role of nitrates in pollution, as follows:

> One morning in April 1983 I came to VKI in the belief that this would be a quite normal day. But it was not. Even outside the main entrance I was met by an agitated secretary who said that I had to telephone to several persons, and especially to two from the Agricultural Advice Centre (*Landbrugets Rådgivningscenter*).

I did this and spoke with [two] Chief Consultants, who immediately set about 'to put things in their proper place' in this matter, and made me the surprising offer to retract everything that I had said and written on agricultural nitrate pollution and throw my report into the waste paper basket (with the understanding that I should then escape from further retribution). I could have accepted if they had questioned what I had said and written. But this they did not do: they rejected outright that agriculture had anything whatsoever to do with nitrogen pollution and offered me an honourable withdrawal if I took everything back again.

...In my contribution [to the radio interview] I said, what everyone in VKI had known for the last ten years and what had become clear to everyone interested in the matter, that agriculture had to be involved in combating pollution if the programme as a whole was to have any effect. From the Environmental Agency (*Miljøstyrelsen*) we (at VKI) had the following reaction: with immediate effect we were to be deprived of all project funds in the area of the aquatic environment. Together with this we were called to a 'Collegial Discussion' (which, apart from physical violence and the threat of physical violence, differed little from what one sees in gangster films) in the Ministry of the Environment, where now it was the turn of the Vice Director and the Office Head to 'put things in their right place' for us, and gave us an 'offer' the content of which was only too clear: 'Shut up, or more sanctions will follow'. In fact, more sanctions were applied, because *Miljøstyrelsen*, through negative commentaries to our proposals, hindered us in obtaining funds from other sources.

It was VKI's founder and director until November 1984 who had made it possible for us at VKI to be open and direct in our criticism, and it was he also who had made my radio interview possible. [However] the record of VKI's participation in the subsequent public debate provides a model of how badly everything can go when an Institute, that is really dependent on the system, tries to behave in the manner that the President of the Academy of Technical Sciences (ATV) and other such persons had long supported and propagated, that true science 'does not aim at political consensus, but is always in some sense politically revolutionary'.

The Institute survived by finding the 'politically correct' direction by changing its director. But it is not difficult to imagine how everything would have gone if it had continued its scientific revolt led by its upright first director. In that case VKI would probably have celebrated its 25 anniversary in 1997 not with 160 staff, but maybe only 16. Maybe there would have been no anniversary to celebrate at all.

To this we must add that Hans Schrøder received much support and encouragement in his attempts to challenge the state apparatus, and by no means least from the director of the Danish Hydraulic Institute (DHI), a sister institute to VKI, who took Schrøder back into its employ in 1985. This was possible because DHI was scarcely dependent upon *Miljøministeriet* or any other government organisation for that matter, while the total of its government funding for research was only 1.5 percent of its turnover. DHI was running for all practical purposes as a private business. Schrøder prepared several proposals in the field of the aquatic environment. However, "Many months and many planning meetings later it was made clear to me that [a particular person in] the Danish Environmental Agency [*Miljøstyrelsen*] had instructed his collaborators that I was to be excluded from all further cooperation with *Miljøstyrelsen*." Since there were no other aquatic environmental projects at DHI upon which Hans Schrøder could be employed, in 1989 he was transferred through the good offices of DHI to AIT in Bangkok, where he remained until 1995.

It has to be emphasised that the President of the Academy, leading professors at the Technical University and of other educational institutes, nearly all colleagues at VKI and DHI, the former covertly and latter at least initially overtly, followed and supported

Schrøder's efforts. He became 'a Mini-Sakharov in a Mini-Land'. However, neither Schrøder nor his supporters could prevail against 'The System' with its thoroughgoing and total 'politicisation' of environmental science and technology in Denmark.

It should be mentioned that so far as VKI was concerned, a direct line can be traced between the situation in which that institute was placed when its new director took over in 1985, and all criticism of government policy by VKI staff was forbidden on pain of dismissal, and the effective bankruptcy of VKI in 1999-2000 and its consequent fusion with DHI. While 'easy money' flowed from government agencies for 'rubber-stamping' their actions, scarcely any attempt was made by VKI to develop commercial software that would integrate with and help provide the services and other facilities that VKI could offer, while almost the only international work in which VKI was engaged was through its association, as a next-door neighbour, to DHI. Beyond this again, VKI lost credibility through its association with a project that was becoming increasingly untenable. As soon as VKI started to loose its credibility as an independent organisation, so it lost its value to the administration and could be 'rationalised' accordingly.

Of course it is easy, especially in retrospect, to accuse the persons who collaborated in a policy that was so obviously and blatantly unfounded on recorded fact and scientific understanding of duplicity and dishonestly. However, the director of an organisation, even though it is an 'independent' foundation, is responsible not only to the high-sounding aims of the organisation to support scientific integrity, as written in its statutes, but also for the livelihood of the persons who work there, and thus their families also. This matter was taken up during the 25th anniversary of VKI in 1997, where it was the intention that the then minister of the Environment should listen to the views of the scientific community, chosen for the most part from outside of VKI, speaking with one voice. As it was, the minister was the last to arrive and arrived late, stumbled through his prepared speech, unable to pronounce many of the words, and left again immediately. He neither wanted to know nor appeared to care at all about the scientific integrity of 'his' plan, leaving such 'details' to his 'public servants'.

(In this respect we may recall Niccolo Machievelli's observation that "Princes should leave to others the enactment of unpopular measures and keep in their own hands the distribution of favours").

The President of the ATV, who was the next to speak after the (by then departed) minister and who had prepared his speech specifically for politicians, and for the minister in particular, observed that "It is not reassuring to take advice from persons who are economically dependent upon you". He then continued, by posing the question: "Are researchers dependent upon political interests?" He led the answer from the side of the assembled research community by saying: "If the path of research is to be determined by political interests, we are back in the Middle Ages".

As another speaker then emphasised further:

> It is of decisive importance that researchers are independent, otherwise politicians can get them to say, or deny, anything at all – exactly like the Church did in the Middle Ages. Public servants (*Embedsmændene*) do what the politicians expect of them, or what they believe the politicians expect of them. And ATV Institutes respect what one is bound to respect, that the customer is always right. And we cannot really blame them for that.
> It is in fact unreasonable to demand that they should behave independently and bite the hand that feeds them.

> ….It is with politicians as it is with [any other] client: they get what they wish, and when they do not want the truth, then they will not get it either. The customer is always right.

Following this debate conducted by scientists and ignored by politicians and their public servants, one is struck by the apparent naivety of the scientific community in this respect. They had clearly not bothered to read at all in political science, as initiated in the modern era by Machiavelli, Hobbes, Locke and Montesquieu. If they had done this they would not be in the least bit surprised by the behaviour to which they were witnesses, and indeed if they had read such more recent critics, running at least from Durkheim to Althusser, they would not expect anything else. Thus, if we just change the word 'Prince' to 'minister' and the word 'minister' to 'public servant' in Machievelli's masterpiece, we may read:

> A man entrusted with the tasks of administration should never think of himself but of his minister, and should never concern himself with anything except the minister's affairs. To keep his public servant up to the mark, the minister, on his side, should pay him honour, enrich him, put him in his debt and share with him both honours and responsibilities. Thus the public servant will see how dependent he is upon the minister, and then having riches and honours to the point of surfeit he will desire no more; holding so many offices, he cannot but fear change. When, therefore, relations between ministers and public servant are of this kind, they can have confidence in each other; when they are otherwise the result is always disastrous for both of them.

We should observe how the Danish administration has followed Machiavelli's advice on the need to reward its loyal public servants most generously. Already, as of 2001, most of the top positions in the government administration were occupied by persons who had collaborated in this way. As for Hans Schrøder, he remains to this day disbarred from all government contracts following his 'kamikaze' activities. Other examples are provide by the two public servants who have exposed the unethical machinations and corruption of the European Commission, the one whose revelations led to the collective resignation/dismissal of the Commissioners and the other to criminal proceedings against the EC agency concerned. The two main 'culprits' in these exposures remain 'suspended'. Similar fates have befallen persons in the UK who have fallen foul of political interests. Clearly, in our time no one can confront any state apparatus in such a direct way and expect to survive professionally: only an indirect approach is feasible at all in such cases. Consequently, almost everyone today understands this and 'keeps a low profile': it is extraordinary how few brave men and women there are who dare to speak out the truth in these matters.

It is time here to conclude this episode from little Denmark, whose 5 million inhabitants had come to spend some 20 billion Danish Crowns by 2001on a programme that should have been completed by that time, but which it came to be accepted, even politically, might perhaps be realised in another 20 years or so, if ever at all. It then came as no surprise when a new government that had fewer vested interests in this matter made drastic cuts in the budgets that supported this and similar programmes.

It remains however important to understand that this problem of the politicisation of science has become more acute over the last century or so. Thus, to take a case from The Netherlands (Alberts, 1986, p. 30-31):

> In the middle of the last [nineteenth] century a Netherlands minister made a statement on the obligations of a civil-servant [*Ambtenaar*] that we find rather strange today. His outlook is expressed in a private correspondence but he appears to have stated it later in public. He thus meant what he said.
> He was a capable man. Ministers were at that time... His staff never sent a replacement to his department: they were very careful.
> The minister thus stood for dutiful responsibility - and then something else besides. One of his friends – political friends we would say today – had asked his opinion about a Mr. So-and-So who had been proposed for a higher position in the administration. So-and-So was already Department Head and so directly under the Minister, so the Minister knew him in and out. His advice was that So-and-So should not be considered for such an appointment because he was not an upright man, and this was because – and here it comes – *he has broken the golden rule that applies to all civil servants:* ' *Whose bread you eat, his words you speak'.*
> Strong language, isn't it!
> But perhaps less strong than it first appears. We know in fact what dreadful crime So-and-So had committed and we can easily imagine what would happen to him today. He was in complete disagreement with the policy exposed by the Minister on fiscal-agricultural matters and had expressed his views in a brochure. That was his personal view of the matter and we can at once add that he was in no way sanctioned for it.
> And what would happen to the man today? What would happen with the top civil-servant who allowed himself to be interviewed on television or wrote an article in a quality newspaper that did not leave much over from the Minister's government policy? He would be forbidden to speak and write anything more and if that did not help the So-and-So would be sent on sick leave. For a civil servant who gets it in his head to attack a ministerial policy appears to belong more in a psychiatric institution.
> The minister of the nineteenth century was more humane. He did nothing, except to say no when asked whether So-and So was suited to a higher position. His negative advice otherwise left the man unharmed.

Happy days indeed! Alberts himself survived a Japanese prison camp, albeit at the last stage before death, and was left crippled with diabetes. Returning to the Dutch Colonial Administration, but in The Netherlands, he suggested to the Minister that the Minister's current policy of reasserting Dutch colonial rule by killing tens of thousands of Indonesian men, women and children was not perhaps the best way to regain their support – and was dismissed on the spot.

There are any number of other examples where politics 'sits in the driver's seat' and science and technology are used only to provide the credibility and thus the public support necessary to pull the political wagon along – and never to criticise that policy. A string of papers in the area of Policy Analysis have dealt with this matter, but it does appear that their only remedy is...even more Policy Analysis! Several highly-critical books on the privatisation of water, together with its treatment and distribution systems, have now appeared. All manner and forms of regulation have been described and analysed in newspaper and television programmes, as have the financial manipulations frequently involved (with Enron still a prime example). The associated connivance and often shady manoeuvres of the World Bank and other such institutions have now also been extensively exposed (e.g. Easterly, 1999; Stiglitz, 2001). The immense damages done to human societies and to nature, and not least to the high-minded principles embodied in the charters and statutes of so many organisations, have also been highly publicised. All the problems that arise in these exposures are in their essence, however, problems of ethics, and so we shall only return to these matters through one particular aspect in the next chapter when we shall characterise situations of the kind described so fully above in terms of *the authentic in the service of the inauthentic*.

3.8 Geopolitics and distance control

Within its specifically European context, sociotechnology is essential for the understanding of *Geopolitics*, understood as political actions proceeding between different language groups. Many of the most obvious and dramatic case studies historically are concerned with just this aspect of politics while some of the most immediately relevant today arise as geopolitics itself now becomes increasingly the norm within the 'Europe of the 25' and also as representative democracy as a whole becomes increasingly moribund and is augmented and reinforced by participatory democracy.

Sociotechnical case studies in this genre usually include the development of constructs intended to maintain the control of processes proceeding at such a distance from the centre of power that some measure of *distance control* becomes essential. The first well known example of this was the Roman road network. Such constructs are regarded in sociotechnical studies as means for changing the space and time scales of processes of power and information/knowledge transmission. The Roman road network still provides not only the paradigm case of a system that was devised to project power/knowledge at a distance by changing such scales of space and time, but also the paradigm case of how this device turned against its originator as the Roman Empire imploded, leading to the repeated incursions of the peoples of the peripheral tribes to plunder, sack and control Rome itself.

Classical studies also include the distance control of the earliest, Portuguese, seaborne trading arrangements with Asia, and specifically with the Portuguese settlements in trading stations with warehouses and factories, whereby an extraordinary level of control had to be and indeed was maintained almost entirely from Lisbon over hitherto unprecedented space and time scales. The development of the great trading companies, from the Dutch East India Company (actually largely initiated by refugees from Spanish oppression in what is present-day Belgium) onwards through its many imitators, provide other case studies again. The era of the *European colonisation* of the entire land surface of the Earth with the exception of China, Japan, Korea and Thailand has provided many case studies in the sociotechnology of distance control.

The relation of this to the very recent accession of North East Asia (China, Korea and Japan) to the position of the world's most highly industrialised region, with the European Union relegated to a second place and North America descending into an ever more distant third place, has its own relevance here, raising in our own time the notion that Europe and Asia are essentially one continent, called 'Eurasia'. Another case history, that may be quite popular at this point, even though it belongs properly to the next section, is that of the development of the British navy, as the first world-encompassing sociotechnical system. The origins of British and Dutch sea power in piracy (albeit if only as a 'sideline' in the case of the Dutch) should be mentioned to indicate the anarchistic element that supported much of this success, as maintained in the British navy by the practice of paying what were often lavish rewards in 'prize money' to captains and crews – and even to their shore-bound admirals also - when they captured enemy vessels and their cargos.

The development of the colonial era into the full-blown *imperialism* of the nineteenth century can be seen as the apogee of these kinds of geopolitical activities, but the sociotechnology of this phase passes over into the next section. It should none the less be observed that sociotechnical developments in such situations turned the movement towards a more extended democracy on its head, in that it made possible the subjugation, and in some cases the physical annihilation, of populations and whole peoples. It has however to be stressed when studying this aspect that the technological component was essentially neutral in these processes and indeed in many cases it was this component that catalysed the process of decolonisation, as exemplified by the use of the Indian railway system by the Indian nationalist movement to spread its message. Similarly, the role of Japanese imperialism in destroying the ethos of European imperialism in Asia provides a particularly remarkable case study of a sociotechnical-geopolitical nature.

Geopolitics in our own time is also increasingly dominated by the transmission of power indirectly, by communication. The major television chains, newspaper and weekly journals have become international, all pumping out the same 'news' and 'analysis', very little of which is constative, but instead overwhelmingly performative. Much the greater part of this is in the English language, with the inevitable result that this language suffers also from distortions of meanings, false definitions and cosmetic phraseology. Thus, just to take one brief item of news from Irak on the day that this is written, when hundreds of innocent people are killed and many hundreds more again are mutilated, and most of these are women and children, this is simply called, as usual nowadays, "collateral damage". This anaesthetisation of language, together with the cosmetic treatment of visual impressions on television through the 'embedding' of reporters and cameramen, is an integral part of the technologies of persuasion that nowadays dominate the 'news media'. It is in this same vein that, when these media profess to be 'spreading democracy' in various parts of the world, they are thinking only in terms of Tweedledee and Tweedledum politics, and whenever some nation throws off this travesty of true democracy these same media are the first to denounce it. It is perhaps because of the immense damage that is currently being done to language – which Heidegger described as "the house of Being" – that some of the greatest contemporary linguists and others deeply concerned with language, such as Noam Chomsky, Jacques Derrida and Christopher Norris, are among the foremost in denouncing the kind of politics that necessitates such deformations. Words like 'liberty', 'terrorist', 'security', 'democratic', 'fanatic', 'anti-Semitic' and so on are nowadays taken out of all their historically-determined and dictionary-established contexts, their true meanings being torn to shreds in the interests of political manipulation. It cannot be our concern to condemn this here, of course, but only to constate it.

It should be obvious, but still it must be said: the true leader can never 'play politics' and should never try. Even if he is tempted to do so, he should always reflect that he would almost certainly fail in it. He would forget which lies he told last time, he would lapse in his deformations of language, and he could never sustain the open, honest expression and beautifully controlled body language of the professional politician. Such deception and dishonesty generally constitute an art, and it is one that the true leader should not so much as try to practise,

3.9 War as sociotechnology

"War", in Clausewitz'dictum, "is the continuation of politics by other means". However, the expression 'War and the Man' points to the strong interaction between the technical means and the human-social arrangements that are even more of the essence of armed conflict than they are of political development. Sound leadership in war has always demanded sociotechnical insights and every armed conflict has been essentially a conflict between sociotechnical systems. This has long been apparent in naval warfare, where a thorough knowledge and understanding of the technical aspects, such as those of navigation, mobility and armament, had always to be closely coordinated with the complex of human functions that 'brought the technical equipment to life' so to speak. As Nelson observed, "Men, not ships, fight battles". Leadership to a high degree has always consisted of the art and science of coordinating the technical equipment and the human resources that were available to the best possible effect and in providing the training that made this highest level of coordination possible. As probably the most widely available because most popular reference describing the high level of ability on both social and technical sides that were held together by a leader of exceptional sociotechnical experience and brilliance, one can do no better than refer to the semi-fictional figure of Jack Aubrey in the 18-volume series of Patrick O'Brian on the role of naval power and naval intelligence in the geopolitics of the period of the French Revolutionary and Napoleonic wars. It is useful to read these alongside a biography of their real-world prototype in the person of Thomas Cochrane, who Napoleon christened "The Sea Wolf" for his daring exploits and who, after being most incorrectly discharged from the British navy, played a major part in the wars of independence of Peru, Chile, Brazil and Greece.

In this connection, the study of war also provides the most valuable insights into that which is called 'chance' and 'luck'. It is still often recalled that Napoleon, on receiving a recommendation to promote a man to the higher ranks of command, always asked in the first place: "But is he lucky?" Chance and luck are often surrogates for something else again, which is an awareness deep within the unconscious mind of the 'lucky' person that is not accessible to the outside observer. It is this that can cause that person to take decisions the outcome of which must appear to depend entirely on 'chance' and 'luck', even though we would find, if we could seek deeply enough, that they are really based upon calculations proceeding below the level of consciousness. We shall return to this when we come to consider the character structure of the *entrepreneur*, as a natural associate of the leader, in the next chapter.

In the case of war, the misleading of an enemy is often as important as the leading of one's own forces and the *arts of deception* have been extensively practised in this field since time immemorial. These arts of deception are also of a sociotechnical nature, involving not only people but also often elaborate technical simulacra, such as the camp fires kept burning in the already evacuated French encampment area on the night before the Three Emperors' battle at Austerlitz in 1805, or the use of dummy trucks, tanks and guns at El Alamein in 1942, or even the extensive modification of an old and largely disarmed British battleship to resemble a new one from 1942 to 1945. Similarly, *stealth* has always been of the essence in the successful prosecution of war.

These examples alone indicate that war is not a business - even though many individuals and organisations have made a business out of it. In practice, business proceeds in ways that are markedly and fundamentally different to the ways in which wars are prosecuted. The study of war is none the less very valuable to the leader in industry, and then not because armed conflict can be equated to industrial competition – these are in fact very different activities – but because of the insight that it provides into matching human and technical-artefactual material in sociotechnical constructs. We study war not because it so much resembles industrial competition – and certainly not because we are in any way 'warlike' - but because it provides us with case studies in sociotechnology that have been far more extensively documented and much more carefully analysed than anything in the area of industrial development.

In particular, the study of war demonstrates more clearly than any other activity the disastrous consequences of introducing a mismatch between the social and the technological components: it provides most of the paradigm cases among the case studies in this field. Indeed, one can formulate the following principle on the basis of a study of military sociotechnology alone:

The more competent and well organised on the social side and the more competent and well organised on the technical side, the greater the disaster unless the technical and social aspects are properly coordinated.

The case study that provides the supreme paradigm case of this principle remains to this day that of the so-called 'Western Front' that stretched across France and Belgium from Switzerland to the North Sea in the First World War. Scarcely ever before in history had there been such effective social arrangements for the recruiting, assembling, feeding, accommodating, basic training and transporting of men and horses – yes, horses were also 'recruited'! – while never before in history had such 'weapons of mass destruction' as barbed wire, machine guns, heavy artillery and poison gas been available in such quantities and of such quality; and yet the consequences of the employment of these unparalleled social and technical resources only provided the greatest sequence of military disasters in history associated with a mutually debilitating military stalemate. The historian Alan Clark said of the British commander, Haig, that (Clark p.186):

> [He commanded] the greatest army that the Empire had ever put in the field in the past, and was ever to amass in the future. A body whose heroism and devotion was such that they could twice in two successive years be ravaged in hopeless offensives, who were to loose in a single day more men than any other army in the history of the world, whom, after twenty seven months of slaughter and exhaustion, he was to leave so perilously exposed that they were nearly annihilated.

Only with the development of the appropriate sociotechnical solution – the tank with radio communications and an appropriate communications and command system coordinating its use with other arms – was the stalemate of the Western Front broken and the war ended.

The sociotechnology of war, or the study of war as a sociotechnology, often emphasises the erection of hierarchies and the development of taxonomies in other ways than those used in other disciplines. It should be emphasised that hierarchies are not only social hierarchies, as exemplified by the allocations of ranks in the armed services, but are always based at some point on a real or at least supposed *sociotechnical competence*.

Competence, however, is itself a Form that extends over many other fields than those of sociotechnology, just as it transcends the social and the technical. Competence, as a Form, constitutes an *existential* category, very much as leadership does also, and indeed sound leadership can be seen as one form or manifestation of competence. For this reason it is better to leave this aspect of 'competence' here at this point, on the understanding that most people have some feeling of what competence is and can recognise it in at least some places at some times. Large parts of official military histories are dedicated to delineations of military competence, even as even larger parts of unofficial histories, as observed earlier here, are given over to military incompetence. The notion of competence is one of the issues taken up in the Second Appendix that concludes this work, where it is seen to be a function of *agency*. [5]

Hierarchies in this military sense are the primary instruments and expressions of organisational structures in which commands are passed in one fixed and prescribed direction and not in others: they define extreme instances of what we have earlier described as *exostructured organisations*. However, precisely in situations which demonstrate the most extreme levels of incompetence and absence of authentic leadership, as in the example of the Western Front in 1914 to 1918, it is observed that endostructures appear spontaneously and, to the extent that anything much was gained at all in many of the battles that were fought within that context, this was largely due to the spontaneous emerging of these endostructural arrangements. Thus, for example, as the massive 'human waves' of infantry were thrown into battle to struggle over barbed wire entanglements that were distorted but by no means destroyed by the preceding massive artillery bombardments, and so were easily mown down by enemy machine guns protected in concrete blockhouses, so a few survivors broke into small groups and leapfrogged from shell hole to shell hole to destroy the machine gun nests with grenades. Such tactics were never accepted at the command level of course and were considered highly irregular and indeed 'unacceptable' because they were regarded as "undisciplined" and "anarchistic".

In much the same vein, the sociotechnical stalemate that characterised that conflict could only be broken by the introduction of new sociotechnical means, as realised by the tank and its appropriate personnel and their communications equipment, situated within a new kind of battle plan coordinating the contributions of supporting arms. Because of the total sociotechnical incompetence of the exostructure, however, the first employment of tank formations proceeded with a total disregard for the communicational and support functions, leading to grievous losses, and it needed two years and some millions more lives to be lost before these lessons in sociotechnology were taken to heart.

This particular lesson from warfare is also important to the leader as an example of the importance of persistence in the face of all manner of reverses administered by persons who oppose and sabotage their efforts at every opportunity. At our present time, for example, it is now clear to some people at least that so-called 'knowledge-intensive' agricultures, aquacultures and health services, which make long-established organic, homeopathic and ayuvedic methods effectively and cheaply viable in all parts of the world, have the capacity to resolve most of the world's food and health problems at a small fraction of the costs of the currently dominant methods. These developments however call for skills that are not those that are available to those commanding the so-called 'development agenda', so they are almost entirely ignored.

In the case of conventional warfare in more recent times, it is only through the development of fast and flexible computation and communication technologies in the competent hands of properly trained and led troops, effectively unrestrained by the constraints of place, space and time, that it has become possible to initiate what are essentially post-modern sociotechnologies within what remain predominantly exostructured organisations.. On the other hand, however, these sociotechnologies are now much better suited to what is still regarded as unconventional warfare, which is associated much more with endostructured organisations, for which *al-Qaeda* currently provides the paradigm case.[6]

Case studies can be taken almost every day now from the pages of newspapers and from television reports. All guerrilla movements and other forms of armed resistance to exostructured military occupiers have adopted endostructures, only passing over to more defined command structures when they succeed in displacing the occupier - and then come to face dissent within their own ranks. Among conventional exostructured armed forces, it has been pointed out that only the British Navy insists on the exercise of personal initiative over and beyond the command structure when this is deemed necessary by the person or persons most directly concerned, so that a 'fall-back mechanism' providing a reversion to an endostructure is accommodated within the exostructure itself.

Military and naval sociotechnologies also provide valuable insights into a whole range of *questions concerning taxonomies*, these being concerned with how organisations are to be divided into interacting parts and how these parts are to be related and connected in exostructured organisations - or how they may be and do in fact come to be related and connected under given sets of sociotechnical arrangements in endostructured organisations. Thus, in conventional military terms, this is about how an army is to be composed of various regiments with corresponding varieties of competences and equipment for realising these competencies, or how a brigade or a division is to be composed with various regiments and their arms for a particular purpose, or how the weapons themselves will be differentiated, such as guns may be differentiated by calibre, muzzle velocity, elevation, range, accuracy, ammunition types and rate of fire, or tanks may be differentiated from heavy battle tanks downward in size and weight of fire, in every case necessitating different tactical, command and manning arrangements. Most of manufacturing industry confronts much the same problems, such as how to redeploy its existing machines and their associated skills to best advantage so as to maintain a required pace of product innovation and development. Such problems are usually 'solved' by some process of reorganisation, such as always poses problems of elaborating new taxonomies, and this must then proceed in a sociotechnical way and not in a technocratic way.

The more obvious case studies include the development of a complex, multinational but highly mobile Swedish army, first under Gustav Adolph and subsequently under Charles XII - with its partial imitation by Peter the Great – and its next successor in complexity and mobility, albeit after almost 250 years, in the form of the Panzer divisions of the Second World War. In both cases these forces won extraordinary victories with remarkably small numbers of men and quite negligible losses on their own side, but then only until their opponents imitated or bettered their methods and equipment, that is, these opponents imitated their sociotechnical arrangements or devised other and even better ones.

The way in which military strategy and tactics have been adapted to what might still best be called 'national character' and the employment of multinational and even multiethnic forces provide further case studies again, and these naturally cast their own light on questions concerning cultural and other forms of diversity in present-day industry.

The sociotechnology of war provides also some of the best case studies in the promotion of invention and innovation in the face of established opposition, and this aspect may also be covered under this heading. These studies indicate how inventors and innovators have worked to realise their projects, usually against formidable opposition, and the lessons that can be drawn from their experiences, such as their seeking out the weakest among a group of competitors as the one most likely to embrace their innovative schemes. The development of the torpedo by Whitehead provides a paradigm case.

Among other studies in this area, those directed to the formation of military alliances and coalitions provide examples of the dynamics of stability or otherwise contributed by the various arrangements that were introduced. Many cases of failed mergers and cooperation agreements in industry only reflect lessons that could have been learnt very easily from the study of military and naval history.

3.10 Creative business as sociotechnology

Technology owes its name to its creative spirit and, to the extent that it brings together people to practise technology in a common enterprise, so it becomes at one and the same time an industry and a sociotechnology. A creative business is one that is driven in the first instance by an urge to create which is natural to most, if not all, human beings. In order that this business can continue its creative activities in our current societies it must of course be financially viable, but that is rarely the primary reason for its existence. From the point of view of the born leader, businesses are not built in order to make money, but money is made in order to build businesses. Other persons than the leader may not necessarily see it that way, but we are here talking about leadership.

In the construction of a creative business, the leader has to balance in practice the relation between the objects of his concern and their social, including money, values on the one hand, and the relation between these same objects and their intrinsic, including personal, values on the other hand. As explained towards the end of the first of the appendices that conclude this book, these two relations are connected by what are there called 'natural transformations', as entities that are irreducible, 'as given at the Creation'. We may then in fact define:

A creative business is one in which the transformation from the objects of the business into their social values is maintained in a right balance with the transformation of these same objects into their intrinsic values.

Our next and last chapter will now take us into the world of the leader in this undertaking.

Chapter 4

THE EUROPEAN LEADER OF INDUSTRY

4.1 To the future leader of industry

As a leader of industry you will have many friends and only one enemy. You have now met this enemy and have been introduced to this 'it-which-is-no-thing' which we have correspondingly call 'nothingness'. Since however this enemy is within everyone, and by no means least of all within your own self, it is the most dangerous of all enemies. Although it is within everyone else, that by no means makes them enemies. They are not in themselves enemies, for only nothingness is in itself your enemy. This is not my own teaching or anyone else's own teaching, but it is the universal teaching of all ages.

Of your many friends as a leader of industry, there is one who will always be the most trusted and reliable, and this is technology. In the myths and legends that have been bequeathed to us, technology is commonly symbolised by the most sociotechnical of all its productions, which is the sword. In the ancient Germanic myths this was the sword *Notung*, driven into the greatest of trees by Wotan himself, and only to be withdrawn from that tree by 'the one' who had the most upright character and thus the greatest strength of character as given by the gods. When broken - but then only through a division within the circle of the gods - it could only be reforged by 'the one' who was again of godly descent in this sense of nobility of character. In the Arthurian legends it was the sword *Excalibur*, driven into a great stone and again such that it could only be withdrawn from the stone by 'the one' with the finest and greatest strength of character. 'The one' was the person who was 'the right person in the right place at the right time', as corresponds to the integration mystery that we have introduced in Chapter 2. Those who are chosen to lead and accept such leadership are, within this generalising metaphor, those who must once yet again draw the sword. They must then aspire in the first place, not to leadership itself, but to the upright character and strength of character that will make them worthy of the trust that is to be placed in them as a leader of industry. And the measure of this trust is the sword that is to be girded metaphorically at their side, as the weapon of technology applied in society. It is in this sense that:

Technology is always on your side.

As a leader then, your most immediate responsibility is to your own self. And this is the whole self, as we have defined it following Hegel and Kierkegaard in the second of the Appendices that conclude this work. This is then not only, or even so much, the intellectual self, but it is the combination of all the modes of existence of the self, as the *existential self*. Thus the development that our Institute seeks to foster is an 'all-round', or, to use a nowadays much overused expression, the 'holistic' development of the self. This is then not only a development of the mind, and in no way at all involves any emphasis on the development of the body, but is something that starts out from or is based upon what we might call a 'mind-body' development. In terms of its problematic it is concerned with the so-called 'mind-body problem' as this was initiated by the phenomenologist philosopher Maurice Merleau-Ponty already from the 1940s onwards. In its more material sense this has to do with the physical and psychological balance and general sense of well-being of the individual person, such as may be developed in part through the training of his or her proprioceptive system. To this end there are many practices and the choice of which is the more suited than the other to a particular individual is already a significant part of this problematic.

Of course all this may appear unduly portentous, but that is because it is meant most seriously. In your activities as an authentic leader you will almost certainly be plunged into stressful situations and you will most likely also have on some occasions at least, like Hamlet, to "suffer the slings and arrows of outrageous fortune". Thus, as Machiavelli expressed the matter and as we shall have cause to emphasise later here: "In times of quiet and peace the Prince makes his preparations for riot and war". Such activities constitute one part of these preparations, and a not insignificant part, and it is our responsibility to introduce you and further encourage you to maintain such activities, as practices, throughout your life, and even under, and especially under, the most difficult circumstances.

Unlike so many 'business schools' our objective is not to raise up your spirits to any sense of euphoria. We may recall again, with Tolstoy, how the old Marshals of the Austrian and Russian armies before Austerlitz sensed the disaster that Napoleon was preparing for them and were aghast at what one of them called "the hip-hip-hurrah!" atmosphere of the young Austrian and Russian Emperors and their entourage of sycophantic younger officers for whom victory appeared already assured. In the actions that you will have to take you will have little room for euphoria, but will promote instead a quiet confidence in the correctness of what you and your colleagues are doing based upon the best plan and the most thorough preparations that you and your colleagues have been able to put together in the time available. You will have to be bold when boldness is required and cautious when caution is necessary and you must be able to distinguish which of these *attitudes* is the most appropriate in a given situation – and of course there are many other kinds of situations requiring any number of different attitudes besides.

As observed earlier, your attitudes are the consequences of your *belief system*, as largely formed by your experience, working upon the *facts* with which you are confronted. The correct attitudes, and following from these the correct decisions, are then formed by the belief system that you have acquired and the facts that you are able to assemble, so that the foremost tasks are, on the one hand, to enrich and strengthen the means by which your belief system may most advantageously develop itself, and, on the other hand, to educate you in acquiring the means to access and select the facts that will be most relevant to your belief system in the formation of your most appropriate attitudes and subsequent decisions.

should be natural

4.2 Your belief system

Your care for your belief-system is your next-most immediate responsibility, for it is this that is in its turn responsible for your sense of what is real and what is not real, and thus of what is true and what is not true. We have to be clear at once, of course, that our collections of beliefs will never form a system in the strict sense established by Kant, as forming a totally ordered and completely consistent whole, but we have the responsibility to approach this 'ideal' as closely as we can even while accepting, and even promoting the understanding, that such an 'ideal' is in fact as impossible in attainment as it is undesirable in practice. And indeed, in the generalised object-value theory established a century after Kant by Meinong, which we shall take as another reference in our courses, 'completeness' is understood in this more relaxed and attainable manner, as also introduced in the first Appendix to the present work. It is for this reason that we persist for the most part in using the term 'system' in this context. [2]

Your beliefs are the products of your experience of events and of the facts that accompanied these events. These experiences and their contextual facts may be acquired either by your direct personal experience or, as is more common nowadays, from communications emanating from others. The first are of course usually the more reliable but the most demanding to acquire, while the second are on average less reliable but easier to acquire.

All belief systems are however accumulative in that, given a certain configuration of existing beliefs, it is easier to introduce or reject a new belief. This propensity obviously also has its disadvantages in that an existing faulty belief system may propagate its faults further by accepting more faulty beliefs again through this same accumulative principle. It is then through this last mechanism that nothingness works in subverting the sense of reality and the intimation of truth of the individual, by seeking out existing false beliefs and building out on these further again. In his masterpiece on the consequence of this process of subversion, Kierkegaard referred to it in his nineteenth century Danish as a *Sandsebedrag*, which translates literally to a "deception of the senses", which sounds at first a little strange, for why should this deception be "of the senses"? But, as always, Kierkegaard was on the right track, for this process of subversion has the effect that even sense impressions as 'mere' data are interpreted differently as they are translated into 'facts' and are conjoined with the faulty belief system to subvert the attitudes and thence the decisions of the afflicted individual. Thus two persons with different belief systems may well observe exactly the same event but take very different attitudes and make very different decisions accordingly, so that the very senses of one of these persons at least must be 'let-down' or *deceived* by the actions that follow from what they have correctly registered with their sense organs. They *look* at one and the same thing, but they *see* different things.

In order to correct a situation of this kind we have to "raise (*ophæver*) a deception of the senses". It is usually quite impossible to do this directly by simply telling the person concerned that he or she is 'wrong'. The effect of such a direct communication is usually only to harden the resolution of the individual in persisting in his or her 'wrong-mindedness'. The approach that has almost always to be followed is the indirect one that we have met earlier when introducing the technologies of persuasion. There we saw how the technologies of persuasion were used by the media and other organs to propagate one or the other form of nothingness, but now we have to consider how much the same technologies can be 'run in reverse' so to say, to oppose and expose nothingness.

Naturally, you may ask, why should your technologies of persuasion when serving the right cause overcome the technologies of persuasion that are in the hands of those who are employed in the service of nothingness? The answer is of course entirely clear: because it was Moses' staff-cum-snake that ate up all the staffs-cum-snakes of Pharaoh's magicians: it is because technology was on his side just as it is always on the side of the authentic.

This Biblical paradigm case of the triumph of technology in the service of the authentic over technology in the service of the inauthentic already teaches us a first lesson about how it is that this triumph *functions* in the service of persuasion. For the story is in its own way *amusing*, which is to say that *it has humour on its side*. But of course for the ancient Greeks humour was the language of the gods and it has always served to distinguish the authentic from the inauthentic. Given the capacity of nothingness to imitate everything, a sense of humour is not an infallible yardstick of authenticity, but on the whole it is a good measure. Thus we observe the great prevalence of jokes on the Internet directed at a current notorious power monger and what he has high-jacked to become a greatly destructive 'rogue state' – so many jokes, indeed, that no further indication of his identity is required! This particular movement indeed reached new heights as this was being written with the award of the *Palme d'Or* at the Cannes film festival to Michael Moore for his film *Fahrenheit 9/11*.

A healthy sense of humour on your own part is then of great value in the positive development of your belief system as something authentic, just as humour is also of great value to you in your efforts to raise the deception of the senses of individuals afflicted by the untruths of nothingness. Humour is then of the essence of the indirect approach in communication as a power capable of exposing the deceptions of nothingness. It is through its power to attain such effects that humour *builds*, and so *creates something*: it also is something poietic, as some kind of 'technology of the spirit' as it participates actively and positively in 'the technologies of persuasion'.

Humour is itself only one of a series of techniques for lifting states of *Sandsebedrag*, of the deception of the senses, and Kierkegaard referred to these restoring techniques collectively as 'aesthetic deceptions'. They are thus deceptions that are made in the service of communicating a truth. The Eucharistic sacrament provides the most powerful paradigm case: the transubstantiation of the bread and the wine through the ritual words spoken by the presiding priest during the consecration induces a state of communion that has the effect of reunifying the body and the soul of the true believer. It thus lifts the deception of the senses whereby the body and the soul have become separated.

The whole field of aesthetics is one of aesthetic deception. Thus, for example, I - for all this has to do with 'the one', 'the individual' - was present at a performance of *Rosenkavalier* in Copenhagen, physically present there in the here and now, but I was transported in every nerve and fibre of my mind and body to the Vienna of the end of the eighteenth century. As the opera concluded, the entire visual scene itself faded as I was enveloped in the magical trio of the Feldmarschallin, Sophia and Octavian:

> *Es sind die mehreren Dinge auf der Welt,*   (There are many things in this world
> *so dass sie ein's nicht glauben tät,*   that you cannot believe at all
> *wenn man sie möcht' erzahlen hör'n*   when you hear about them.
> *Alleinig wer's erlebt, der glaubt daran und*   Only when experienced, do you believe them
> *weiss nicht wie -*   not knowing why -)

This kind of aesthetic deception transports one to an emotional understanding of a profound truth, and in this case of the truth of the relation between true love and renunciation, such as no amount of written text can ever do. This is then aesthetic deception in its most evident form.

To take a more prosaic example, consider this from Fishman (1981, p.73):

> ...why did IBM'ers wear blue suits and stiff collars? Simply because my father had the feeling that, if we could looked the part of a successful corporation...if we could look the part of intelligent corporate business men...then we would slowly and inevitably become known in the eyes of the public as a smart corporation with intelligent, dignified, above-average personnel...and this, I submit, came to pass. Clothes don't make the man – but they go a long way to making the successful businessman.
>
> Long before we really had enough money to get off Broadway, we established an unusually fine showroom on Fifth Avenue. If we were to decorate a showroom today and use as much of our income to do it as we did relatively in those days, our Directors would tell us we were crazy...yet again we were carrying the corporate image far out in front of the size and reputation of the corporation in order to increase the velocity of its growth.

Similar in its theme, but passing into another era (Moritz, 1984, p.190-195):

> Since nobody had expected that Apple would sell more than five thousand of its second computer, Jobs and Mannock chose the [cheap and low quality] reaction injection method [for molding the case].
>
> The first cases that were extracted from the molds were rickety. The surfaces were uneven, the lips were bowed, and the edges lapped over the keyboard. At Apple half a dozen people used trimming knives, sandpaper, and putty to camouflage the worst blemishes and sprayed the cases with a beige paint which gave a light look. They decided to muddle through the fair without air vents on the sides of the cases that weren't cut cleanly.
>
> Because Jobs had made one of the first commitments to appear at the show, Apple had pride of place in the front of the hall. Markkula organised the design of the booth – ordered a smoky, backlit, large and illuminated Plexiglas sign carrying the new company's logo and a large television screen to display the computer's capacity. Three computers lay on three counters. These gave the impression of substance and bulk even though they were Apple's only assembled machines. Meanwhile, Markkula and McKenna paid attention to sartorial graces, guiding Jobs to a San Francisco tailor and persuading him to buy the first suit of his life.
>
> The spray of a public splash is made up of facades, gestures and illusions.

We should observe that indirect leadership can often be construed as proceeding through aesthetic deception. Thus all the physical facilities of IKEA are such as to create the situation described earlier, in Chapter 2, which we can now regard as an aesthetic deception whereby the customer is led to take on the rolls of the transporter and assembler of IKEA's furniture.

These then are all examples of 'aesthetic deception', which is such just so long as the objective of the deception is one of building or inculcating something of real value. It is then the antithesis of 'the technologies of persuasion' as these are most commonly employed to an entirely opposite effect. Both, however, are directed to your belief system.

Moving on now from these last, more mundane examples, we return to the so-called 'religious criterion' in the development of your belief system. This is called 'religious' – although some would prefer 'spiritual' - because it relates back again to the development of the individual self as associated with the individual soul. This criterion can be expressed by the following *existential question*: how far are you prepared to go in your search for truth? How much time and effort are you prepared to devote to this? We emphasise that *this is not a demand, but only a question*. Since it is not a demand you are only obliged to yourself to answer it, but to the extent that you do thereby feel obliged to yourself it becomes one of the most important questions that you have to answer: you have to answer this question *to yourself*.

It has then my duty, and thereby my obligation, to indicate one of the ways that you may choose to pursue in your search for truth, but then as a preparation for industrial leadership. Of course you may choose to follow any one of any number of other paths or none at all, and you may well follow one of these that will be of great benefit to you as a person, but I believe that no other path will promote your abilities as a leader of industry within our contemporary European context as well as the path that I have already introduced and upon which I should now expand.

Truth, as we have seen, is an intimation, being associated with a very peculiar kind of deeply felt pleasure that arises when we experience the oneness of our inner and our outer worlds. Now of course that may seem to be a rather restrictive definition of truth, since it not only excludes outer-world-to-outer-world oneness, which however must always pass through our inner world so that it is implicitly accommodated, but it also appears to exclude inner-world-to-inner-world oneness, such as arises in our experiences of logic and pure mathematics for example. But then, we may ask, is such an oneness really, or if you will 'truly', so separated from what goes on in our outer world?

This kind of question, which may at first appear as so abstract and so far removed from everyday affairs as to be apparently irrelevant, is in fact one of many that arise when we seek to understand the ways in which we are ourselves thinking, so that it constitutes a kind of 'thinking about one's own thinking', as one form of *secondary reflection*. The concept of secondary reflection, as developed by Gabriel Marcel, is not concerned with problems arising from outside our own selves, but with the mysteries proceeding within our own selves. At one time, during the nineteenth century, it was considered that such activities belonged to the domain of psychology, but it soon became clear that psychology was itself constructed using only the intellectual resources of primary reflection, so that it could not so much as touch the deeper-going problems that it sought to solve. And moreover – which is not at all so obvious, even though Schopenhauer had foreseen it - that every *science* was plagued with the same, essentially self-referential, problem. Inseparably from this, since many persons, personal events and other private happenings have together formed these mysteries within us, and indeed continue to do so, we are obliged to treat all of these, not as objects, but as subjects that are in some way like, or have become part of, ourselves, and in this case we speak, again following Gabriel Marcel, of *intersubjectivity* (See Troisfontaines, 1953/1968).

Chapter 4

[It was my privilege as a young boy to witness one of the great and decisive battles of history, fought high above me over a period of two months between anything up to two thousand aircraft at any one time. The battle was fought high above, often in the stratosphere, but everyone knew that the consequences of this battle would have the most serious repercussions for all of us on the ground if it went the one way rather than the other. Despite my tender years, it all left a very deep impression on me. This leads directly to the studies of the kind that I should recommend: they appear to fight their battles in the stratosphere of thought, but the consequences that follow from these studies are those of life and death, and most immediately here for the future of European industry and thus for the peoples of Europe as a whole.]

Some of you at least at some time or the other will have to fight your battles in the stratosphere.

The first of the studies that provide the path that I have been obliged to recommend is that of the development of classical European philosophy that we have already introduced as *Phenomenology*. Whenever we think about the world we think in terms of *objects*, such as houses, blades of grass, mountains, legal agreements, customs and so forth. Everything else that operates in our minds, including that which brings objects to presence in our mind, operates with these and discards them again, is called in object-theoretical terms *content*. It is a consequence of content working on and through existing objects that not all of us come to view any particular object in the same way. For the one person a particular house may be very precious to him as his home, while for another person it may be just a nuisance, as something that blocks his view. Put very simply, but not too simplistically:

An object that is seen from a particular point of view is called a phenomenon.

Thus phenomenology has to do with the different ways in which we regard objects and so operate with them as conditioned by what we have here described, but then very simplistically, as 'our belief system'. [1] Phenomenology is then at the same time the study of how we build our belief systems on the basis of experiences and facts within a context of current predispositions, prejudices, likes and dislikes and other such 'content'. The first great phenomenological study which founded this movement, namely Edmund Husserl's *Logische Untersuchungen//Logical Investigations* of 1900-1901, was given over to analysing the functioning of human states of consciousness in which logic comes into being and goes to work, whether directly or indirectly, during a wide range of thinking processes, and thence how what we are here calling 'a belief system' is formed, or forms itself. This book followed and overlapped with two different but related works of Gottlob Frege which, despite their critical importance to European thought, cannot be followed in this précis, but whose import can only be given in reference through the works of Dummett.

Phenomenology often starts out from the proposition that we are all part of a tradition, which is usually the tradition into which we have been born and raised. We cannot normally choose this tradition and we can even less commonly leave it to adopt another tradition again. As explained earlier, we Europeans belong to a predominately Christian tradition which includes a tradition of modern-scientific thinking. As also accepted earlier, many of us will probably not consider ourselves as Christians, but on the other hand, because of the tradition that has fostered us, we continue to behave as though we did.

As the founding father of what we nowadays call 'Phenomenology', Husserl later wrote about this influence of tradition as follows (1973, pp42,43):

> The world in which we live and in which we carry out activities of cognition and judgement, out of which everything which becomes the substrate of a possible judgement affects us, is always pregiven to us as impregnate by the precipitate (*Neiderschlag*) of logical operations. The world is never given to us as other than the world in which we and others, whose store of experience we take over by communication, education and tradition, have already been logically active, in judgement and cognition. And this refers, not only to the typically determined sense, according to which every object stands before us as a familiar object within a horizon of familiarity, but also to the horizon-prescription....The sense of this pregivenness is such that everything which contemporary natural science has furnished as determinations of what exists also belongs to us, to the world, as this world is pregiven to the adults of our time....In other words, for this world which is pregiven to us, we accept the following idea as a matter of course on the basis of modern tradition, 'that the infinite totality of what is in general is intrinsically a rational all-encompassing unity that can be mastered, without anything left over, by a corresponding universal science'....
>
> This *idea of the determinability 'in itself' of what exists* ...is so much a matter of course for us that ...this 'objectivity' is from the first accepted as self-evident.
>
> In this way, the world of our experience is from the beginning interpreted by recourse to an 'idealisation' – but it is no longer seen that this idealisation...is itself the result of a function of cognitive methods, a result based on the data of our immediate experience.... 'Judgements of experience' or, to speak more clearly, judgements which are obtained only from original operations in categorical acts purely on the basis of experience...are not judgements of science in the precise sense – that is of science that works under the idea of definitive validity.... Thus, by their nature, the logical activities of idealisation and of mathematisation, the latter presupposing the former,...are distinguished from other categorical activities.

It is a long quotation but a very important one, for it already makes the vital distinction between what is to be taken as scientific and what is not, which is one of the most difficult decisions that you will have to take when deciding what you will believe and what you will not believe. For nowadays almost everything is passed off as 'scientific' and thus as something completely determinable. For example, it is loudly proclaimed that pension benefits will have to be cut because people are living longer, and all manner of statistics are provided to demonstrate this – but with no account taken of the development of technology that, if properly led sociotechnically, will necessitate no such action and, to the contrary, will obviate the social demoralisation among currently-working people that such a prospect will otherwise induce. Similarly it is demonstrated with all manner of numbers and graphs that working hours will have to be extended and incomes reduced in order to increase competitiveness, and these numbers and graphs are accurately measured in comparative money-valued outputs per employee – ignoring the need for fit, attentive and unstressed, because secure, operatives in the kind of production facilities that a future Europe must have precisely in order to compete. And so we can go on apparently indefinitely. The numbers to n decimal places recording growths in GNP, that are really only recording how many more bureaucrats are producing nothing, how many more lawyers are wasting everyone's time and money and how much junk food is fuelling spirals of increased obesity and an ever growing pharmaceutics (and for once the US has the appropriate name: 'drugs') industry are little more than a joke – at least for those with the sense of humour to overcome their revulsion at the whole nonsense.

It is because of this passing-off of every decision as one involving 'scientific computations', usually all employing the one common denominator of money, that the business management school has been so successfully established and so long sustained. In the never-never world of this kind of 'business', all of whose workings can be finally described in money terms, all major decisions can be reduced in the last analysis to computations conducted with this single dependent variable: 'money'. Within this ideology, the nature of the organisation in which the manager is employed is of minor importance: all that matters is that he should be able 'to read the accounts'. We recall the words of Schopenhauer given already in the notes to this work: "Where calculating begins, understanding ends".

Now such a money-restricted view is bound to be anathema to anyone who has been at all exposed to phenomenological studies. The very watchword of phenomenology is *"Zu den Sachen selbst"*, translated as *"To the things themselves"*. Thus from a phenomenological point of view, money-based evaluations can play only one part, and in the final analysis only a secondary part, in the belief system of a leader of industry. The leader is much more concerned with what is going on at the human and the technical levels, and thence at the conjoining sociotechnical level, within and around the organisation for which he is responsible.

Let us give an example of a business-school classroom case study to illustrate this. In this case study, it is supposed that the shareholders of one brewery are talking with the shareholders of another brewery about either a merger or a takeover. The class is divided into two groups, with the one part representing the shareholders of the one brewery and the other part representing the shareholders of the other brewery. All that they have available to make a decision on their preferred courses of action are some very general indications of the market segments to which the companies belong and the financial reports of the two companies. On this basis, and effectively on this basis alone, they should work out their positions on the course that they wish to follow in their negotiations in an attempt to reach an agreement. This great economy in the knowledge that is mobilised has the advantage that it is possible to carry through this exercise in a single day.

From a phenomenological point of view, all this is a snare and a delusion: the leader confronted with a problem of this kind must, before all else, establish 'the position on the ground' in both of the organisations involved. In the case of such a proposal, presumably involving several millions of euros, he will spend many months of his own time and the time of some others that he can trust explicitly on a very thorough investigation of the human, technical and sociotechnical features that characterise the functioning of the two enterprises. Following Foucault, he may start at the most direct or 'lowest' point at which knowledge/power is applied, presumably at the level of the most basic, and thereby most central process or processes. He will study the actions of and talk with the person or persons responsible for this process or these processes in order to ascertain the specific agencies and associated competencies that are thereby brought into play over a wide range of operating circumstances. He will watch how the one may smell the bouquets, taste the liquors, study the colours of liquids and their precipitates, test the temperatures, often directly with the hand, and listen to the various sounds that the individual processes produce, even as he is piecing all of these impressions together to provide the pattern of the creative whole. This leader will then be particularly attentive to such *intuitive behaviours* of the key operators, trying to give expression to their actions and thereby trying to understand something of their underlying intentions. In this respect he situates himself within a philosophy that, although closely related to phenomenology, is none the less distinct from it, which is that of existential philosophy, as the study of human existence, as 'the human condition', that passes by the name of *existentialism*.

Accordingly, the second of the studies that I have to recommend to you as a future leader of industry is that of *existential philosophy*.

The leader who is only so much as acquainted with such studies will already be especially alert not only to the creative capacities of the persons with whom he is working within their working environment, but to their attitudes towards the company and the proposed merger. He will naturally be wary of all attempts on the part of certain persons to obfuscate his view of the real situation. At the same time he will talk as openly and frankly as he can with these persons, recognising not only their central value to their companies but their qualities as persons. He will be especially concerned to 'keep them on board', and especially sensitive to the possibilities of their retirement, let alone their leaving for other reasons. He will do this for both organisations so far as he is allowed to do so and thereby relate the capacities of the two organisations at this most basic level.

Alongside these investigations, he will be studying the physical equipment with which these key personnel are working, estimating its present condition and its expected longevity and the ways in which this equipment, in the hands of the key staff, provides the *qualities* upon which each of the two enterprises depends for its survival and longer-term prosperity. This is then not only the condition and capacities and other characteristics of the pumps, piping systems, filter systems, electrical systems, communication systems, buildings and all else of this physical kind, but how this is suited or fitted to the persons who are working with it. As we shall see shortly, it has not only to do with its *presence-to-hand* (its *Verhandenheit*), as equipment that is ready and available for use, but something much more again, which is its *readiness-to-hand* (its *Zuhandenheit*), as equipment that fits together with the persons employing it like every well-designed tool fits the hands, and thereby the senses and the mind of its user, while at the same time this user learns not only the actions but also the reactions of the tool as, so to say, 'it fits itself to him'.

Working out from these central, productive and creative cores of the two organisation, the leader will proceed backwards to study the two companies' supply chains, looking for and assessing the various risks and to which each of the companies may be subject from that side alongside the opportunities, such as may be implicit in their futures' contracts for their raw materials. He will as well work his way forward to study the packaging and distribution chains of the two companies, identifying the risks and opportunities that are inherent there too.

Alongside these investigations into each of the companies, he will be assessing their market situations, trying to explicate their relative strengths and weaknesses, relating these to the different perceptions of the companies and their products that their respective clienteles may be induced to express.

It is only on the basis of such a very thorough analysis and careful synthesis that the leader of industry would normally proceed to make assessments of the possible synergies that a merger or a takeover would provide if it proceeded in each one of several possible ways. Thus he would attempt to arrive at the most attractive strategy accompanied by the most suitable tactics for realising the takeover or merger – or for not proceeding with any such action at all. The leader of industry thus does all this not only or even so much in order to grasp the situation as it is, but primarily in order to conceive of the situation as it might be.

But now let us return to the more personal *you*, as the leader-to-be, and question our way further forward together. For if we pose the question of its adequacy relative to *your* intentions we at once see that, although everything that we have just described is necessary, *it will be in no way sufficient for you as a leader of industry*. For this 'you' has not only to perform as a leader, but has *to live as a leader*. This is then much more than a social demand; it is now also an existential one. And in response to this, something much more is required by you of yourself. You have to *live* what has always been called in religious terms *the passion*, but then this is much more a passion of integration and much less a passion of renunciation. The leader of industry in a Europe that is under an ever increasing stress from the encroachments of nothingness has the means to express this passion as a *love of the product*, and this is as necessary to the product as it is to the individual self of the leader. Referring forward to Kierkegaard's definition of the self as given in our second Appendix, it is through this process as it occurs in his most everyday existence that the leader "relates himself to himself" through what we have here described as his belief system.

(For those with a more mathematical bent, we shall see in that Appendix that Kierkegaard's definition, that was based upon a formulation of Hegel, defines, as *def(s)*, a self *s* as a mapping which has the unique property that it indeed "maps itself into itself", so that:

$$def(s) = \quad s{:}s \to s,$$

which certainly expresses the uniqueness as well as the compactness of this definition.[3]). Of great importance to the development of this self is *the experience of failure*, as touched upon in the Introduction, but we can better take the influence of this up later here when we speak about the person of the entrepreneur, in whose case it is often of decisive importance.[2]

What follows is something that 'management' does not normally like to hear, which is that if you are not imbued with this passion within your own self for the product which far surpasses a mere enthusiasm, you should not get involved in its production as a leader at all. In whatever you do, you should do this with genuine enthusiasm, and that is not possible if you are not genuinely enthusiastic. Thus, in the case considered here, unless you have a certain passion for beers and their brewing, you should not be leading a brewery. The process of selecting leaders should in this sense be a self-selection, in that each enterprise should fit with its leader's own 'leading passion'. This is in fact not as difficult as it may at first seem: there is a kind of 'natural law of attraction' that works in such cases, and once again phenomenological and existential studies provide us with the means to understand something of the workings of this 'law'. We in fact introduced this notion in Chapter 1, where we described it in terms of *an integration myth*, so that, like any other 'natural law' as expressed as myth, it always has this sense of timeless mystery about it.

Arriving at this point, however, it will be clear that, whatever one can or cannot do with numbers representing quantities, and no matter how necessary these may be, *the use of numbers exclusively can never be sufficient for leading an enterprise successfully*. Other, much more basic, realistic, intuitive and instinctive capacities, working with qualities, are necessary for the success of every enterprise. It is essentially for this reason that one can never replace leadership by mere management.

4.3 The Facts

After technology and your own belief system, the next among your closest friends are the facts. Like all close friends these need your attention, but in a Europe where nothingness is encroaching so rapidly upon the sphere of communication, the facts need more of your attention than ever before. In a world swamped, not so much at all any more with information, but much more with 'disinformation', ascertaining the facts has become one of the most demanding of activities. For this purpose you depend again on your intuitions, but for the purpose of distinguishing between what is true and what is untrue you are now concerned more specifically with *the training of your intuitions*, and for this purpose you need to make recourse yet again to certain applications of the results of phenomenological studies. In these studies, extensive use is made of the criteria of *coherence* and *intelligibility*. This is not the place to go into these criteria in any depth, and certainly we do not have space in this précis to enter into the techniques evolved in phenomenology for identifying whether statements are indeed coherent or incoherent, and are indeed intelligible or unintelligible, but only to introduce these notions by one particular but highly relevant example.

Our example at this point concerns the veritable barrage of propaganda that currently seeks to show the inherent superiority of the so-called 'Anglo-Saxon' model of socio-economic development over the also-so-called 'continental-European' model. This is currently being concentrated upon a denigration of the more recent development of the German economy whereby Germany is depicted as "The sick man of Europe", a phrase originally invented to describe the parlous economic and political state of Turkey as it stumbled into the First World War on the side of Germany and Austria-Hungary, and consequently lost its entire empire and slid into an economic and military catastrophe. The innuendo is obvious enough.

This great deception starts out by creating a false image of the US economy, as something that has performed and continues to perform so much better than the economies of continental Europe, while even the British economy is held up as a model, although admittedly trailing somewhat behind its transatlantic 'big brother'. The renowned Swiss economist Fredmund Malik described this as "a masterpiece of disinformation" and analysed how it was engineered: how it became possible for the Anglo-Saxon media - and not only these, but much of the media in continental Europe as well – to produce so many numbers and graphs and charts showing such tremendous advances in US production, income and consumption. In fact, as he showed, hardly any of this had actually happened, the only real factor being a more recent and particular kind of consumption that was, as he and many other economists have documented, fuelled almost entirely be accumulating debt in every possible way, superimposing the resulting new debt burden upon an economy that was already by far the most heavily indebted in the world. But we shall return to that later.

The first trick employed for this deceptive purpose has been to employ different measures in calculating indices that should describe production and productivity. Since the mid-nineties the US has used what is called 'Hedonic Price Indexing' which is supposed to reflect an increase in quality on the dollar price as a multiplier on the actual sales price. Thus if a 2000-model computer provided ten times the speed and ten times the hard-disk capacity of a 1995-model computer, the volume of sales of computers measured in dollars can be multiplied by a factor of ten in the statistics of computer production. Malik quoted the example of how the physical numbers of dollars invested in the computer business, that actually increased from 23 to 87 billion during the so-called "technology boom' that really did occur between 1995 and 2000, became through the hedonic effect an increase from 23 billion to 240 billion in the statistics used to calculate the BNP of the USA. He calculated that if one stripped out this kind of 'growth' in the financial and computer sectors of US industry - neither of which are really so preponderant in the total US economy as they are commonly made out to be - the real rate of growth of the USA in the complete decade of the 1990s was zero. Despite this, such devices have allowed the new so-called 'neoliberals' to show an increase in productivity in the USA of 23.9% over the period from 1991 to 2002, while Germany, using more traditional methods of accounting, showed only an increase of 16.4% over the same period. Moreover, this growth of productivity in the USA was associated with an increase in employment of 14% in the USA, albeit largely through new immigrants taking lowly paid jobs, as opposed to 1% in a Germany, with this last result primarily a consequence of the economic and financial burdens imposed following the reunification of West and East Germany in an environment where minimum wage conditions were much more widely upheld.. This recorded difference, however, naturally inflated the differences in BNP even more, with the USA showing an average of about 3% year-on-year growth over this period as opposed to Germany showing only about 2%.

In order to arrive at a true picture – in order to arrive at *the facts* – we need to apply the criteria of coherence and intelligibility using the forces of our intuitions. Even before advancing to these facts, however, we can already *intuit why* the so-called 'neo-liberals' are spreading such 'information' - what are their *intentions* in doing this - and thereby we can already anticipate that their productions are sure to be composed for the most part of disinformation. Using the theory of nothingness we can see that the deception starts with the deception of the name, introducing something that calls itself 'neoliberalism' even while it has *in fact* nothing to do 'liberalism' in any normal understanding of the word. The reason for this – that which makes it coherent in its deception – is a play on the other buzzword of these 'neoliberals', which is *the market*. Liberalism believes in markets and market forces, but on the whole it is suspicious of an ideology built around the concept of 'efficient markets'. In an article in *Der Spiegel*, (36/2002, 132-135) Malik explained that thinking as a Liberal in no way implied an unconditional faith in a market that would always point in the right direction and would be consistently intelligent. In fact it had to be accepted that the market always runs behind events, so that it does not tell us how we should trade, but only how we should have traded. Thus the market does not prevent mistakes; it only punishes them. Great liberal thinkers like Friederich von Hayek knew that the market was highly imperfect - but that all other solutions were much worse again.

An old English saying goes that "A fool and his money are easily parted", and the device required to separate 'the fools' from their money was in this case already *present to hand*, and all that was required was to make this device more *ready to hand*. The money was in the form of the savings of the population as a whole, and then for the most part in the pension funds that had been set up to provide the means for this population to enjoy a reasonably commodious retirement. The device was the existing share-trading or stock markets, reinforced by some other markets besides, but this market had to be popularised so as to extend its appeal much more widely, and so advertised in the new ways that had become opened up through the growth of the new media, such as those supported by commercial television and the Internet. Indeed, in this respect, this development had definite socio*technical* dimensions too.

Thus was inaugurated the era of round-the-clock 'business news' and 'chat shows' with 'leading business personalities', all directed to promoting 'investment opportunities', and for this purpose it was and remains essential to have *success stories* and *business heroes*. All this in its turn fuelled a business in providing success stories and heroes, and for this purpose such devices as Hedonic Price Indexing was and remains a godsend. Of course with some recent scandals involving the manipulation of numbers leading to financial disaster some of the gloss on these activities has been tarnished, but the business of providing disinformation continues unabated. It is in this way that this phenomenon then already starts to become coherent.

Since we see in all of this the hand of nothingness we understand that it will not form any kind of system and that its acolytes will be just as much the victims of their disinformation as those to whom they purvey it. It is in no sense a conspiracy, but then as Malik explained in reference to the 'technology bubble' of the 1990s:

> No conspiracy was necessary. It was enough with the *Zeitgeist*: the belief in a never ending profitability, ever increasing productivity and practically eternal growth. It was a self-amplifying process that led first to an enormous flight into the skies and then to a crash. This development was comparable to that of the 1930s. At that time instead of a 'New Economy' one spoke of a 'New Era'.

What was happening here was that an intention was being translated into 'facts' that were not factual at all. In order to understand this phenomenon, *qua* phenomenon, however, we need to proceed deeper into its origins within the context of the spread of nothingness in the societies involved. At the most physical level we can identify this with the different natures of the US and UK economies on the one side and the German economy on the other side. The US market is in most respects self sufficient and, below all the talk of 'competition', large sectors are not subject to competition from outside the USA. As one among several analogous examples, the USA is not at all internationally competitive in most areas of industry, and such competitive potential as it can still muster has to be protected and reinforced politically, and then on the inside by a constant stream of legislation concerning subsidies, tax breaks, tariff walls and other forms of protection, and from the outside by all manner of diplomatic and international-trade interventions on the part of the US Government and the US Congress, as described earlier. The German economy on the other hand is export-orientated by necessity and remains highly competitive in almost all international markets. For this purpose it has to concentrate on maintaining high standards of quality and innovation, and for this it relies in turn upon a well educated and highly skilled working population, such as necessitates high levels of education and health care, and a well-founded sense of social security.

It follows from this analysis that, if we must rely on measurements at all, we can better measure the competitiveness of these two 'systems' in terms of their export potentials and accomplishments and, with these, their relative financial strengths as measured by their balances of payments. If we turn to the much more reliable statistics concerning these measures we see that whereas the USA registered an increase in exports of some 35% between beginning 1995 and end 2003, Germany registered an increase of some 70% over the same period (*Die Zeit*, 17/2004, p. 25). The UK did slightly better than the USA, but since such a large part of UK industry is foreign-owned and operated, this does not necessarily mean so much.

If we turn to the balance of payments of these nations, the situation becomes that much clearer and coherent again, and also starts to become more intelligible. There we see that Germany, with some 80 million inhabitants, is the greatest exporter in the world. If we take account of German products and services exported through the Netherlands and Belgium, this lead over the second-biggest exporter, the USA with 300 million inhabitants, becomes much greater again. Japan, China and France come in after this, with China (with 25 times the population of France) only pushing France from fourth into fifth place in 2003. In terms of balances of exports relative to imports, Germany had a positive balance in 2003 of some 150 billion euro, while the USA had a negative balance of 580 billion and the UK a negative balance of 85 billion, but this last is reduced by the immense incomes – some 20 billion euro in 2003 - accruing from The City, which make London, on paper at least, the richest region in Europe, even when it is surrounded by an industrial wasteland (*Le Figaro*, 7.04.04, p. III).

Thus an article by N. Elliott in *The Guardian* (July 5, 2004) popularised a University of Sheffield report which drew upon a 2001 census to describe the negative influences of The City on the UK economy as a whole. "Our conclusion" the report said, "is that the country is being split in half. To the south is the metropolis of Greater London, to the north and west is the 'archipelago of the provinces' – city islands that appear to be sinking demographically, socially and economically. The UK is looking more and more like a city state. It is a kingdom only united by history, increasingly divided by geography". Elliott's conclusion was that the north-south divide had actually widened under the Labour government so that the City wielded more power than ever, making for ever greater financial, and thence economic risks.

All this is in stark contrast with the view of continental European societies, where industry is held in the highest esteem as the principle producer of wealth. Thus, just to take France as one example, the prime minister Pierre Raffarin continues to affirm the necessity of "avoiding the development of economies founded only on the tertiary sector: powerful industrial sectors are essential", while to the political left, the former economics minister Dominique Strauss-Kahn says much the same: "It is necessary to get away from this crazy idea that one can transform France into an offshore platform for financial and other services". For his part, the present finance minister, Nicholas Sarkozy, has given the assurance that in this matter: "It is necessary to retake the initiative: France, like

Europe generally, cannot become an industrial desert". And those who know the French *dirigisme*, which for all its many and often glaring faults has delivered successful industrial sectors, excellent infrastructures and sound public services, know also that these men are serious. (Quotations from *Le Figaro Économie*, 16 May 2004). Whether they are going about things in the most effective way is of course debatable, but the intention is clear. The slogan of 'interventionism without protectionism' is seen to be converted into government policy, even as it is often presented less fortunately as *le retour du patriotisme industriel* // 'the return of industrial patriotism'.

This difference in views concerning the roles of industry and finance has the most profound social consequences: we are in fact here in the presence of a sociotechnical phenomenon. The obsession with 'making money' as opposed – because it is an opposition! – to the passion for 'creating value' is observable on every side. Continental Europe is concerned about maintaining and creating values in a way that much of the UK is not. Thus, as the FT's Prowse recently observed, Britons who have been living for some time outside the UK agree that Britain sets standards of what he called 'yobbish conduct' that are largely unacceptable in continental Europe, with its football hooligans particularly violent and abusive and its holidaymakers close behind As one who had himself lived in the USA and continental Europe, Prouse was struck by how squalid a place much of Britain had become, as a place where people have become so taken up in themselves that they no longer know how to behave in public in an acceptable way.

These observations, which will be familiar to everyone visiting the UK from continental Europe, do not square at all with the numbers that are regularly presented for the gross domestic products (GDPs) of the UK, as also of the US, as compared with those of continental Europe. Thus a statement like that of Martin Wolf (FT, 20.07.2004, p 11)) that the English-speaking countries generate close to 40 percent of global GDP, the eurozone another 23 percent, Japan 12 percent and the rising economies of Asia only another 11 percent, must be terribly misleading in terms of the real standard of life of the respective peoples. How is it possible that in the UK and the USA, as compared with continental Europe, a major part of the population is so obviously in such indifferent health, is so poorly dressed, living in such low-quality housing, wasting so much time and energy commuting, working such longer hours for such lower real incomes, is so ignorant and poorly educated and badly spoken, has access to so few cultural amenities…and so on and on again? Clearly there is a massive mismatch between the numbers that are supposed to represent their wealth and the true wealth of these nations.

We may then trace this mismatch back to a difference between societies that have turned their backs upon industry and instead embraced 'services' that for the greater part provide no service at all and societies that continue to value industry and are determined to develop it further. The great media machines of persuasion have had their success in the so-called English-speaking world and are now turning their attention to subverting continental Europe with their siren songs of quick profits and the other virtues of untrammeled markets. But then continental Europe is resisting, and indeed is counter attacking by building up its industries together with the social structures within which these industries can best prosper, thus creating other kinds of societies than those of the so-called English-speaking world. The difference here is one between two different ways of Being-in-the-world (the Heideggerian *in-der-Welt-sein*). For his part, Elliott explained that although there were 1.7 million more people working in banking in 2001 than a decade earlier, most of this growth has been in and around London, even while, under Labour, 700,000 jobs in manufacturing had been lost, making the north-south divide even wider. He expressed the widespread view that the City now exerted more influence in Westminster and Whitehall than ever before. Within this context, and despite what he considered genuine attempts to construct a stronger regional policy, he saw the primary task of the UK government as one of making Britain safe for the financiers and rentiers.

The UK as an independent state has of course its own good right to take this path, as does the USA in a similar way, but we in continental Europe are on a quite other track again.

It is often observed that the USA and the UK have strong economies even if they do have weak indigenous industries, but this again does not take account of the nature of the 'strength' of their economies. For us in Europe, they have such large 'national-economic' bodies because they carry so much dysfunctional fat at the expense of so little functional industrial muscle, so that they cannot possibly compete internationally. There is then only one way that they can continue to survive, which is, once again, *by running up bigger and bigger debts*. Both countries correspondingly continue to pile up debts at every conceivable level of society. There are unprecedented levels of household debt, both with and without property being included; there are unprecedented levels of debts of towns, cities and states in the USA, quite apart from unequalled Federal budget deficits; and there are hidden debt burdens in the form of promises to pay the present general population for health care and pensions for which there is no prospect of the assets becoming available to fulfil these promises. Thus, the US Treasury Secretary estimated that this implicit debt of the US central government alone to its presently living citizens was 44 *trillion* dollars, or seven times its explicit sovereign debt, and this was over and above all other US government debt, and stated that there was no plan whatsoever for how this was to be financed. Shortly afterwards this estimate was revised upwards to 72 *trillion* dollars, and increasing at the rate of some 2 *trillions* a year (J. Liebermann in the FT, 25.05.04).

In the case of Germany and other Continental European countries there are also large implicit debts, but at least some investments have been and are being made to provide the means to finance such deficits in the future. For example, the 1.2 *trillion* euros invested by the West German *Länder* to rebuild the infrastructure of the former DDR constituted such an investment, made as a gesture of solidarity, and so something which would be unthinkable at this scale in the UK or the USA. We can easily criticise the way in which this was invested – disgracefully arrogant and correspondingly technocratic instead of sociotechnical again! – but the intention was certainly correct. As we observe these financial aspects, the intelligibility of the phenomenon becomes so much more evident.

This extended example illustrates how we can arrive at facts by following the criteria of coherence and intelligibility: the facts, if they are truly facts at all, must fit together and they must make sense. The faculty of intuition that makes this possible, and which develops its own subtle logic correspondingly, has however to be trained, and, like every exercise in phenomenology, it is develops precisely by exercising it. This in its turn requires a certain very broad kind of attitude, or perhaps we can better call it a state of mind. It calls for our concentrated attention, for our 'being with it' to use a more colloquial expression, or simply with our 'being there' when evaluating what is truly factual. Since we do not have a specific word in English for this condition and underlying attitude, we follow a common practice in existential philosophy by calling this state of Being by its German name, as *Dasein*, which is compounded from '*Da-Sein*', which is indeed just 'being there'. When evaluating whether something is a fact or otherwise as just exemplified, we are not seeking a fact in the sense of identifying whether something is simply the case, such as for example when naming something or the other, but we are endeavouring to ascertain a fact that is bound up with our own Being-in-the-world, with our own 'state of mind'. The fact that I have to be 'with it' while writing this, and that you (hopefully!) are 'with it' while reading it is something different from the fact of an accidental coming across something. [4]

The phenomenon that we have introduced earlier here, whereby millions of people were persuaded to invest their savings, and in many cases their life savings, into the most improbable adventures, only to lose a large part of these savings, as happened in the so-called 'dot-com bubble', is only one example among any number of others of the consequences of 'not being there' or 'not being with it'. The 'Business School Phenomenon' provides another example that may well serve also as a case study. In all such cases (Heidegger, 1927, p.127//1962, p.165):

> The distantiality, averageness, and levelling down, as ways of Being of the 'they', constitute that we call 'publicness'. Publicness proximally controls every way in which the world and Dasein get interpreted, and it is always right ...because it is insensitive to every difference of level and of genuineness, and never gets to 'the heart of the matter'. By publicness everything gets obscured, and what has been covered up gets passed off as something familiar and accessible to everyone.

The basic concept that follows from this, which again goes by a German name, there being no appropriate English equivalent, is called *Gerede*. We can only translate it into English as 'gossip, chatter and idle talk', which has the effect of trivialising what is really something quite sinister and potentially highly dangerous. Dare we return to Heidegger once more? We really have no alternative (ibid, pp. 168-179//pp. 212,213):

> In the language which is spoken when one expresses oneself there lies an average intelligibility; and in accordance with this intelligibility the discourse that is communicated can be understood to a considerable extent, even if the hearer does not bring himself into such a kind of Being towards what the discourse is about to have a primordial understanding of it. We do not so much understand the entities that are talked about; we already are listening only to what is said-in-the-talk as such. What is said-in-the-talk gets understood; but what the talk is about is understood only approximately and superficially.
> ...What is said-in-the-talk as such, spreads in wider circles and takes on an authoritative character. Things are so because one says so. Idle talk is constituted by just such gossiping and passing the word along – a process by which its initial lack of grounds to stand on [*Bodenständigkeit*] becomes aggravated to complete groundlessness [*Bodenlosigkeit*].
> The groundlessness of idle talk is no obstacle to its becoming public; instead it encourages this. Idle talk is the possibility of understanding everything without previously making the thing one's own. If this were done, idle talk would founder; and it already guards against such a danger. Idle talk is something that anyone can rake up; it not only releases one from the task of genuinely understanding, but develops an undifferentiated kind of intelligibility...
> ...The fact that something has been said groundlessly, and then gets passed along in further retelling, amounts to perverting the act of disclosing [*Erschliessen*] into an act of closing-off [*Verschliessen*]. For what is said is always understood proximally as 'saying' something –   .

> that is, an uncovering something. Thus, by its very nature, idle talk is a closing-off, since to go back to the ground of what is talked about is something which it *leaves undone*.
>
> ...The dominance of the public way in which things have been interpreted has already been decisive even for the possibility of having a mood – that is, for the way in which Dasein lets the world 'matter' to it. The 'they' prescribes one's state-of-mind, and determines what and how one 'sees'.

All of this will be familiar enough from the interminable 'management meetings' which contribute no improvement whatsoever in management but only increase existing muddles, the column-kilometres of print in newspapers which never arrive at any fast conclusion but leave everything in confusion, and the endless wafflings of 'commentators', 'analysts' and so-called 'panels of experts' that provide the regular diet of television programmes and which leave one more disorientated at the end than one was at the beginning. But at the same time of course one must not underestimate the great success of all this in 'forming public opinion', manipulating the minds of this 'public' to acquiesce in the one or the other political, economic or whatever other objective.

Gerede can express itself in another way again, however, and in order to describe this we need another metaphor. We have earlier spoken about 'recognising the signs', or even, in our introduction, of 'reading the signal flags' of nothingness. An inability to read is a case of *dyslexia*, and when this is shared more widely we refer to a *collective dyslexia*. It clearly corresponds in the most direct sense to the Kierkegaardian *Sandsebedrag*. In a recent popular-political book, Miller (2003, p. 14) refers to 'a corporate version of dyslexia' as follows:

> Thus we are the victims of a new national disorder. It is as if the US body politic were itself afflicted with a corporate version of dyslexia. The individual dyslexic cannot learn to read because he is unable, for whatever reasons, to translate letters into sounds. Because he cannot decode those printed symbols for their phonetic content, the writing on the page can make no sense to him. Today our body politic is comparably disabled, although it is not written language that is the problem. The head that drives that body forward is, of course, the media machine – the busy neural network of producers, editors, reporters, anchors, pundits....While it has no trouble scanning press releases, or providing copy for the cameras, that swift collective mind is fatally dyslexic when it comes to reading the very spectacle that it presents to us. Unable to perceive the glaring daily evidence of absolute hypocrisy and cynical manipulation, it cannot read the writing on the wall – which, meanwhile, is crystal-clear to many of the rest of us. The dyslexics at the top may be extremely savvy, yet they lack (to quote Orwell...) that all-important knowledge 'in the bones' whereby we try, down here, to make our way. Seeing that it's all gone wrong, yet always hearing, from on high, that everything is perfectly all right, we each feel – whether we can read or not – as helpless and perplexed as any undiagnosed dyslexic faced with signs, menus, newspapers and exams.

The problem then presents itself as one not only of reading the signs oneself, but of curing states of dyslexia, as a collective dyslexia, in others so that they may come to read the signs also. The problem of reading the signs ourselves is a problem of *hermeneutics* in the traditional sense, and this translates into a problem of *deconstructing a 'text' in order to arrive at its hidden significance, its motivations and its intentions*, within this more modern context.

Many of us will already be familiar with a situation within an organisation whereby we 'read the signs' of untidiness, slovenliness, poor quality of work, lack of discipline, personal indifference, all kinds of time-wasting activities and other symptoms of demoralisation, even as most persons employed in the organisation cannot read any message into these symptoms even if they notice them at all, and are genuinely shocked, being totally unprepared, when disaster strikes the organisation and everyone who is employed in it. They cannot read 'the writing on the wall' no matter how large and how clearly this appears to others.

Very much has been done to facilitate the processing of facts through a belief system to arrive at judgements, and as already indicated this process can in some cases be automated through the construction of judgement engines. Only some knowledge of linear algebra and linear programming, fuzzy set theory and working with Java is required. Similarly, the simple processes that used to pass under the name of 'operations research' have now been incorporated into more general business-planning environments with a multitude of simple tools. However, the processes of arriving at the facts themselves has become a much greater problem than earlier, in part through the sheer quantity of data that is now available, to a large extent chaotic, in another part again through the performative intentions that have already been worked into the data so as to bias it when it becomes available, and in another and increasingly important part again by the need to make the facts available as soon as possible and where they are most needed. Thereby, although the powers of calculation can still be utilised to good effect, the most significant problems today, being essentially sociotechnical, are those of communication, and these require entirely new approaches.

To use military metaphors, you as a leader of industry must never be outgunned technologically and never outmanoeuvred sociotechnically. You will almost certainly be leading much smaller groups than your competitors initially and therefore you must have the best technology on your side and the knowledge of how best to deploy this within its social context. Attention has then to be given to technologies for mining data for knowledge discovery and value creation on the one hand, and for the timely and well-targeted dissemination of knowledge and value-enhancing judgements on the other hand. Just as competitiveness in the first industrial revolution was a function of the power of the machines placed at the disposal of producing operatives, so today it is a function of the quality of the knowledge resources made available at the ultimate point of their application.

This programme calls for a fairly substantial mathematical background, but so much is now encapsulated into products that a deeper knowledge of this background is usually not essential. You should understand enough to know what can and what cannot reasonably be done with the tools available. The so-called 'mathematics of non-mathematical objects' that is so useful for formalising sociotechnical processes will be largely restricted here to a few elements of category and allegory theory such as have already been well exercised in such areas as computer science. We shall take these last matters up in the Appendices that conclude this work, there being now sufficient material to introduce the notion that fact, its factuality and its facticity are not trivial matters for you as a future leader, but will always necessitate your most careful attention.[5,6]

4.4 Among friends: your colleagues

Your colleagues should be your friends. Few will ever become your close friends, and in the usual way of things very few will become so, but the bonds of friendship are vital to holding any organisation together. This has always been the case, but it has rarely been as important as it is today and rarely as vital as it is at this moment in European industry. The reasons for this have been introduced earlier here: our European societies are moving, or perhaps one should rather say drifting, into a post-modern condition, understood where people become less and less 'knowers' and more and more 'consumers of knowledge'. As I have been constantly emphasising, this is a sociotechnical phenomenon the most visible technical manifestations of which are the computer, the Internet and the mobile telephone. The Information and Communication Technologies, or simply ICTs, provide the technical means to realise new kinds of societies with new kinds of industries, while without the realisation of these new kinds of societies with new kinds of industries the ICTs can never be applied successfully.

These interacting, interweaving social and technical, technical and social and so-on-and-on processes require a constant attention to innovation, which is a particular form of creativity. They also call for initiative and well-orientated activity, and thus for *poiesis*, at all 'levels' in all industries, where at the same time the very notion of 'level' becomes ever more diffused, unclear and ultimately opaque. Even as they call for new skills and new knowledges – understanding that skills and knowledges are by no means the same things – so they also call for the rehabilitation of old skills and old knowledges, and this is again of the essence of *the post-modern condition*. In this condition of society we treasure our inheritance from previous generations, as currently manifested by our conservation of historic buildings, restoration of ecosystems and in our nurturing of old and even ancient crafts and competencies.

It is then however in the very nature of this kind of industrial activity that much of it, and indeed most of it, cannot be planned in advance, but instead *situations must be created* whereby the different creativities of the persons involved may be fostered and encouraged to develop in cooperative and collaborative ways as semi-autonomous and almost autochthonic developments. Structures can then become less and less pre-planned and imposed and more and more emergent and thus anarchistic in the strict sense introduced earlier here. They thus increasingly generate their own endostructures, as introduced in Chapter 2.

In such a mode of development, working groups form and reform to meet changing environments as self-managed entities, so that there is less and less place for 'managers' as persons who are not themselves directly involved in the immediately-productive activities. The notion of someone who just 'manages others' as an overhead on the productive labour of these others, such as could be justified in the now fast-receding modern condition of exostructured organisations, becomes increasingly redundant, and such persons must correspondingly be retrained to carry out productive work in the new post-modern environment. The shifting of millions upon millions of 'managers', whose activities become ever more harmful in that they themselves become ever more parasitic in these new self-structuring environments, and of shifting them, not to the ranks of the unemployed, but to socially useful activities, is one of the greatest challenges facing our European societies today. Even as our populations 'age', a vast reservoir of recruits to productive industry becomes available, and this is certainly sufficient to obviate all the dire prediction of those whose ideas are still stuck in the old and increasingly moribund exostructured industrial paradigm.

Such a development does however also pose new and demanding challenges to leadership. In the very first place and for you personally, it then poses all manner of questions and problems concerning *your* relation to *your* colleagues – and their relations to *you*. What, after all, is a leader in an 'anarchistic environment'? What will you be in such an environment? How will you select, develop, train and test your fellow leaders, that you collect around you and who you support even as they in turn support you? We have seen something of the qualities required in Chapter 2: such a person should be a disciplinarian and a humanitarian, but he should not be authoritarian. You need these qualities and must be free or be able to free yourself from their negativities.

Clearly, this leader has to be appointed and provided with the requisite authority to lead – he still has to be in this sense 'the boss' even within the self-organising business entity - but he has then necessarily to lead by his own force of character, through his own personality. You, as such a leader, cannot lead by fiat, so that you must lead by 'force of personality', but this 'personality' must be backed by great competence, by a passion for the creative business that you are constantly building together with your colleagues, and a love of the product that this business is itself creating and providing. You must care for every aspect of the business, but at the centre of your caring must be your colleagues, and in the first place among these your fellow leaders, both actual and potential. You are responsible, and in the last analysis you are always in a very direct sense responsible, for their wellbeing, their further development, the security of their employment that is essential to their active, innovative engagement, their material prosperity that should always surpass that of your 'competitors' and the surety of the retirement and other pensions that they have the right to expect and enjoy. It is in this sense that you must be their friend, and it is on this basis, which is essentially a basis of trust, that they will be for the most part your friends This is a friendship that cannot be built upon the quicksand of bonhomie and other forms of publicness, but must be built on the rock of personal integrity, decency and fairness. It is then a friendship that will become mutual, being constructed upon this rock of what is true.

Of course there will always be those who will see you as their enemy and attack you accordingly, but as long as you lead effectively and are seen to lead effectively, you need fear nothing from these manifestations of nothingness.

4.4 Among friends: your competitors

Really? Yes, really! Without good strong competitors you are unnecessary, redundant, without purpose. Why should anyone care to appoint or accept a leader at all if there is no competition? Your competitors are your very *raison d'être*. Precisely to the extent that they are good strong competitors, you should praise them and honour them. Without them you are nothing as a leader; with them you are everything that you are intended to be. It is they who keep you on your toes and you who keep them on theirs. And your competitors are in exactly the same position as yourself. So in this sense you and your competitors are already implicitly cooperating.

It is then in this sense that we see that:

There can be no competition without cooperation, no cooperation without competition.

It is this that runs as a leitmotif through all your relations with what we shall now call your *authentic competitors*. These are, in their essence, organisations that share with you one and the same ethic. They are as serious about their work as you are, they take just as much care of 'their' people as you do, they put just as much effort into preparing and promoting younger leaders as you do yourself; they also love their products and they share your passion for the business. It is with such competitors that you *build an industry*, making what is new and unfamiliar and regarded suspiciously into something everyday, familiar and widely accepted. It is together with these competitors that you fight the inauthentic, as that which drags down quality and degrades its employees by rendering them insecure and anxious and survives only by false advertisement, by 'pressuring' its suppliers and distributors and politicking for tariff walls and other forms of protection. Sometimes people from another authentic organisation may come over to work with your people, or vice versa, and there can never be any bad feeling about this from either side; or sometimes you and they will combine forces in acquiring a project and executing it together. In the limit you may yourself, on your retirement or moving on to another challenge, recommend one of 'their' people to replace you. When dealing with authentic competitors, almost everything is possible, while when dealing with the inauthentic very little, if anything at all, is possible.

The relation with your authentic competitors is then essentially one of a friendship founded upon mutual respect and this naturally leads in some cases to cooperative ventures. These may include consortia engaged in doing business and cooperating with organisations that are already established clients or customers of one or more of the organisations participating in the consortium. Much attention must then be given to maintaining ethical standards within the consortium, following up on every event that might tend to sour relations within the group and this is all but impossible unless the leaders concerned have good friendly relations, so that they may speak openly in good faith and with complete trust. Matters of this kind and several others concerning the dialectic of cooperation and competition, and especially in relation to the new international order in industrial development, with its dominance of the China-Korea-Japan axis and associated reorientation of trading relations, will be taken up at length in the EIIL courses within the context of 'Eurasia'.

4.5 Among friends: the entrepreneur

Very good leaders can sometimes be very good entrepreneurs and very good entrepreneurs can sometimes be very good leaders, but these correspond to essentially different and distinct forms of human initiative and creativity and need to be carefully distinguished. We have seen what a leader is, but what is an entrepreneur?

The word comes from the French verb, *à entreprendre*, composed in its turn from *entre*, or 'between', and *prendre*, or 'to take'. As a noun it is applied to someone who serves as a 'go-between in order to undertake something'. In French itself, and in some other languages besides, the term is commonly used for what in English is called a *contractor*, as one who serves as an intermediary between labour and capital, but that obviously does not catch the meaning that we usually associate with it nowadays and with which we wish to associate it here. So: what *is* an entrepreneur?

Let us try to answer this question phenomenologically. A phenomenon, we have seen, is an object seen from a particular point of view, and so as something subject to the belief systems and the accumulated facts and Facts of the viewer. We are then led to ask *how the entrepreneur shows him or herself to us*, or *how entrepreneurship manifests itself*. When we do this we proceed to 'the things themselves' by actually observing entrepreneurs closely and critically in their everyday environments. As soon as we follow this path, however, we are at once struck by *the attitude of the entrepreneur towards risk*, which we may characterise as one that is not based upon the ordered, the numbered and the countable that we have identified as the basic traits of modern technology in its present-day deprived states of Being, but is instead based upon a drive for a *self-expression* in some enterprise that is particularly suited to the mode of expression of this *self*. It is once again an expression of the mystery of integration. The risks may or may not be apparent, but they are anyway not determinate or do not play a really determinate role in the decision of the entrepreneur to proceed with his or her enterprise. They may be assessed intuitively, but they are rarely if ever calculated. This is to say, however, that the entrepreneur is one who does not count all the risks, or in some cases does not even count the risks at all, but relies more than most persons upon 'chance', or rather *luck*.

We have already touched upon the peculiar properties of this phenomenon that we call 'luck' in the previous chapter and have there already intimated that what appears as luck may in fact be otherwise construed as a deeply subjective, pre-scientific, pre-predicative, pre-linguistic and essentially unconscious estimation on the part of the 'lucky' person of the risks inherent in the situation in which the event that we call 'luck' arises. We now need to take this further, indicating how this intimation may be extended to an unconscious assessment of the risks inherent in sociotechnical initiatives.

In phenomenological terms, 'luck' has its own kind of Being and is even *existentiell* – as one form of understanding of oneself - in its own right. In this sense, the entrepreneur is an inspired gambler, but then his or her gamble is conducted in the casino of the world of business enterprise and the stakes are the capital, in money and in time and effort and love that the entrepreneur commits to the enterprise. Thus entrepreneurship is *a state of mind*, and as such *a Fact* that interacts with and modifies the belief system of the entrepreneur, leading this entrepreneur to make quite other judgements on the nature and extent of the risks involved in the entrepreneurial enterprise than would a more 'rational' person. *Entrepreneurship is a kind of faith, and indeed a form of passion.* But then, in the words of the French philosopher Jean Wahl (1959, p. 67):

> The ideas of passion and uncertainty are interrelated for Kierkegaard; it is the unsure thing that solicits our passion. We are not impassioned by certainties, but by things involving a risk. The subjective thinker is not in possession of any universalisable truth in the rational sense of the word; rather, he always has the sense of being in danger, of being on the high seas amid a storm. It is this uncertainty as regards what he believes that heightens and intensifies his subjectivity. He is on a stormy, bottomless sea. In the sphere of existence, in the sphere of subjectivity, there are no proofs, no demonstrations. When he has come to know this risk the individual is thoroughly transformed; there are no results in the sense that science gives us

results, but the individual is *internally* transformed and, in this sense, everything is transformed.

It is in this way that the entrepreneur acquires another and thereby deeply connected characteristic, which is that of *opportunism*. There is on the one hand this deep inner sense of purpose that is at least related to faith, and so *consistently maintained* through thick and thin through every situation, but then on the other hand, and apparently inseparably from this, there is this totally incongruous, because *often outrageously opportunistic and risky behaviour* in so many of the activities of the entrepreneur. So what are you, as a leader, to make of this person called the entrepreneur? Even more difficult: what are you to think of this person called the entrepreneur who is an inseparable part of your own person? Can you work with this person, or will you be ill-advised even to try? The answer is then already clear however: *you can work constructively with this person if he or she is your friend, and the closer the friendship the more successful your combined enterprise will be.* So, just as one consequence, if you are both leader and entrepreneur in one person, you had better stay very good friends with yourself!

When discussing leadership we took a little time off to introduce the logic of leadership. What then, correspondingly, is the logic of entrepreneurship? We see at once that this has again a logic of obligation to one's own self, but it is not leadership because there is no corresponding obligation towards 'the others' in the venture, and none again necessarily from 'the others' to take on the obligations, manifest as commitments, of 'the led'. To the extent that 'the led' become present as such alongside the entrepreneur, then we are back with leadership and this entrepreneur becomes also a leader.

This distinction becomes of critical importance nowadays in Europe because of the correctly perceived need to create new businesses, almost all of a small to medium size. The need to promote such small-to-medium sized enterprises (SMEs) is already at the centre of interest of governments and of the Union as a whole, but this interest has been high-jacked, like most other such initiatives, to promote the notion of the superiority of the *hard* 'Anglo-Saxon' model of capitalism over the *soft* 'continental-European' model. It is then argued that the level of social security, including unemployment benefits, provided by the 'soft' model is much too high to be affordable by those starting new businesses. In the 'hard' model, the employer can pass a great part, and in many cases the greater part of the burden of his or her financial risk onto the employees, since in the event of failure he or she has relatively few obligations towards them. These employees must, *de facto*, share the risks of failure of the enterprise even as they cannot be expected to be able to gauge the magnitudes of these risks and can only expect a much lower level of social security on average in the (statistically quite likely) event of *failure*. In the 'soft' continental-European model, many, and probably most potential entrepreneurs are dissuaded from building their businesses because of the exponentiation of their own personal risk by the risk of paying much heavier compensation to employees in the event of failure. In the case of industrial developments where the nature and employment of technology plays a significant role alongside the employment and social-security aspects, the problems involved become essentially sociotechnical and the outcomes of entrepreneurial activities correspondingly less predictable again.

This matter takes on another aspect again, however, when seen within the light that existential philosophy throws upon *the notion of failure*. The German religious-existentialist philosopher Karl Jaspers especially, emphasised the essential role of failure in the development of the self. In existentialist philosophy from Kierkegaard onwards, failure is intimately related to *repetition*, and especially in cases like those experienced by the entrepreneur who has to 'pick himself up again and start all over again' after the failure of an enterprise. Of course one can always learn something practical from every failure, but this kind of learning is not at all the main point, let alone the purpose, of failure. The essential point in this case is *the transformation of the self* that occurs when one 'picks oneself up and starts all over again': we then overcome our failure by becoming conscious of that failure, by accepting it, and by so doing we 'transcend our earlier self', making of it another self again. The person who has passed through this is not the same as the person who was there before it happened, and the myths, legends and sagas provide many examples of this particular *drama*, and it has been depicted in many recent films besides. Thus (Wahl, 1959, pp.74, 75):

> Jaspers' interpretation of the idea of *repetition* is different from Heidegger's and a little closer to Kierkegaardian repetition: our failures, he believes, are nothing but the affirmation of transcendence. The fact that we fail is an indication that there is some greater thing, a sphere higher than existence. We become aware of this sphere in what Jaspers calls 'boundary situations'.
> Thus failure makes it possible for us to mount from existence towards transcendence, and for this reason, in so far as it conducts us to repetition, it is the supreme 'cipher', the supreme symbol of transcendence....
> It is thus that the two ideas of failure and repetition are not so opposed as they seem at first, since in both Heidegger and Jaspers it is failure that brings about the possibility of repetition, it is failure that leads us to triumph and to authenticity.

This notion is accepted almost instinctively in a former 'frontier society' like the USA, but it is less understood in European business circles. It needs to be understood more clearly in our European societies and its consequences for those caught up in the entrepreneurial adventure as employees needs to be reconsidered accordingly. The legislative initiatives necessary to ameliorate the social consequences of entrepreneurial failure are reasonably clear and some efforts are being made in this direction, and a more dynamic, better-informed and better-educated leadership can already devise means to counteract such negative features as these are currently associated with entrepreneurship in the 'continental European' model. Even so, it has to be said that about one quarter of all German companies now trading were established only during the last ten years, so perhaps the situation is not nearly so critical as some persons would like to present it.[7]

4.6 Among friends: the inventor, the innovator and some others

These are other invaluable but often difficult friends of the leader in industry. Industry, we have seen, drives and is driven by technology and technology is all about creation. The inventor and the innovator are among those who functions at the level of creation itself, albeit in different ways, and to these we can add the facilitator, the venture processor and some others, each with another way again. These may be creators of products, of services, of new organisational forms, of business models or any number of other objects and arrangements. We shall concentrate here on invention and innovation, each of which is obviously something different again to leadership, even though the leader must often be inventive and innovative, and something different yet again from entrepreneurship, even though here also there may be overlaps. Invention and innovation are always concerned with something new and new-born, and as such their first need is protection, and after that nourishment and encouragement. As soon as they are not in the care of those who parented them, invention and innovation have to be fostered; they needs fostering, and then in the first place by the leader. From the point of view of the leader, the entrepreneur is his eyes and hands and heart looking outwards into the outer world of the enterprise, while the inventor and innovator are his eyes and hands and heart looking inwards, tending the very life-giving forces of the enterprise. The leader needs the entrepreneur to grow the enterprise towards the outside, in its outer world, while he needs the inventor and the innovator to grow the enterprise from within, in its inner world. Only when there are good relations, mutual trust and a deep understanding between the inventor, the innovator, the entrepreneur and the leader, so that they are on good friendly relations, can the enterprise succeed. The responsibility for realising and maintaining this situation remains of course that of the leader.

If we take up the difference between the inventor and the innovator, we may at once observe that, just as the life of the entrepreneur is in some ways more difficult than that of the leader, so that of the innovator is more difficult again and that of the inventor is the most difficult of all. And then there is the golden rule, that the more important the invention for the society in which it comes to presence, the more difficult the life of its progenitor. History is saturated with examples of the struggles of inventors to bring their inventions to fruition against every kind of discouragement, ranging from the total indifference of those with most to benefit from the invention to the most tenacious opposition of those who feel in the one or the other way threatened by it. Everyone who is anybody nowadays says that what our societies *need most of all* is innovation supported by invention as advanced by entrepreneurs and led by true leaders, even as the inventors, innovators, entrepreneurs and leaders all know that this is precisely what our present-day societies *want least of all*. There is nothing like the invention and the innovation to 'upset the applecart', that is, to upset the status quo. Accordingly the leader has to protect and encourage the authentic inventor and support the efforts of the genuine innovator to the limits of his capabilities, even as he guides the true entrepreneur in his efforts to bring the products of invention and innovation to market at the most propitious moment. The history of the Sony Corporation provides several case studies in itself. [8]

4.7 Among friends: your clients and customers

These do appear to be arriving here exceedingly late in the day. In the world of the inauthentic I should never be allowed to leave the clients and customers until last-but-one. This does not suit the publicness of such a book, which is to say that it is not 'politically correct'. Any and every publicly-aware reviewer would jump on this implied relegation at once and insist that it should be 'corrected'. "The clients and the customers came first!" the reviewers will all cry...because that is what everyone is *supposed* to say. But *in fact* the clients and customers do come in this order among your *friends* in any conventional personal way, for it is these that you must *serve* if you will ever build a business and those who you serve can very rarely also be your personal friends. They may become personal friends with some of the staff of the organisation who are especially helpful to them, but friendship rarely goes beyond this at the personal level.

But they are your friends at another level again, and one which I shall take up in the last Section here, for *they are among your best teachers*. In this sense they can perhaps best be characterised as *your impersonal friends*. Rather like the entrepreneur, they can be difficult and on occasions vexing friends, but friends none the less. You must listen as carefully as you can and so in every way that you can to your clients and customers, and you must encourage everyone in your organisation to do so too. But "The customer is always right" is only true in the world of publicness, and certainly it is 'politically correct' to tell the client or customer that he or she is always right as often as possible, but it is rarely a fact. Every successful organisation is aiming to produce what the customer *does not want* at the time when the service or product is being projected, but what he or she *will come to want* as the service or product becomes available. If the customer or client already wanted it, you would already be far too late in satisfying the new need and your authentic competitors would already have taken the market. The direction of this process is of the essence of good leadership, and the art of your leadership in this sense will be, on the one hand, to listen to your clients and customers with a view to explicating *what it will be* that they will want by the time that your new services and products can come to market and, on the other hand, to be following social and technical developments sociotechnically in order to satisfy this future need. After that, of course, all is opportunism and serendipity, for there is no telling how the market will develop as the service or product is accepted and matures through its use and application.

To this it must be added that as a client's or customer's society moves into a postmodern condition, so the client or customer will in many cases want to produce what you are selling rather than simply buying it from you, and in this case you are again involved in cooperative ventures. These and many other aspects of 'the dialectic of cooperation and competition' are themselves functions of the new industrial order associated with the rise to industrial predominance of the China-Korea-Japan axis and the reorientation of trading patterns more towards an East-West axis and less towards a North-South axis. It is developments of this kind, involving factors that are rapidly changing and which you may help to shape, that lead us to take a much different and more differentiated view of such earlier-established practices as those of 'Product Life Cycle Analyses'.

4.8 Among friends: your teachers, including your family

But now even I have to be 'politically correct' and mention these friends just before the very end of the story - which is often and most unfortunately where they finish up in real life! There are teachers in the traditional sense, like myself, and there are teachers among all the categories of friends already mentioned. There are friends in the authors of the books which you read, authors who, even when they are not still living, are immortal just so long as you read them. These two classes of friends are connected because your living teachers will constantly be referring you to the immortals and your reading of the immortals will keep bringing you back to interrogating your living teachers. One of the functions of the EIIL is to maintain a service of 'life-long learning' along these lines, currently supported by e-mail and similar devices. Speaking dramatically:

The training, education and development of the leader end only with his death.

Which brings us to the real heroes in all this, namely those who make up the family of the leader. It is these who have to support the leader in all his travails, and indeed without this support the leader is like one with his right hand tied behind his back. One who is solicitous of 'his people' therefore endeavours to ensure that they enjoy good family lives…or at least good lives. This intrusion into such private affairs may sometimes appear patronising and otherwise undesirable, and so it is to some extent, but it should be understood that it is well meant when it is directed to realising the inherent abilities of the born leader.

4.9 The authentic in the service of the inauthentic

This situation is so much the rule that it might appear that it scarcely deserves mention: you will almost inevitably have to work at some time with and 'under' persons who are in no sense genuine leaders, and so are no real leaders at all – which is why it is mentioned in the last place, below the level of your friends. It is all rather like Hemmingway's 'death and taxation' in that there seems to be no way of avoiding it. Even if this is not the situation in your employment, it must sometimes be the case in your dealings with your clients and customers. The inauthentic produces nothing, or at least nothing of any value, so that it is totally dependent upon the authentic for its very survival, let alone its success. Indeed it is of the essence of the power of the inauthentic, of nothingness, that it must contain within it and exploit the most authentic. At the productive centre of the greatest evil is the greatest good!

As one of the authentic, the classical solution is of course for you to build your own 'pocket of competence' within the organisation and among your clients, constantly manoeuvring to maintain the integrity of this pocket under the assaults and attacks of nothingness emanating from certain of those around you. Since your colleagues are by and large your friends, these pockets sometimes, and even often, link together to form alliances of competent groups within an otherwise inauthentic organisation or market.

But even when they have clearly declared themselves your enemies, the victims of nothingness are still your friends in the sense that you can learn from direct observation how nothingness has taken hold of them and so how to recognise this hold in your future career. This attitude corresponds in fact to a quite other way of looking at the inauthentic, which is that of seeing it as an essential part of your training as a leader. Your time spent in the service of the inauthentic plays in this respect something of the same role as the dissection room in a teaching hospital: it is there that you pursue not only the study of anatomy as such, but specifically the study of pathology, a study that will be of inestimable value to you as you proceed further. Among other things, it will 'toughen you up' emotionally so that you are better prepared to confront future negative experiences. This is then *your training in the diagnosis of nothingness*. To return to the article of John Berger quoted earlier, in Chapter 2, "Bacon brings together the pieces …of the human anatomy and arranges them as assemblages of body parts on the dissection table".

Your present employment is then in part, and hopefully only in a lesser part, a training in the ways of inauthenticity, of nothingness, and one that you can end, or at least reduce, when you locate an organisation that is more authentic in its operations. So long as you can keep your sense of humour, this experience of the inauthentic should provide an excellent training in spotting all manner of platitudes, hyperbole, bullshit, nonsense, deceptions, falsifications and the other hallmarks of the inauthentic: it teaches you, again, to read the very signal flags of the kingdom of nothingness. You will learn to recognise the rhetoric of lies and manipulation much more quickly and more surely. Like all forms of hard training, it is often painful and tedious and uncongenial, but it is essential in its own way to your future survival and effectiveness as a leader.

It is an immediate consequence of this training that, paradoxically enough, the ways of a nothingness that has no order and no plan and no system become eminently predictable. This is because nothingness proceeds entirely opportunistically, so that it is only necessary to identify the latest gimmicks and buzz words that are currently circulating to know in which direction the inauthentic will turn. One only has to look for the 'opportunities' as these will appear and appeal to the inauthentic to predict what it will do next. This closely resembles identifying the symptoms of a disease so as to diagnose the type of a malignancy, so as to treat it appropriately whenever you are able, and otherwise to protect others as well as yourself from its depravations and further dissemination.

Of course you have to be very careful about this so as not to become infected, possibly irreparably, with the diseases of nothingness yourself. I have to repeat the warning, contantly emphasised in theology, that you should not spend too much time on studying these matters and so should not give them too much of your attention and effort. Under no circumstances should you find them 'interesting'! But then the EIIL is intended to 'inoculate' you with knowledge in such a way as to give you a good chance of avoiding such diversions and so not succumbing to these diseases yourself. And on this cheerful note it is time to wish you:
Good luck!

So wandle du – der Lohn ist nicht gering –
nicht schwankend hin, wie jener Sämann ging,
daß bald ein Korn, des Zufalls leichtes Spiel,
hier auf den Weg, dort zwischen Dornen fiel:
Nein! streue klug wie reich, mit männlich stäter Hand,
den Segen aus auf ein geackert Land;
dann laß es ruhn: die Ernte wird erscheinen,
und dich beglücken, wie die Deinen.

Goethe

NOTES

These notes are primarily intended to link the text more closely with the references. As observed earlier, the text provides only a very partial and incomplete coverage - no more than a Précis - of the theoretical and philosophical part of the EIIL Course. Correspondingly, a major part of the material to which reference has been made when preparing the Course as a whole cannot be connected to this Précis at many points, and hence the need for the present linkage as some partial compensation. The last dates and editions are those to which reference has been made when writing this book. Since most participants of the EIIL Course may be expected to have a good working knowledge of French and German, the originals in, and in some cases translations into these languages have also been referenced.

INTRODUCTION

(1) Liddell Hart, 1970/1983, p.236.
(2) Kant, I., 1781/Second Ed. 1787, refers to the *Critic der reinen Vernunft von Immanuel Kant etc.* as published by Hartknoch at Riga. Let me on just this one occasion explain something of the problems involved when citing such works and quoting from their translations, even while promising not to repeat such pedantries. The course will be taught using parts of the unchanged revision with intercomparison of various earlier editions made by Raymond Schmidt in 1924 and as published by Reklam at Leipzig in 1972. Ignoring several other revisions and reprintings, I have also availed myself of the less completely annotated Suhrkamp edition of 1956/1976. The 'standard' English translation seems to have become that of N. Kemp Smith, 1929/1933/1987, which however I find distinctly 'wooden' and sometimes clumsy, even though it drew upon the earlier translations of J. M. D. Meiklejohn (of 1855) and Max Müller (of 1881) and is said to be more accurate than these. Kant was certainly 'difficult' in this work, and indeed he apologised for just this and explained the reasons for it in his own preface; but he was always elegant. Goethe observed that, certainly previously to this first of the *Critiques*, taking up and reading Kant was "like suddenly walking into a brilliantly lit room". The difficulty in this work, whether in the original or in translation, was indeed inherent in the whole 'Copernican Revolution' in modern thought that it inaugurated, and Schopenhauer wrote a wonderful appreciation of this. Personally I prefer the Meiklejohn translation, as republished by Dent in 1934 and subsequently reprinted several times. Thus the central notion expressed already in the Introduction to the Second Edition (p.13) – "*Sie begriffen, daß die Venunft nur das einsieht, was sie selbst nach ihrem Entwurfe hervorbringt*" - is quite beautifully translated by Meikeljohn (p.10) as "They learned that reason only perceives that which it produces after its own design", which however Kemp Smith (p.20) mangles into "They learned that reason has insight only into that which it produces after a plan of its own...". In other such cases of markedly different approaches to translation, I have given references to more than one translation,

without however expressing my personal preference. The present note thus marks the only exception to this rule.

(3)   We shall have much to say about ideology and ideologies later, but just a short note is required to connect already to the references. We shall here refer to an ideology when certain ideas have taken over and have come to control at least some aspects of the behaviour of the person rather than the person having taken over and coming to control the ideas. This is accordingly a situation in which the person has lost some part of his or her individual freedom of thought, and thus of action as well. Such a situation has then to do with the very existence of the individual, *qua* individual, so that it raises issues of individual human existence, or 'existential issues'. It has to do most immediately with the relation between 'the one', as one's own self, and 'the other', who may or may not be seen or regarded as another self of the same kind as one's own self. Ideologies then serve to divide persons one from another by separating 'the we' who are like our own self in subscribing to the ideology from 'the they' who are not like us in that they do not so subscribe and are otherwise in some way different from 'us'. To the extent that management becomes an ideology, so it divides humanity into 'those who manage' and 'those who are managed', and it is this ideology that is the primary driving force of many, and indeed most, business schools, leading further to a veritable cult of management. It must then appear that leadership could be infected by the same virus of ideology and it is an important part of the work of the EIIL to prevent this happening by showing that developing leadership as an ideology must lead to even more unstable and unsustainable situations than it does in the case of management. A recent book of James Hoopes (2003) makes much the same point. As we shall demonstrate, just as *ideologies*, even as they gather together their ideologues, have the overall effect of separating by differentiating socially, so they are opposed by *doctrines*, which have the effect of bringing individuals together around a nucleus of shared values, without excluding any others, who are free to adhere or otherwise to the doctrine. Ideologies thus differ from doctrines in that ideologies integrate in order to differentiate, while doctrines have the capacity to integrate without differentiating. Clearly this distinction is not accepted universally, but it is one that we adopt here on the basis of common theological practice, while in all of these matters we are also in the philosophical and theological environments of phenomenology and existentialism - and our references follow accordingly. Here already we introduce the person of Søren Kierkegaard as the founder of existentialism, both in its philosophical and in its theological dimensions. Kierkegaard expressed the greatest admiration for Schopenhauer who, although most unjustly described as 'pessimistic', in fact contributed greatly, albeit indirectly, to the foundations of both of these movements and remains an essential point of reference.

(4)   My own most direct encounter with this movement was in relation to the (3.8 billion euro) motorway and rail link between Denmark and Sweden in which the time allocated for on-site supervision by management was reduced by 80 percent as compared with earlier projects, such as the closely related (4.2 billion euro) Great Belt link which was very similar in concept but less environmentally sensitive. Once again savings were not only, and even not so much, realised through the reduction in management time – although that saving was still substantial - but more, and much more, through the greater flexibility and effectiveness that was obtained when the different teams engaged on the project worked out their own spatial and temporal arrangements as the work itself

proceeded. This was also necessary in many parts of the construction because the project was 'working with nature' in that the associated construction processes were designed to coordinate with meteorological, oceanographical and associated near-field current and wave conditions. Thus, for example, the very fine (chalk and clay) dredging spoil was stored when conditions were unfavourable for its discharge and air-lifted into suspension when the density currents in the Sound were favourable to the transport of the spoil over the greatest distances – usually between 80 and 120 kilometers - with the greatest lateral dispersion, thus reducing the subsequent sedimentation to ecologically sustainable levels. This of course necessitated the most accurate and reliable numerically-modelled predictions of the usually strongly-stratified flows and, in the shallower regions, of the sediment-stirring short-period wave fields. It also called for similarly accurate and reliable networks of instruments with on-line radio transmission of their data streams, as well as many other devices, providing on-line assimilation of data directly into the models. Simultaneously, all the resulting information and knowledge that was relevant to the individual self-managing teams was being transmitted in appropriate formats through radio internets to the self-managing teams as the work proceeded (See Torkildsen and Dynesen, 2001 and, for example, Gimsing and Iversen, 2001). There could then be no preset schedules, such as are still generated in conventional PERT-defined formats, but an opportunistic self-management that constantly adjusted itself to conditions dictated by nature herself. The result was that the link was completed and has since operated satisfying all the stringent environmental conditions imposed and closely monitored both by the Agencies of the Danish and Swedish governments and by the many non-governmental organisations that were involved directly in the acceptance and on-line supervision of the project, while it was also completed within budget and six months ahead of schedule. This was in the starkest contrast to the Channel Tunnel project, which was of the same scale as the Sound and Belt projects combined, in which environmental constraints were less onerous but which overrun its budget more than two times over and the completion of which was considerably delayed, with financial consequences that are still with us today.

There is now so much written and anecdotal evidence from so many places to support the view that a sound leadership can achieve exceptional increases in efficiency and profitability in this way that a whole string of case studies can now be presented on this theme.

(5)   See again Gimsing and Iversen, 2001, and Torkilsen and Dynesen, 2001.

(6)   It must be added that the melancholic state, as something apparently inseparable from a heightened state of awareness and exponentiated insight, although accepted because understood within the Christian Church, was not considered inevitable in men of some genius. From Saint John of the Cross onwards, this condition of the spirit was seen as a preparation for something higher that transcended mere genius, whereby the condition was overcome and indeed transcended by faith, as accompanied by divine grace. Kierkegaard spoke memorably of the 'leap of faith' through which this transcendence proceeded. He described this leap as proceeding through two movements, the one being an infinite movement in which a man became conscious of God, suffused in the light of God, and the second being a finite movement in which this man returned to the world of name and form again with no outward sign of his transformation other than his loss of melancholy: see also Lambotte (1999, pp.35 *et seq*).

(7) The works of Jean Baudrillard are particular revealing of the downside of the 'postmodern condition' and the possibilities that it provides to flee from an unacceptable reality into a wide variety of pseudo-realities, often of a damaging nature. These works seem to have influenced some 'alternative' filmmakers, such as Michael Moore in his 'Bowling for Columbine' and 'Fahrenheit 9/11' and Morgan Spurlock in his 'Super-Size Me'. For our present purposes, Baudrillard's works can be treated together with these films to provide excellent case-studies in inauthentic leadership, but then of course taking due account of their propagandistic intentions. The critique of the 'downside' of postmodernism of Christopher Norris is also recommended even though it is very one-sided in its almost total neglect of the 'upside'.

(8) Case studies should be actual as well as historical and the actual should resonate with the historical if a deeper understanding is to be attained of both. Teaching of this kind is always a form of preaching along the road and at the roadside (*theologia viatorum*) strongly conditioned by the interaction between the teacher and the taught, whose positions change from teacher to taught and back again during the interaction, whereby the historical and the actual come to interact in another way again. Classical historical studies include those of the *socio*technical view of the development of maritime navigation and naval warfare in the age of sail, of the coming and development of the age of steam with its need for a network of bunkering arrangements, and thence of the development of networks of all kinds (as introduced later, in Chapter 3, as the iconic instruments of the ideology of modernism).Specific examples may continue with the *socio*technical view of the torpedo, the torpedo boat, the submarine, the machine gun, the tank and so much other paraphernalia of naval and military history, and some specific examples of these (such as the T34, the Il-2 or Stormovik, the Katusha and the Kalishnikov, just to mention some specifically Russian military contributions with important *socio*technical dimensions). Other specific product developments which occurred with profound social interactions, whereby the product could not have succeeded without the social development and the social development could never have taken place without the technological development encapsulated in the product, provide much further material. Current developments, such as the ultra low-cost, highly-reliable and durable Renault saloon car, being constructed under the Dacia and Renault brands, initially in Romania, Iran, Russia, China, Morocco and Columbia, provides an excellent contemporary example in which widely varying social transformations are being carefully integrated with the overall production process. These include the use of a low initial level of robotisation as a sustainable way of reducing immediate local unemployment, the formation of a special team for the retraining of 11,000 former employees into persons supplying motor-car related services – maintenance, coachwork repairs, taxi operations, etc. – besides setting up personally-owned businesses in other areas so as to provide much-needed local artisinal services, together with trade-training facilities and many other infrastructural contributions. The Airbus 380 together with its airport terminal requirements, transport hub restructurings and other sociotechnical-infrastructural arrangements, while taking account of the consequences for the structure of long-haul mass-transport operations generally, provides another important contemporary example. The construction of by far the largest passenger ship of all time, the Queen Mary II, in 30 months and within budget employing sub-contractors from a wide variety of cultures, and, once again, the Denmark-Sweden motorway and high speed

rail connection connecting, together, with the similar Great Belt project, Scandinavia to the rest of Europe (and so now exemplifying also the so-called 'geopolitical dimension' of sociotechnology) provide excellent case studies of multi-knowledge, multi-language and, most generally of all, multi-cultural operations.

(9) Through phenomenological studies, which have to do with the way in which different individuals can come to see and understand one and the same thing in different and often very different ways, and existentialist questioning, which delves into the essences of our individual and our collective modes of existence, we come to understand something at least of the functioning of the doctrine and the nature of the miracle. The Encyclopedia review article of Antony Flew continues to provide an excellent introduction to the notion of the miracle which draws upon the celebrated – Flew called it 'notorious'! – Section 10 of David Hume's *Enquiry*, but probably of necessity he omitted the conclusion of that part:

> Mere reason is insufficient to convince us of its veracity. And whoever is moved by *Faith* to assent to it, is conscious of a continued miracle in his own person, which subverts all the principles of his understanding, and gives him a determination to believe what is most contrary to custom and experience.

Thus a person or persons of faith may undertake a task that seems quite impossible by the norms and standards of the time, but there may be just one person, or at most a few persons, with the faith supported by knowledge – which knowledge will usually be itself highly subjective and 'emotional' - often nowadays unfortunately called 'emotional intelligence'- to make a success of the venture, and then everyone will speak of 'a miracle'. Kierkegaard saw that such a usage was self-referencing and expressed this aspect in his formula that "Faith is a miracle, otherwise it is not faith". Correspondingly again, the miracle does not reside in the event itself, but in our perception of the event, so that, when seen philosophically, it is phenomenological. This point of view was in fact adumbrated already by John Locke, but in a lesser and mostly neglected work.

It follows further from this however that, as Hume contended: "a miracle can never be proved so as to be the foundation of a system of religion". Since the 'foundation of a religion' is commonly expressed in the form of a doctrine, this repeats Pascal's earlier formulation: "*Les miracles sont pour la doctrine, et non pas la doctrine pour les miracles //* The miracles are there for the doctrine, not the doctrine for the miracles" (Lafond, 1992, p. 433).

(Further to this note, I should be remiss if I did not point out here at once that 'emotional intelligence' in the sense that has become popular nowadays is essentially an oxymoron - even if a most appealing one to those who do not care so much about the meaning and use of words. Emotion has to do with a movement of the feelings, while intelligence has to do with the faculty of understanding and these are two very different and even contrasting things. The first is limbic in its origins and the second cerebral. The one is, at most, 'of the heart' and the other is essentially 'of the mind'. Putting the matter just as simplistically, it is our own emotions that attempt to steer us while it is we who attempt to steer our own intelligences by way of compensation: the first cannot properly function as an adjective to the second's noun. One could just as well talk of a 'hearing eyes' or a 'handy head': at least these might conceivably have some poetic application. This distortion of language may become clearer if we introduce the term 'intelligent emotions', which most persons would probably find highly desirable in some cases even as such emotions would be generally unrealisable and actually undesirable, becoming in some extreme cases psychopathological. The consequences of the confusion that follows from such conflations in the present case become clear in the book of Daniel Goleman, Richard Boyatzis and Annie Mckee (2002) which starts with "...the primal job of leadership is emotional. We believe that this primal dimension of leadership, though often invisible or ignored, determines whether everything else a leader does will work as well as it could. And that is why emotional leadership – being intelligent about emotions – matters so much for leadership success."

As so often nowadays one has to ask all the time "what on earth are these people trying to say?" And the answer is not at all clear. Sometimes they seem to be talking about intuitive knowledge and at other times about innate intelligence, both of which were distinguished and analysed long ago by Locke, and other times again simply about common sense, or possibly 'gut feeling' - another oxymoron which has however attained at least to some poetic license.

But once such an expression as 'emotional intelligence' gets established there seems to be little to be done about it except to use it circumspectively oneself, if at all, and not to be oneself carried away by its rhetoric. Reading through such current books about leadership I am irresistibly reminded of one of Kierkegaard's many amusing anecdotes, in which while taking his daily constitutional he saw a sign in front of a shop saying "Laundry taken in here". So the next day he brought along some clothes to be laundered, but was promptly informed that the shop did not take in laundry at all, but was only trying to sell a sign saying "Laundry taken in here").

CHAPTER ONE

1) We have to do here with what we can perhaps best describe as *cultural aggression*. Among so many studies of this phenomenon, the lectures given by Michel Foucault at the *College de France* in the 1970s are of a particular relevance in this place. Cultural aggression occurs when nothingness subverts one culture so as to serve its own nefarious ends of damaging and in some cases destroying other cultures and their civilisations, even while seriously degrading the aggressive culture and its civilisation at the same time. The history of cultural aggression is inseparable from the history of Europe and its extentions outside of Europe, and in terms of its extentions this history is still being written large at the present time. What has changed is the attitude of the peoples of Europe itself – although not that of all of 'their' governments by any means! - towards such 'adventures'. These peoples have for by far the greater part turned their backs upon cultural aggression, at least in the form of the naked brutality of overwhelming military force, having been made aware of its consequences on the persons of their own parents and grandparents. The prosecution of programmes of cultural aggression by economic rather than by military means, primarily through certain (but by no means all!) processes of globalisation, continues of course, but even this is nowadays widely recognised and opposed within the aggressor societies themselves. In some cases this is opposed in a spirit of altruism, but it is increasingly also understood that, even

though cultural aggression may suit the interests of some in the aggressor society, it is harmful to the society as a whole in which the culture of aggression has been implanted.

At the same time it has to be said that in the absence of this so-called aggression as perpetrated by economic and financial means, the prosperity of the 'first world' would be seriously degraded unless it could introduce a much higher level of leadership, and in the first place in its industries. One of the more implicit aims of the EIIL is then in fact that of so increasing the quality of European industrial leadership that much fairer and more equitable relations between the peoples of Europe and those of the 'third world' can be realistically introduced and sustained.

2) The integration mystery was treated by Schopenhauer in his first major work, where he described its occurrence as follows (1813/1960//1974, p. 113):

> Every simpleton has the faculty of reason; give him the premises, and he will draw the conclusion. But the understanding supplies primary, and therefore intuitive, knowledge, and here we find the differences. Accordingly, the pith of every great discovery as well as every world plan of importance is the product of a propitious moment when, through favourable outer and inner circumstances, complicated causal series or concealed causes of phenomena seen already a thousand times, or obscure paths never previously followed, [this] suddenly reveal itself to the understanding.

Schopenhauer spoke of 'empirical intuitive perception' and 'intuitive apprehension' – again, roughly what has just been castigated as 'emotional intelligence' - whereby the leader and the led come together at the propitious moment in the propitious place. As Kierkegaard in his first great masterpiece allowed his Æsthete to express this matter, "Everything is in the coincidence and the coincidence is everything". Kierkegaard emphasised that one cannot possibly calculate such events and the laws of probability have no relevance in such situations. In the words of Schopenhauer (*op.cit.* p.112): "It can even be said that *where calculation begins, understanding ends*". A more recent view of this is provided, albeit from a very different perspective, by Dupuy, 2002.

3) The relations of the theological concept of nothingness to its philosophical counterparts were set out with exemplary clarity by Karl Barth in the *Church Dogmatics*, where he contrasted the theological view with the views expressed by Heidegger and Sartre (Vol. 3, Part 3, pp. 334-349).

4) Since it will be the fiftieth anniversary here next week of the signing of the Geneva Accords that marked the end of French colonialism in Vietnam, it may be apposite to quote two commentaries originating from two opposite sides (*Le Monde Diplomatique*, July, 2004, p.21). The first is from the Algerian Nationalist leader, Ferbat Abbas, writing just after the hard-won independence of his country in 1962:

> Dien Bien Phu was not only a military victory. That battle remains a symbol It is the Valmy [where the French revolutionary armies defeated the invading armies of Prussia and Austria] of the colonised peoples. It is the affirmation of Asiatic and African man in his confrontation with European man. It is the confirmation of the rights of man at the universal scale.

The second is from a senior officer of the French army, Jean Pouget, who fought to oppose this independence movement:

> The loss of Dien Bien Phu marked the end of the times of colonisation and inaugurated the era of the independence of the third world. Today, there is never, whether in Asia, Africa or in America, a revolt, a rebellion or an insurrection that does not relate itself to the victory of General Giàp at Dien Bien Phu.

Today in Europe, we should all of us be eternally grateful to the Vietnamese people and all those who followed their example for ridding us of our own worst selves, for releasing us from our own 'slave-owner mentality' as colonists, which was our own subjection to nothingness.

CHAPTER TWO

1)   Some understanding of the ineffable element of leadership is essential to our present enterprise, and it is first necessary to explain why this is so in our case even though it may not appear to be at all necessary in other cases. Leadership does not normally appear this way in most 'business studies' because their teachings portray the world only in terms of its outer appearances and so in a way that is instantaneously recognisable to their audiences, who can immediately identify with this world. For the present Course, on the other hand, the picture must pass from the outer world of appearances into the depths of the person, and essentially into the 'inner world', of the leader, being 'processed' there before proceeding back to the 'outer world'. Thus the centre of our concern here is the inner world of the leader from which his leadership emanates, and the outer world is, so to say, the environing field of action of the leader where his leadership is exercised. Many people accept this in principle in other fields– it is after all the very *conditio sine qua non* of the martial arts for example – but they have difficulties in accepting its didactic consequences in this case.

The acceptance or rejection of the present approach depends upon the situation of the person judging it. As will be indicated later, if that person is situated in what commonly passes as 'the modern condition' of present-day society, then it must appear as totally unnecessary, while if in 'the post-modern condition' such a position will appear just as obviously as essential. The origins of such an approach can be traced far back in time, but it's most immediate expression for our present purposes was in the work of Schopenhauer, in the nineteenth century, where he showed that such considerations were necessary even in the case of natural science, understood as the scientific study of the natural or created world. In his great masterpiece, *Die Welt als Wille und Vorstellung // The World as Will and Representation*, he observed more than eighty years before Husserl introduced Phenomenology in its modern form, the principle that (Schopenhauer, 1818/1960//1974, p.28):

> At bottom, the aim and ideal of all natural science is a materialism wholly carried into effect. That we here recognise this as obviously impossible confirms another truth that will result from our further considerations, namely that all science in the real sense, by which I understand systematic knowledge under the guidance of the principle of sufficient reason, can

never reach a final goal or give an entirely satisfactory explanation. It never aims at the innermost nature of the world; it can never get beyond the representation; on the contrary it really tells us nothing more than the relation of one representation to another.

Or, as Spinoza had so concisely expressed this much earlier again, "The aim of science is to reduce the whole world to a tautology". But then, as Schopenhauer had expressed this matter in another and earlier of his works (in 1813/1960//1962, p.140), "The universal, the common reality, of all phenomena of a definite kind ... is the universal force of nature, which must remain a *qualitas occulta*..."

The long-dawning realisation of this situation, whereby so long as we stay in the outer world of appearances we can only keep saying the same things in different words, to produce tautologies even in the case of the natural sciences, had been reinforced before Schopenhauer by Kant to provide the notion that the 'essential natures' of phenomena must always remain as *noumena*, as belonging to the unknowable, as, so to say, 'essentially mysterious'. Ludwig Wittgenstein expressed this repeatedly at the greatest depth of philosophical understanding. Leadership, through its ineffability, has also apparently to remain a *qualitas occulta*: leadership then has its own mystique and this appears to be impenetrable. However, it was this kind of notion before all others that was relativised and modified by the phenomenological and existential movements, or at least by some parts of these movements. Although much of this challenge had earlier arisen from the East, from where Schopenhauer found his inspiration, it has perennially also found its counterpart in the West through the thinking and writings of certain Christian mystics, such have been subject in our own times to another kind again of 'rehabilitation'.

Now let me explain at once that the mystics generally have been regarded for the most part with great mistrust by the Christian churches. For Karl Barth, as expressed in his immensely influential and almost definitive *Kirchliche Dogmatik // Church Dogmatics*, mysticism is considered as just as great a deviation on the right hand of the church as atheism is on its left hand. This is because both species of deviants claim a special relation to God such as is improper, the one of excessive affinity and the other of excessive disparity. At all times, however, there have been defenders of mystics and mysticism, in the Christian as well as in other religious traditions. In more recent times, moreover, the developments of phenomenology and existential philosophy have provided a conceptual apparatus and a language with which to express the mysteries, albeit always and exclusively on their own terms, as mysteries in their own right. The more recent supporting elements may be present explicitly, as in the works of Karl Jaspers and Gabriel Marcel, or they may be more Christological, as in the writings of Joseph Milne, or more Judaic in their origins as in the works of Martin Buber and Emmanuel Lévinas. In any event, the devices thus developed allow us better to understand and appreciate the teachings of certain mystics, although by no means all, in the language of our own time. Thus, from Milne (p.11, with italics added):

> [There] is no meta-language of religion because each religion is itself a meta-language. In particular the sacred scriptures of each religion are the holiest and fullest manifestation of the ultimate truth, and understanding these sacred scriptures requires that *we listen closely to their manner of speaking, and such listening is only possible if there is reverence and piety. The attitude of mind determines what may be understood.* If we are listening to the Lord Buddha, then we must listen to what the Lord Buddha intends us to hear, not according to what we elect to make of his words. The same holds for the Koran, the Gita or the Bible. It is rather

> like listening to music. If we listen to a symphony of Mozart we shall not hear it if we are comparing it to an Indian raga. *Only if we listen to it on its own terms are we touched.*

The consequence for the leader himself of accepting this ineffability of leadership is that he has constantly to question his own behaviour, but then always in a positive, creative way. He must be self-critical without being self-denigrating: he must engage in a healthy introspection. He must analyse his mistakes and his failures most carefully, trying to understand himself better through each such analysis. He is, as will be emphasised especially in the last chapter here, most directly responsible for himself and his own behaviour. He must always try to follow the Oracular Injunction, to "Know Thyself!"

We are treating the subject of leadership here at the most basic level of the mode of existence of the individual leader, which is to say that we are treating it existentially. Then, as Mary Warnock explained in her introduction to the English translation of Sartre's *L'Être et le Néant // Being and Nothingness* (p. xii) "Existentialism does not recognise the boundary between ethics and epistemology, nor between either and ontology (and as for logic, it has no interest in it)". Our own ethical responsibility is thus to provide the future leader with the conceptual instruments for realising this programme, even while knowing that whatever we do will only pass in the mundane and average world as one directed to 'self improvement'.

(This is of course itself an ethical position and it is because we approach leadership here so much 'from the inside out' that no specific treatment of ethics is included in this work. Any such a treatment would invariably have to take the form of a discourse, and as Louis Martin (1997, p. 30) has expressed this matter, "The only possible discourse open to a Christian is not a discourse of language, and even less one of knowledge, but that of his own personal existence". Indeed, the subject called 'Ethics' itself, when understood as a philosophical discourse on morals, can only ever really make statements about itself: all ethics is then in one way or the other metaethics. The *Encyclopaedia of Philosophy*'s sections on the branches of ethics, presented by several different authors, provides an excellent introduction: the section by Kai Nielsen is probably the most relevant here. Those who first tried to 'philosophise' about ethics following René Descartes, such as Baruch Spinoza and Nicolas Malebranche, were consequently led into the greatest difficulties, but this did not prevent many others from attempting the same. However, being essentially pre-logical, or pre-predicative, in practice the essence of ethics can usually best be intimated aphoristically in works on morality itself, such as in the collection of Lafond (1992) and we must again refer to the excellent Marin for a clear explanation of why and how this must be so. A generally good philosophical work in English on post-modern ethics is that of Zygmunt Bauman (1993) but it is unfortunate from the present point of view that it largely lacks a theological dimension, although there is a clear presentation of the crucial insights of Lévinas.)

Passing over so much that we cannot possibly treat here, we observe a further essential point concerning the ineffability of leadership: that it is this which places leadership in action in the world in an authentic way so long as we treat it on its own terms and do not confuse it with other Forms. In the words of Milne (p.65):

> Although the mystics are often thought to dwell in some region far from ordinary life, as if they were outsiders, the truth is that they dwell right at the heart of our civilisation. Their pursuit of the ultimate truth, of the ineffable, has grounded all the culture and institutions of

the West in the common quest of man to live fruitfully and in freedom. The arts, the law, ethics and philosophy all take their ground in and have grown from the meditation on the ineffable....

There is a correlation between the human quest for ultimate truth and the form civilisation takes in any age or epoch. The civilisation that emerges from that quest is the articulation or manifestation of that quest, the concrete form it takes. The human quest for truth does not end in dumb silence but rather in prolific creativity and affirmation of truth in every walk of life.

Thus it is just this ineffability of leadership, such as we associate with its mystique, that is at the centre of leadership in its totality. Leadership is then one way out of many of seeking after an ultimate truth and thereby providing ethical action. We shall return to another manifestation of this ineffability of leadership when we develop the so-called 'integration mystery', of how the leader and the led come into conjunction, later in the main body of the text. It may sound very strange indeed to consider the leader as some kind of mystic and leadership itself as a mystery, but no serious study of leadership can avoid this issue. Another and less deviant view of this matter is again that provided by Louis Marin (1997; see especially pp.169-196).

2)   We should present the rules applying here even if only to explain why we do not follow them. It is accepted that when referring to the Godhead one should use the upper case; so that it would appear that we should use 'Himself' instead of 'himself' in this context. However we are here speaking of the *historical* Jesus, as seen at the time as a human being among human beings, and for that reason we keep to the lower case. In something of the same vein, we have so far used 'self' instead of 'Self' when referring to 'the essential self', which is not the normal usage, but this has been done to simplify the reading, where such a distinction has not so far been essential. We shall return in a moment to the nature of this 'essential self' and to its definition.

3)   There is a very different way of looking at these matters, but one that proceeds in the diametrically opposite direction to that so far followed, no matter how much it may itself deny this. It is the domain of 'esoteric studies' that have proceeded over all times but which can be dated for our present purposes from the division identified by Carl Jung (1944//1953, p. 430) whereby the great alchemist Theophrastus Paracelsus and the popular mystic Jakob Böhme "between them split alchemy into natural science and Protestant mysticism". This left an open space into which another form of esotericism inserted itself. One of its earlier landmarks was the *Arcana Cælestia* of Emanuel Swedenborg, which introduced the notion of the systematic analysis of texts, including the in-depth analysis of metaphors and the utility of 'word counts'. Such 'esoteric philosophy' became ever more influential during the nineteenth century, drawing increasingly upon Eastern mysticism and esotericism, and attained to considerable respectability in the form of the Theosophical Movement, gathered around its Society, as founded and led by Helene Blavatsky. This subsequently divided and extended into several other, but still related movements. All of these sought 'a higher reality' and 'a higher truth', as compared with which our everyday reality and everyday truth was merely average, mundane and even vulgar. Mankind was, so to say, 'asleep' and had to awaken to 'higher levels of consciousness'. In church-dogmatic terms, all of this corresponded to idolatry, and specifically to an idolatry of truth and its close relative, an

idolatry of reality. However, new psychic forces came into play in Europe through these means and these were not to be underestimated.

The danger with all such movements was that their teachings were open to every kind of abuse and moreover, as expressed by Carl Jung: "One cannot possess this kind of knowledge oneself without being possessed by it". Such knowledge subverts the self even as it subverts the selves of others, and it was for this reason that all the major religions have eschewed such studies from the earliest times, and have warned against their potential dangers, not uncommonly forbidding their teachings. For his part, Kierkegaard introduced a complete category, of *the demonic*, to characterise persons subject to this condition and also expressed the tragedy inherent in it.

This danger became so much more acute again in the aftermath of the First World War and the danger was expressed by the great French sanskritist and Vedic philosopher, René Guénon, in his *Le Théosophisme, histoire d'une pseudo-religion*, published in 1921. Guénon clearly saw the risks entailed as and when this kind of knowledge came into the wrong hands at a time of deep social crisis, such as in fact came to a head following the great stock-market crash of 1929 and the subsequent economic depression. And indeed, already in 1923, Adolf Hitler and Rudolf Hess, at that time still only small-time local politicians, were studying just these techniques and the knowledge that supported them in the *Thule* group in Munich. Hitler developed into a national figure accordingly and ultimately, exploiting the effects of the great depression in Germany and in Europe generally, into an international figure. The 'integration mystery' thereby asserted itself and, as the saying goes: 'The rest is history!' An excellent description of the working out of esoteric philosophy into the ideology, idolatry and consequent practises of Nazism was provided by Hermann Rauschning in a book that was so precisely entitled *Die Revolution des Nihilismus*, which was translated into Swedish – Rauschning then having sought refuge in Sweden - as *Nihilismens Revolution* in 1940.

The view taken here is that, although studies of this kind are unlikely to fall into the hands of an inauthentic leader of any such education and competence these days, the 'integration mystery' must still remain in place, so that such studies should still remain 'ring fenced'. Thus we shall not proceed beyond 'the technologies of persuasion' in their current and much less potent forms in the teachings of the EIIL, regarding 'esoteric philosophy' as a potentially pathological deformation from which nothing positive is to be learned and to which much can be lost, so that it must be avoided completely. Its works have not been referenced accordingly.

4) Ivan Illich (1993: see also Cheetham, 2002) wrote of this event as follows:

> Reading is experienced by Hugh as a bodily motor activity. In a tradition of one and a half millennia, the sounding pages are echoed by the resonance of the moving lips and tongue ... the sequence of letters translates into body movements and nerve impulses. By reading the page is literally embodied, incorporated.

As Cheetham himself observed however:

> In Western culture none of this was to last. We no longer hear or speak words this way. We do not taste them or perceive their complex sensuous auras, or feel our way among the complexes that they carry. The alphabet coagulated, fixing the meaning of the literal, canonical text. The passionate, breathing reader receded, displaced by the rational mind

searching for a changeless impersonal Truth. Our soul withdrew to reside, finally, Descartes tells us, in the pineal gland, for lack of a suitable habitat elsewhere.

This was then another part of the sacrifice that Europe had to make at the alter of modern science: see also HRH The Prince of Wales, 2000/2001. Louis Marin also treated this matter (*loc. cit*, p.194).

5) This naturally raises the problem of why in our times engineers and leaders of industry do not command the attention of historians and commentators of current affairs to anything like the same extent as do political, military and other leaders. Those with a penchant for Kierkegaard will recognise the reason for this in his introduction of the category of *det Interessante*, literally 'the interesting', which had its origins and received its name in earlier studies by Friedrich Schlegel (see Koch, 1992). Put most simply, we should say that there is so little recorded in English about engineers in general and leaders of industry in particular because in the English-speaking world engineers and leaders of industry are *not interesting* and indeed *have been considered less and less interesting for well over a century*. Thus if we wish to understand why so little is recorded, and especially if we wish to change this situation, we have to understand *why* engineers and leaders of industry are not considered interesting in Anglo-Saxon societies, and have been considered ever less interesting in recent times. What is it that happened and is still happening, at least in these societies, to create this situation, and can the analyses of Schlegel and Kierkegaard help us to understand what it was that happened and is still happening - and can they point a way to retrieving this situation?

The word 'interesting' can be used in three different ways. At its simplest, it just applies within such contexts as 'the interest on a debt', where it is a synonym for 'rent'. In most everyday use, 'to be interested in something' is to be taken up by and to be attracted to or seeing a use for something. It has however a third denotation which is the one that we are using here, whereby 'something, or more usually somebody, *is interesting*' to someone. If we have to do with a somebody A who is interesting to a person B, A becomes 'the interesting' to B. Of course a person may find himself interesting so that $A = B$, and in that case we say that this person is 'narcissistic', but we shall only consider the situation where A and B are different persons. In that case B may find A so interesting that he can identify himself with or 'live himself into' the life of A. We can of course observe this basic character trait in many of our fellow creatures here on Earth: it is at the origin of learning as of leadership as well, and within these contexts everything that is experienced as interesting can be seen to correspond to a self-interest.

From the time of Schlegel onwards, however, 'the interesting' took on increasingly more of a moral and cultural-philosophical connotation, and indeed for Schlegel 'the interesting' became a new category as the hallmark of the modern age: "Whereas the beautiful in all its timeless ideality was the ideal of antiquity, in the modern world this ideal is the interesting" (loc. cit. p. 35).

Kierkegaard agreed with this view, but saw not only the aesthetic benefits accruing from this transformation but also the social dangers that it introduced, in that in this modern world it was likely that the general public, the undifferentiated crowd (if not the mob!) would be likely to find the creative person much more interesting than it would find the fruits of his creative activity. "In our times", he observed, "the crowd is running amok in whatever is interesting, whereas the movement should be towards the simple, the direct, the innocent (*det Eenfoldige*)" (*loc.cit.* p. 12)..

As a well-educated, handsome, entertaining and rich young man, Kierkegaard saw himself, in the words of Koch, as "eminently in possession of 'the interesting' and was, as an author, 'the interesting' par excellence: both his person and his authorship attracted the inquisitive, at any rate for an hour or so. If he had maintained that role he would have been 'The hero and idol of the moment', but he remained true to himself in his faith and became instead 'The martyr of the moment'" (loc. cit., p. 12). The greatest danger of all for Kierkegaard was that he himself should become the centre of interest instead of his productions having this pride of place absolutely.

So it is with all persons who are genuine and serious about their life's work, that they never let an interest in their own person stand before the work itself. Consciously and unconsciously, such persons recognise that their productions, when authentic, constitute a continuation of the Creation, whereby they have the privilege and honour to be the agents in the creative work, which is more than recompense enough. They must therefore always place their productions in the position of 'the interesting' and never their own persons. It is in this spirit that engineers and leaders of industry direct interest to their productions, so that they consciously deflect it from their own selves. There is of course always the temptation to promote an interest in one's own self as a means of promoting one's productions, and this can lead to the phenomenon of the 'charismatic leader', but this is a dangerous game to play on the part of the authentic leader and generally he will abjure it. A recent book of Andrew and Nada Kakabadse discusses this point (1999, pp. 199-206). Some recent BBC series, such as those dedicated to the ancient engineering wonders of the world and to the achievement of Isaac Kingdom Brunel, appear to indicate an understanding of this in that they have concentrated upon the aesthetic and ethical issues that these raise as means of expressing admiration for the productions themselves - and thus doing the only justice to their progenitors that these would have wished.

This underlying principle of placing the product before the producer is so essential because it has to do with authentic productions, and of course all of this transforms into its opposite as soon as we enter the sphere of the inauthentic. This is a world of 'personalities', 'celebrities' and other 'interesting people'. These are persons who have achieved a certain worldly success even while the largest possible audience can identify with them simply because these 'interesting people' have little more to say and are almost as vacuous as the members of this audience themselves. Various arrangements, such as 'chat shows', are then used to facilitate the resulting 'meetings of no-minds', and these are prepared and reinforced by newspaper articles with their piquant details of the latest activities of these 'interesting persons', and the great arsenal of 'glossies' that celebrate every triviality that occurs around them. After all, if these people 'can make it', why not the millions of like-minded others? By way of the most immediate example to hand, this weekend's F.T. (7 and 8. 08. 04) carries an article by Vanessa Friedman on 'Why we care what our leaders wear'. The leaders concerned are composed however almost exclusively of US and UK politicians, with in fact the only exception being Queen Elizabeth II, and so, with that honourable exception, these are only the erstwhile leaders of the political worlds of Tweedledum and Tweedledee. The real question for Ms Friedman, however, was why we should be remotely interested in the first place. Why indeed?! In answering this she quotes from a psychiatrist with the portentous name of Darien Leader, and then from her book that is so appropriately named *Why People Get Sick*, namely: "As ideologies merge more and more, politicians become like celebrities. They sell their images as a point of differentiation", to which Ms Friedman adds that we all know what we want to know about celebrities when it comes to image: what it is they are wearing. But nowadays, in our celebrity-clogged world she explains, the way leaders are dressed is seen as a clue to the nature of their persons, to which we must add that, as a consequence, these clues are now most carefully selected and orchestrated to maximise the public empathy with the image of the politician concerned. This is then just one more component among the many 'technologies of persuasion' discussed elsewhere in this book.

Obviously all this is light years away from the world of the authentic engineer and the leader of industry, and the way that this world of the authentic must present itself has to be entirely different from the way in which the inauthentic proceeds. The authentic announces itself by its deeds and it is by these that it is judged. Since we are talking about the UK anyway, why not take as an example one of the most familiar of all the manifestations of engineering and more general sociotechnical leadership in the UK, namely that of the shaping of the London Underground and its surface extentions under the leadership of Franck Pick, its chief executive from 1928 until 1939 (following Halliday, 2001)? Among the many tributes paid to him upon his untimely death, that of the great architect Nikolaus Pevsner must be the most remarkable:

> For he was, to add a last word, the greatest patron of the arts whom this century has so far produced in England, and indeed the ideal patron of our age.

Many, and maybe most Londoners still meet his image every day, in the railway stations and workshops, bus terminals and garages that are still functioning as beacons of good, honest design, and it is impossible to exaggerate the positive effect of these upon a city that is otherwise so beset by every form of aesthetic and ethical degradation. In Pick's own time also, again in the words of Pevsner:

> It can be safely said that no exhibition of modern painting, no lecturing, no school teaching, can have had anything like so wide an effect on the educatable masses as the unceasing production and display of [Underground] posters over the years 1930-1940.

It was a consequence of Pick's indirect – but entirely regular – leadership that the overcrowded and unhealthy centre of London lost half a million inhabitants, while *Metroland*, the colloquial name for the area served by the Underground, gained two and a half millions, which provided in its own time a marked improvement in the lives of the great majority who changed their environment in this way.

He *created the situation* whereby this became possible, and it became a physical reality because it was so desirable. He was as a person, however, in no way 'interesting'. He was an austere, teetotal Quaker who said of himself: "I have always kept in mind my own frailties – a short temper, impatience with fools, quickness rather than thoroughness. I am a bad hand at the gracious word or casual congratulation".

One anecdote connected with Pick is essential to drive home the essential point that is being made here. When the war approached, Pick was appointed to plan the evacuation of London, which he did very efficiently, and several other government positions followed. However, this brought him increasingly into contact with politicians and, as he confessed to a good friend, "I fear my new venture may be hazardous. Political waters are full of wrecks and shoals". In fact he came into conflict with Winston Churchill himself, over the issue of dropping leaflets over Germany that contained false news, or 'disinformation', and he was so naïve as to admit to Churchill that he was not in the habit of telling lies. He was told to 'get out' at once and was dismissed shortly afterwards. He died the following year.

But then Churchill was pre-eminently 'interesting', and Pick was not 'interesting' at all.

(Churchill's behaviour contrasted strangely with the recognition of Pick's influence in receiving and aiding a series of Soviet delegations from the group led by Nikita Khrushchev that was building the Moscow underground in the 1930s: Stalin awarded Pick the Honorary Badge of Merit of the USSR, a most unusual distinction for a Western leader. Pick received no such recognition whatsoever in the UK.)

Before leaving this we really must pick up one further insight of Kierkegaard, that just so soon as the authentic person recognises that someone has joined the ranks of 'the interesting', he himself looses all interest in him or her: the 'spell' is then, so to say, 'broken'.

(So much more could be said about making engineering and industrial leadership more interesting and more popular – there are so many historical and contemporary examples - but it should now be clear that this cannot proceed through the persons concerned themselves joining the ranks of 'the interesting', but only by promoting a better understanding of their productions. Let us then in conclusion at this point give one example of how engineering and industrial leadership should be promoted in this way. Just at this moment, the design and construction of the new Peugeot 407 and the new Volkswagen Golf so as to minimise injury to pedestrians and cyclists in event of a collision with them, and the way that such collisions have been studied and the studies transformed through the specification into choices of materials and their forming and mounting, leading further into the substantial rethinking of the distribution of space within the vehicle that also becomes necessary, and so on, would make for an excellent television programme. Interviews with the engineers and leaders concerned, interspersed between views of the physical aspects, would do far more for the status of engineers and industrial leadership than any amount of 'interesting waffle'. Contributions from some staff of an emergency ward, of a surgeon and an insurer would also be essential to introduce the *socio*technical aspects, but still it would be clear that it was the engineers and industry leaders who, so to say, 'made it all happen'. If anyone was seriously interested in 'the status of engineers', this is the way that they would go about things.)

6) There is overwhelming anecdotal evidence of this and at the same time a great difficulty in accessing the numbers that would support the reasons advanced for it. The destruction of the traditional university is clearly inseparable from the massive bureaucratisation of university education, and indeed of education generally, that has been such a feature of the second half of the twentieth century, whereby the traditional university, which was at the origin of, and provided the ongoing centre of modern science from the twelfth century onwards, has been effectively suppressed in most places. The traditional university was a self-managing, self-organising body whose structure emerged

from interactions within its own body and between this and its immediate social environment. Such a structure then constitutes an *endostructure*. It was largely independent of the state and, especially, of political processes occurring within the state apparatus. Thus, for example, in many European countries professors were appointed by the Crown in order to establish and maintain their independence from political influences. In engineering, medicine and many other fields besides, the professor was expected to teach and research within the university and to practise his or her discipline outside the university. Most of the great international civil engineering companies of the first half of the twentieth century were developed as a consequence of the synergies thereby released, as the careers of the great civil engineers, hydraulicians and others of this period bear witness.

The subversion and suppression of this arrangement that occurred in the second half of the twentieth century is a story in itself (e.g. Larsen, 2003). It coincided with a 10- to 40-fold increase in student numbers, a large – but never commensurate - flow of money from the state to the universities, a rapid multiplication in the number of these universities with the increased total student intake, a burgeoning administration to supervise this process and a corresponding imposition of hierarchical-bureaucratic organisational structures, constituting *exostructures*, upon the original endostructures. The negative consequences of this have been exacerbated by the various attempts, by successive political administrations in most countries, to create a 'market' in research, even when this was financed almost entirely through state agencies. Correspondingly, the traditional market mechanisms whereby knowledge passed backwards and forwards between the university and practice through the agency of the independent professor were largely dismantled. Instead there arose a competition for university financing that was no longer driven by the needs of practice, but by the needs to satisfy the selection committees of the fund-providing state agencies. Unlike the earlier arrangement, which bred whole new industries, this produced for the most part only a zero-sum game, where projects were acquired primarily to keep university departments operational under an increasingly heavy bureaucratic burden, almost inevitably to the detriment of some other departments elsewhere. The anecdotal evidence that I have personally collected from many universities in some ten countries is remarkably uniform on this point: that today only some 20 percent of all funding in university education is really used on academic activities and the remaining some 80 percent is devoured by non-academic and essentially bureaucratic activities. All of this is driven by the politicisation of education that has become so pronounced over the last thirty or so years. It is characterised by persons holding leading positions who are totally devoid of leadership capabilities, the formation of exostructures composed of incompetent managers who are totally beholden to the pseudo-leaders for their jobs and the 'parachuting-in' of these *above* the professors and other academic staff. This process has naturally led further to the appointment to chairs of persons who can most readily accommodate themselves to this situation, holding no allegiance to their discipline having so little understanding of it anyway. These pseudo-professors have also become permanent fixtures in the academic landscape. The resulting power structure has the effect of inhibiting, frustrating and stunting the education and research of universities, so that their primary purposes of education, research and learning generally is frustrated. The consequences for the universities and with this for the society generally are nothing short of catastrophic.

One further example may exemplify this. In the resulting situation, of a market with no genuine market mechanisms – a pseudo-market in fact - it became inevitable that a competition should arise between the various parts of a discipline, such as has occurred for example in hydrology. Since there could be no real competition between the sciences that contribute to hydrology – glaciologists could scarcely compete with plant physiologists or agronomists with meteorologists - competition became concentrated between the various instrumentalists, whereby each proponent of a particular *instrumentalist methodology*, applicable within certain parts of hydrology, endeavoured to promote his or her speciality over all other contenders. The temptation to 'hype' one's wares then became almost irresistible for anyone with no other sources of funding than those of the state. To the extent that this becomes a 'competition in ways to save the appearances', and so a competition in instrumentalisms, so the different *methodological sub disciplines* come into 'competition': those applying probability theory come into 'competition' with those promoting fuzzy set theory, those pushing artificial neural networks become 'competitors' with those with a penchant for genetic programming, and many other divisions arise between methodological sub disciplines that are, in principle, complimentary . Some of these instrumentalists have indeed joined forces, but then often only in order to oppose distributed, modern-science-based hydrology, which in turn continues to draw most of its inspiration, as well as its financial strength, from engineering practice. It seems to appear to some instrumentalists that if this particular essentialist development could be discredited, then more and alternative sources of financing would become available to the instrumentalist 'competitors'. From the point of view of an essentialist, modern-science-based hydrology, on the other hand, some at least of these methodological sub disciplines clearly have something of value to offer, so that there can be no such discrimination: the exaggerations of certain methodological sub-disciplines were and continue to be considered regrettable, but of no longer-term consequence.

The essential thing for a leader in this field is to set up new business arrangements to which universities can subscribe without the fruits of their labours being consumed by an ever burgeoning bureaucracy. This is not the place to go into such matters, but it will provide an extensive case study in the EIIL Course.

7) There is of course a very good reason why leadership is treated in the way that it is here, in what is commonly called 'continental Europe', and what are really the very different ways that it is treated in the 'Anglo-Saxon' societies. This is because there is a real difference between the two cultures that are in play here and this difference nowadays runs much deeper than is commonly realised. Of course there are bound to be those who will call for following both treatments 'so that they meet in the centre', but the essential point is that there is no such centre at which they could ever meet, in that the approach followed here already has its own centre which has now been identified, while the 'Anglo-Saxon' approach has no centre at all, since it has no need of one. Even if the one were to be set up against the other in some kind of 'debate', they would simply go straight past one another, leaving the adherents of the one quite unmoved by the arguments of the other. However it is necessary to be most wary of these labels, in that many persons in the UK and not a few in the USA will recognise what is said here as applying to their own beliefs and behaviours, while there are already too many in our part

of the world who are eager to emulate the exploits of those in the UK and the USA who have amassed and are still amassing very substantial private fortunes very rapidly at the cost of those who they were and are still supposed to lead. Of course, those who look at leadership 'from the outside' will surely not condone this last kind of behaviour any more than we do, but I believe that unless one does view and teach and train leadership 'from the inside' this behaviour will be difficult if not impossible to avoid. Those seeking the grounds of this belief may find them everywhere in European culture, as represented here by the many philosophers, theologians and religious writers. Concerning this matching of the manner of presentation of the material to the aim of this material in out present-day world, we can do no better than refer once yet again to the 1997 book of Louis Marin.

CHAPTER THREE

1) This view naturally finds its most enthusiastic acolytes in such fields as politics, journalism and 'public relations'. For example, in a review included by way of promotion in a book by Jacqueline Moore and Steven Sonsino (2003), we read: "With this book Jacqueline Moore and Steven Sonsino support the view that leadership is theatre and that effective leaders are scriptwriters and editors, theatre stars, producers and directors who change discourse and model the discourse they want repeated and realized in the daily action of others. From the idea of the new renaissance of value propositions we can see how we might experience the ethics of a leader through their performative theatre."

2) We return to the point that it is not the event that creates the miracle, but the perception of the event. The visual impression of the collapse of the Twin Towers projected as seldom before in history the vision of the apocalypse: it was itself apocalyptic. The miracle was not one for the so-called 'first world', for which the perception was restricted to that of a tragedy, but it was so for the so-called 'third world', for which it was the very symbol of the downfall of a deeply detested order, being one that was seen to divide and continues to be seen to divide the world into two parts through a process of so-called 'globalisation' that is commonly seen in the third world as an ongoing act of cultural aggression. It was in this sense that it was a revelation. The consequences for the leadership of the USA were equally catastrophic of course, in that this event gave the much needed excuse to the US government to attack and overthrow a regime that was the greatest rival and enemy precisely of those who planned and carried out this action. This was thus a quite extraordinary exercise in indirect irregular leadership on the part of those who planned, organised and led it. It also provides a paradigm case of the Kantian *sublime*, such as was developed further again by Lyotard (2002).

3) We have to do here with what Sartre popularised in his *L'Être et le Néant* (p. 661) // *Being and Nothingness* (p.600) as "the psychoanalysis of things", explaining that "[This] psychoanalysis will not look for images but rather will seek to explain the meaning which really belongs to things". Thus we need to proceed beyond the images of things to arrive at the thought processes that made them the way they became, and beyond this again to the states of mind within which these thought processes came to presence, as concepts. This is of course essential to the leader of industry, who must be able to 'read the signs' around him in order to judge what is coming to presence in his domain and outside of his

domain of immediate concern. These signs, as already indicated, arise at all kinds of levels and the profiling of successful products, for example, necessitates a conjunction of readings at as many of these levels as possible. It is nothing like enough only to study 'the competition', let alone 'benchmarking' one's own developments against the developments of others: this is merely 'rear-mirror', pseudo leadership. In the examples employed here, the social, the architectural and the engineering aspects have to be woven together into sociotechnical constructs in order to enter into the collective-unconscious environment within and through which the physical object or event comes to presence. (Also in the case of the Twin Towers, the structural-engineering aspects played a critically important role in the structural failure, so that we have to do here also with a socio*technical* phenomenon, but it cannot be our business to discuss this aspect here.) Only in this way can one glimpse the essential nature, the very noumenon, that lies at the core of the phenomenon.

4) Augustine has had a remarkable influence upon philosophy even though he evinced no great interest in it after his conversion. As background to the definitions given here, reference is made to the *Confessions*, and then to sections IV.15, X.23, XI.3-7 and XII.25-32. A particularly sympathetic appreciation of Augustine was written by Karl Jaspers in his 'Great Philosophers', who drew attention to Augustine's 'practice of theology in a philosophical style'. Augustine was in this and in several other ways the natural precursor of Pascal, Kierkegaard and Nietzsche.

5) Concerning two contrasting views of authentic military and military-style leadership and its absence in this area, compare the books of John Adair - e.g. 2002 - with that of Norman Dixon and his many references: the differences of views in this case are really quite flagrant!

6) It is remarkable that such a more traditional-conservative, Kantian philosopher as Jürgen Habermas has recognised this and expressed the crux of this matter so accurately. In an article in the *Süddeutsche Zeitung* (18. 06. 2004, p. 15) he wrote "The empirical objection raised against the feasibility of the American vision derives directly from the fact that world society has become too complex to be steered from one political centre supported only by military force."

CHAPTER FOUR

1) The concept of 'system' is both an extremely valuable one and a highly restrictive one at the same time. Its utility should need no justification, but its restrictions may be less obvious. In simple terms, the concept is of inestimable valuable when we are ourselves thinking logically, so that no one proposition comes into disagreement with any other proposition or combination of other proposition within our immediate field of thought. It is restrictive when we are considering objects outside our own field of thought, objects which are, so to say, 'out there', beyond the range of our immediate comprehension, such as occurs in our observations of nature, of human society or in sociotechnical studies. In the case of nature, as a product of the creation, we often speak instead of 'environments', intuiting that at some level of understanding, such as we personally cannot attain, they are in some sense systematic, while in the social and

sociotechnical cases we do not even so much as expect this, since both are tainted by nothingness, so that we often then speak of 'constructs'.

2) The question has to be posed of whether and how one should teach a theory of objects and values. It now seems clear that this is necessary and that it should be taught in a unified way. This leads us almost automatically nowadays to the unified object-value theory originated by Meinong between 1880 and 1920 and very greatly extended and developed since that time. The recently republished work of Findlay (1963/1995) provides an excellent survey of Meinong's work and its development up to 1963, while the commemoratory volume edited by Haller (1995) brings this material considerably more up to date. Dölling's (1999) biography of Meinong describes the social-institutional environment within which this theory developed, such as should be understood also when treating such a 'value-laden' subject. Both Appendices draw upon this theory, albeit in a fragmentary way, as it is exposed in the first two of the above references.

Meinongian theory comes as rather a shock to many persons, and often this is a salutary shock. As one important example, if we express the fact that an object exists in our external material world of name and form by writing that it *exists*, then we can easily see that money and numbers, the two pillars of modernism, do not *exist*. Money is a purely mental concept which accepts coin, precious objects and such paper as banknotes, bank statements, share certificate holding statements and so on as surrogates, as signs that point towards the mental concept but which cannot reify it. Similarly we have numerals of very many kinds that serve as signs pointing towards the mental concept of number, but number itself cannot *exist* in our outer world. The Bourbakist attempt to define 'the number one', which necessitated statements involving strings of tens of thousands of symbols if fully expressed, as described by Manin (1977, p.17) provides an amusing but instructive consequence of this point. To take another graphic example, but in a different vein, when it is said that when all the shares listed on a certain stock-exchange index 'lost two trillion dollars' over one year, this is entirely possible because this quantity of money was 'only in the mind' anyway, and indeed on two counts at the same time, both as money and as a number. The shock concerning the non-*existence* of money and numbers may well be salutary in that dealings with these objects can become obsessive, and especially in our present-day societies, whereby they pass beyond the objects of an ideology to become objects of idolatry. Money and numbers are social realities of course, so that we have to do here with particular cases of a more general *idolatry of reality* - but then of course 'reality' must be understood in its more circumscribed, Augustinian form, 'as *a* reality to *that* person', and in no way as '*the* reality', which exists only in the mind of God. Such an idolatry arises when there is no spiritual reality to balance out the materialistically-experienced reality. Because of the connection of reality and truth by definition, we may similarly speak of an *idolatry of truth*, such as arises when the forces released by a fascination with a personal truth are not counterbalanced by the spiritual forces within the same person. From the religious-dogmatic point of view, the persons so possessed, as idolaters, are only worshiping the reflections of their own misplaced and unbalanced beliefs. The would-be leader who is caught in this kind of 'deception of the senses' or *Sandsebedrag* so as to become himself an idolater, is of course inevitably doomed to failure as a leader.

3) There really is a problem here and we had better try to explain it and resolve it even when we must once again appear pedantic - and so go back on our earlier promise. For it necessitates going back to Kierkegaard's original formulation in his nineteenth century Danish as:

> Mennesket er Aand. Men hvad er Aand? Aand er Selvet. Men hvad er Selvet?
> Selvet er et Forhold, der forholder sig selv til sig selv, eller er det i Forholdet, at Forholdet forholder sig til sig selv; Selvet er ikke Forholdet, men at Forholdet forholder sig til sig selv.

Now what can one make out of this when translating it into English? Being presumably Danish by origin, Hong and Hong made of it:

> A human being is spirit. But what is spirit? Spirit is the self. But what is the self?
> The self is a relation relating itself to itself or is the relation's relating itself to itself in the relation; the self is not the relation but is the relation's relating itself to itself.

The problem is with taking the noun *Forholdet* and translating this as *a relation*, and taking the reflexive verb *at forholder sig* and translating this as *to relate itself*, for then whenever one hears the English verb *to relate* within such a mathematical context one no longer thinks about *categories* at all, but about *allegories*, and then one is with another axiom system and thus a quite other mathematical environment again than that employed at this point and in the appendix (following the division of Freyd and Scedrov, 1990). It nonetheless appears that our treatment of Kierkegaard's definition may still be justified because *at forholder sig* does not necessarily translate directly into *to relate itself*, in that *at forholder sig* has an active sense of carrying out an action which we can formalise as a mapping operation, which the English reflexive verb *to relate itself* does not normally possess. Thus the identification of this as a category can be maintained. In fact Sartre (1943, p. 265 //1958, p. 221) has given a very graphic - and much more popular - example of this differentiation, which does seem to work in English translation also.

4) In German one can in this case make the distinction between *Tatsache* and *Faktum*, the one applying quite generally and the other with this connotation of 'being a fact for you and me about our own state of mind'. The English words 'factor' and 'factum' both have something of this connotation. In the construction that we have used above, whereby our belief system operates on 'facts', it is implied that these include our own states of mind: they include facts about our own Dasein. We shall follow convention by using 'fact' with a lower case 'f' for *Tatsache* and 'Fact' with an upper case 'F' for *Faktum*. Then, returning to Heidegger: "Wherever Dasein is, it is as a Fact; and the factuality of such a Fact is what we shall call Dasein's *Facticity (Faktizität)*". Thus the reality of leadership for each of us personally – how each of us experiences it within his or her own person – is the facticity of our own Dasein's being delivered over to the tasks of leadership as something that concerns us deeply and about which we care greatly. Heidegger described an experience of this kind quite generally as one of being 'thrown into something', as one of *thrownness (Geworfenheit)*. More generally (Heidegger, 1927, p. 56//1962, p.83):

> Dasein's facticity is such that its Being-in-the-world has always dispersed itself or even split itself up into definite ways of Being-in. The multiplicity of these is indicated by the following examples: having to do with something, attending to something and looking after it, making use of something, giving something up and letting it go, undertaking, accomplishing, evincing, interrogating, considering, discussing, determining.... All these ways of Being-in have *concern* as their kind of Being....

In existential philosophy however, 'concern' is recognises as something that is bound up inseparably with our very existence, so that it functions as an *existentiale*, and as such it makes itself visible as *care*. Thus the 'facts' that integrate with the belief system of the leader are primarily those appertaining to his own concern, so that they enter as Facts, and it is these which determine his attitude and everything that follows from it in any particular case, as expressions of care. It follows that the leader should give a proper and often special attention to these Facts, always questioning their facticity.

This is in some instances already a well established practice. Thus, when it is said that "fear is the worst councillor", this is to warn you that if it is a Fact that you are afraid, you should take a very careful account of this Fact in reviewing any decision that you may make. This example in turn tells us that we should not make a judgement by following only the schemata of the kind exemplified in Equation 3.1 in Section 3.4, but we should also proceed further to analyse how we in fact reached our judgment, following a schemata of the kind exemplified in Equation 3.2 in that same Section. This is to say that, so far as possible, *our judgemental processes should be transparent to ourselves*. This process will be familiar to engineers through the long-established division between design and analysis: first one *designs* a structure or a mechanism or whatever and then, only afterwards, does one *analyse* it.

This is however only one precaution among the many that are necessary when assembling facts together with Facts. As another of the more important aspects is the way that Facts are modified in our dealings with others and indeed in public dealings most generally, whereby *we get distanced from our own selves and come more under the influence of others*. Thus, a statement like "Let's discuss this over a few beers", or "over dinner" or "over the weekend retreat in the Country Club Hotel" is a common introduction to just such a process. In general, the more inconspicuous this kind of influence is, all the more stubbornly and primordially does it work itself out. Heidegger called this *distantiality (Abständigkeit)*. He explained how (H126) "This distantiality, which belongs to Being-with, is such that Dasein's everyday Being-with-one-another, stands in *subjection*...to the other. It *is* not *itself*; its being has been taken away by the Others. Dasein's everyday possibilities of Being are for the Others to dispose of as they please." However, in the very nature of nothingness, "These others...are not definite Others. On the contrary, any Other can represent them. What is decisive is just that inconspicuous domination by Others....One belongs to the Others oneself and enhances their power....The 'who' is not this one, not that one, not oneself, not some people, and not the sum of them all. The 'who' is the neuter, *the 'they'*. " Or, as we should say following the theological tradition, this is in truth an *it*-which-is-no-thing, which is what is called by the name of *nothingness*.

5) The works of Jacques Derrida are exceedingly valuable in the analysis of information and its processing into authentic knowledge as facts: all three works given in

reference are highly recommended and must appear prominently in the EIIL's taught course, even though they scarcely figure at all in the present simple précis. One example may suffice to indicate this value, being an article in *Le Monde Diplomatique* (February 2004, p 16) on the emotion-laden issue of the meaning of the word, and with this the legal status, of 'the terrorist'. Derrida showed how this meaning had been subverted to specific political and geopolitical ends over the last several decades. Thus, in historical terms:

> In what way does the terror that is organised, provoked and instrumentalised differ from that 'fear' that a whole tradition from Hobbes to Schmitt to Benjamin takes as the condition for the authority of the law and the sovereign exercise of power, as the condition for politics itself and for the state? In the *Leviathan*, Hobbes not only speaks of 'fear', but of 'terror'. Benjamin says of the state that it tends to appropriate by threats precisely the monopoly of violence. Some will certainly say that every experience of terror is not necessarily the effect of terrorism. No doubt, but the political history of the word 'terrorism' largely derives from the reference to the *Terreur* of the French revolution, which was exercised in the name of the state and which supposed precisely the legal monopoly of violence.

Following the basic rule of asking first why some person or group is saying something and then only afterwards what they are saying, Derrida explained the great utility to certain political powers to leave definitions of such words as 'terrorist' vague, open and easily manipulated, since then almost anything can be justified in the name of 'combating terrorism'. In the true Derridian style he observed of such 'justifications': *Au contraire, plus un concept est confus, plus il est docile à son appropriation opportuniste* // 'On the contrary, the more a concept is confused, the more docile it is to opportunistic [mis]appropriation'.

6) Only two references are given to the works of Wittgenstein, which make up in their quality all that they lack in quantity. The German popular philosopher Hannah Arendt drew attention to the extraordinary intensity, expressed as 'density', of Wittgenstein's writings, which much surpasses that of almost all the other works cited here as they analyse the relations between what can be experienced and what can be thought on the one hand and what can be expressed and communicated on the other. Wittgenstein's writings proceed at a level that is far above that of the present work: we may here venture occasionally into a metaphoric stratosphere, but then by comparison Wittgenstein's work has to be moving in outer space!

But there is quite another problem hiding here again, which is a taking into account of the first part of the *Tractatus* and the associated thinking of the younger Wittgenstein as one associated with the so-called Vienna circle and the school of logical positivism that came to be identified with it. The point is that there was a major development in the history of thought in the first part of the twentieth century that finds scarcely a mention here, even as this development arose from out of developments in modern science and the need to understand better the ways of thinking of modern science. Although this movement has long since gone into decline, due at least in part to the geographical dispersion of its adherents, it has left an important heritage in such areas as logic, studies of the logical structure of scientific language and the way that this is used to describe the physical world, as well as in some parts of computer science (See, for example, Papadimitriou, 1994). It is usually regarded as the antithesis of existentialist philosophy and as far removed as possible from the Heideggerian movement in hermeneutics and phenomenology. Indeed on the rare occasions that there was any contact at all between the logical positivists and the twentieth century philosophers whose work has been employed so extensively in this book, it was marked by a mutual incomprehension (See, for example, the article by the Polish philosopher Jan Woleński in Haller, 1995, pp. 113-127).

It would appear that the logical positivism of such as Rudolf Carnap (e.g. 1937 and 1954) and the empiricism that was associated with it, of such as Alfred J. Ayer (e.g. 1940 and 1956) proceeded not so much in another world, but in another universe than that of the existentialists. These two streams of European philosophy appear indeed to be 'worlds apart'. For myself, I can 'click' into the one and 'click' into the other, but I can make no connection between them: my situation, at least in this respect, is entirely schizophrenic! Although a familiarity with this other universe of logical positivism will never make anyone a leader, a leader should nonetheless have at least some acquaintance with this very different view. For the purposes of the present book, although I personally appreciate the work of some among the logical positivists – Willard van Orman Quine (e.g. 1960) springs to mind as a kind of successor to Carnap - as also of some parts of the Anglo-Saxon empiricism that has come to absorb the logical-positivist movement, I have not thought it fit to enter into their universe here. Their work is not properly applicable in the present context and its introduction would simply confuse things, and this book is quite complicated enough as it is!

7) The classical treatment of the function of failure, as a means of transcending the existing Self through the overcoming, including the coming to terms with the failure, remains that of Karl Jaspers, although Gabriel Marcel also treated this matter in some depth as described most conveniently in the two-volume work of Roger Troisfontaines. The book of Jean Wahl reviews some of this material, albeit necessarily in a summarily manner.

8) A particular significance accrues to invention and innovation in times of crisis, and the more acute the crisis the greater this significance. Once again, the histories of warfare provide the best researched and most dramatic examples, and in this vein I may recount a personal anecdote in concluding these notes.

I spent a long winter at the Chuo University in Tokyo in the mid 1960s and travelled extensively in Japan during this period, meeting various Japanese scientists and engineers and lecturing at the former Imperial universities. Among the places visited was Sendai, where I was introduced to the two leaders of the design and production teams that had produced the *Ohka*, an aircraft specifically designed and built initially for kamikaze attacks on the enemies of Japan that were then already threatening an invasion, prepared by widespread destruction. The logic of such a device was clear to me: the industries of Japan were already being bombed by the new Boeing B29s when the Ohka was designed and first went into limited production. However, since this bombing was having little immediate effect, by 1945 the USAAF was resorting more to the systematic fire-bombing of the civilian population in their cities and towns and more than two million Japanese civilians, mostly women and children, were killed or mutilated as a consequence. On March 29, 1945 alone, some 185,000 were killed or wounded in a single day when a quarter of the city of Tokyo was burnt to the ground (Liddell Hart, 1970/1983, p.721). It was not difficult to understand the reaction of those young men who volunteered to sacrifice their own lives to alleviate this misery, and for these a suitable weapon had to be provided. The first remarkable feature of the Ohka was that it was designed in one month and was first put into (limited) production one month later again. It was the kind of design that has never ceased to appeal to me: a combination of the simplest means and the most advanced thinking. It was built partly of wood – although the team eschewed the prestressed concrete wings of their wire-guided German opposite number! – and was powered by a simple but effective rocket engine which could take the device up to 1,000 kilometres an hour as it approached its target.

I naturally asked why it was necessary to wait so long before introducing such a weapon and was informed that there had been no interest at all in it until Japan itself was being threatened, by which time it was simply too late to perfect the machine and to produce it with sufficient reliability and in sufficient numbers. It was then explained to me however that, as the fire bombing increased, the intention changed to one of equipping the Ohka with a jet engine, and I have still not forgotten my embarrassment when I unthinkingly expressed my supposition that this would have been a simple pulse-jet of the kind used by Germany in its first, unpiloted *Vergeltungswaffe* (called the *V1* by the Allies) and was met with the most awkward silence. Obviously however my hosts were accustomed to such implicit denigrations on the part of Westerners and politely took out the drawings and the photos of their pre-production Ne-20 turbojet, showing me that it was by no means inferior to the BWM turbojet of the same time and far ahead of anything that was in any way near operational in the allied arsenal. We were all three of us silent while the implications of such a development sunk into my consciousness, for it was obvious that with this motor the Ohka would have been armed and used as an interceptor, with surely disastrous consequences for the B29s.

But, as Philip II of Spain said after he was informed of the destruction of The Great Armada, "Ah well, it was not to be". Such weapons as this joined with Heinkel's He 162, *Salamander*, and Messerschmitt's Me 163, *Komet*, and, in another league again, his Me 262, as illustrations of weapons that were simply too late and so never developed to attain to anything like their full potential. All these examples, which can be greatly extended of course, only show what occurs when the greatest authenticity is brought into the service of the greatest inauthenticity: they only demonstrate time and time again both the destructive and the self-destructive forces of nothingness.

BOOK REFERENCES

These references are intended to list the background reading to the complete EIIL course on the theory and philosophy of leadership, although particular participants in the course will normally only refer to a relatively few of these works, their particular choices being dependent upon their special interests. Correspondingly, the body of the text outlining this speciality, provided here as a précis, does not refer to many of these works at all, and the notes only partially compensate for this lacuna. The many newspaper, magazine and journal articles to which reference is made in the main body of the text are maintained as a 'scrapbook' that is regularly updated as attention is given in class to specific contemporary issues.

HRH The Prince of Wales, 2000, A Reflection on the Reith Lectures for the Year 2000, BBC Radio 4 broadcast, 17 May / 2001, *Temenos Academy Review*, London, pp. 13-19.
Abarbanel, H. D. I., 1996, *Analysis of Observed Chaotic Data*, Springer, Berlin.
Abbott, M.B., 1993, The electronic encapsulation of knowledge in hydraulics, hydrology and water resources, *Adv. Water Resources*, 16, pp. 21-39.
Abbott, M.B., 2000, The gender issue in hydroinformatics, or Orpheus in the Underworld, *J. Hydroinformatics*, 2.2, pp. 87-104.
Abbott, M.B., 2001, The democratisation of decision-making processes in the water sector, Part I, *J. Hydroinformatics*, 3.1, pp. 22-34
Abbott, M.B., 2002, On definitions, *J. Hydroinformatics 3.1*, electronic version only.
Abbott, M.B., and Jonoski, A., 2001, The democratisation of decision-making processes in the water sector, II, *J. Hydroinformatics*, 3.1, pp. 35-48.
Adair, J., 2002, *Effective Strategic Leadership*, Macmillan, London.
Addis, W., 1990, *Structural Engineering: the Nature of Theory and Design*, Horword, New York.
Alberts, A., 1986, *Inleiding tot de Kennis van de Ambtenaar*, Van Oorschot, Amsterdam. (In Dutch)
Althusser, L., 1959/2003, *Montesquieu, la Politique et l'Histoire*, Quadrige/PUF, Paris.
Anderson, P.B., 1990, *A Theory of Computer Semiotics*, Cambridge Univ., Cambridge.
Arendt, H., 1971, *The Life of the Mind*, Harcourt, New York.
Augustine, $398^{+/-}$//e.g. 1961, *Confessions*, Trans, Pine-Coffin, R. S., Penguin, Harmondsworth, U.K.
Ayer, A. J., 1940, *The Foundations of Empirical Knowledge*, Macmillan, London.
Ayer, A. J., 1956, *The Problem of Knowledge*, Penguin, Harmondsworth.
Baudrillard, J., 1968, *Le Système des Objets*, Gallimard, Paris.
Baudrillard, J., 1970/2003, *La Société de Consommation*, Denoël, Paris.
Baudrillard, J., 1972, *Pour une Critique de l'Économie Politique du Signe*, Gallimard, Paris.
Baudrillard, J., 1981, *Simulacres et Simulation*, Galilée, Paris.
Baudrillard, J., 1985, The ecstasy of communication, in Foster, H. (Ed.), *Postmodern Culture*, Pluto, London.
Baudrillard, J.,2002, *Power Inferno: Requiem pour les Twin Towers; Hypothèses sur le Terrorisme; La Violence Mondial*, Galilée, Paris.
Bauman, Z., 1996, *Postmodern Ethics*, Blackwell, Oxford.
Bennis, W., 1989, *On Becoming a Leader*, Addison Wesley, Reading, Mass.
Bennis, W., and Namus, B., 1985, *Leaders*, Harper, New York.
Boulier, J., 1982, *Jean Hus*, Editions Complexe, Brussels.
Brentano, F.,1930, *Wahrheit und Evidenz : Erkenntnistheoretische Abhandlungen und Briefe, ausgewählt erläutert und eingeleitet von Oskar Kraus*, Meiner, Leipzig.
Buber, M., 1945, *Moshe* (originally in Hebrew) // 1946 and 1952, *Moses*, in German and English translations // Mozes, Trans. Miranda, P. de, Servire, Wassenaar (in Dutch).
Callon, M., 1986, Some elements of a sociology of translation: domestication of the scallops and the fishermen of St. Brieuc Bay, in Law, J. (Ed.), *Power, Action and Beliefs: A new Sociology of Knowledge*, Routledge, London.

BOOK REFERENCES

Carnap, R., 1937, *The Logical Syntax of Language*, Trans. Smeaton, A., Countess Zeppelin, Routledge, London.
Carnap, R., 1954, *Einführung in die symbolische Logik*, Springer, Vienna.
Carey, J., 2002, Etymology and time, *Temenos Academy Review*, 5 , London, pp. 85-100.
Chisholm, R. M., 1982, *Brentano and Meinong Studies*, Rodopi, Amsterdam
Cheetham, T., 2001, Consuming passions: the feast, the stars and the science of the balance, *Temenos Academy Review,* London, pp.117-136.
Chomsky, N., 2001, *Propaganda and the Public Mind* // 2002, *De la Propagande: Entretiens avec David Barsamian*, Trans. Villeneuve, G., Fayard, Paris.
Clark, A., 1961, *The Donkeys*, Hutchinson, London.
Copleston, F., 1962, 1963, *A History of Philosophy, Vol. 3, Ockham to Suārez*, Doubleday, New York.
Derrida, J., 1967, *L'Écriture et la Différence*, Seuil, Paris // 1978/1990, *Writing and Difference*, Trans. Bass, A., Routledge, London.
Derrida, J., 1972, *La Pharmacie de Platon*, Seuil, Paris.
Derrida, J., 1972, *Marges de la Philosophie*, Minuit, Paris // 1982, *Margins of Philosophy*, Trans.Bass. A., Harvester, New York.
Dilthey, W., 1976, *Selected Writings* (Ed. and Trans. Rickman, H. P.), Cambridge Univ., Cambridge.
Dixon, N. F., 1976, *On the Psychology of Military Incompetence*, Futura, London.
Dölling, E., *"Wahrheit suchen und Wahrheit bekennen", Alexius Meinong: Skize seines Lebens*, Rodopi, Amsterdam.
Duhem, P., and Brenner, A., 1997, *L'Aube du Savoir*, Hermann, Paris.
Dupuy, J.-P., 2002, *Pour un Catastrophisme Éclairé : Quand l'Impossible est Certain*, Seuil, Paris.
Dummett, M., 1973/1981, *Frege : Philosophy of Language*, Duckworth, London.
Dummett, M., 1991, *Frege: Philosophy of Mathematics*, Duckworth, London.
Durkheim, E., 1924, *Sociologie et Philosophie*, Alcan, Paris / 1996, Quadrige, Paris
Durkheim, E., 1930, *Leçons de Sociologie,* Presse Universitaires de France, Paris / 1997, Quadrige, Paris.
Durkheim, E., 1930, *De la Division du Travail Social*, Second Edition, Presse Universitaires de France, Paris/1998, Quadrigue, Paris.
Easterley, W., 2001, *The Elusive Quest for Growth: Economists Adventures and Misadventures in the Tropics*, MIT Press, Cambridge, Mass.
Findley, J.N., 1963/1995, *Meinong's Theory of Objects and Values*, Second edition, Gregg Revivals and Ashgate, Aldershot, UK, and Brookfield, USA.
Fishman, K. D., 1981, *The Computer Establishment*, Harper and Row, New York.
Flew, A., 1967, Miracles, *The Encyclopaedia of Philosophy*, Ed. Edwards, P., vol. 5, Macmillan, London and New York, pp 346-353.
Foucault., M., 1966, *Les Mots et les Choses: Une Archéologie des Sciences Humaines*, Gallimard, Paris// 1970, *The Order of Things : An Archeology of the Human Sciences*, Routledge, London.
Foucault, M.. 1972-1977/1980, *Power/Knowledge: Selected Interviews and Other Writings* (sic!), Ed. Gordon, C., Pantheon, New York.
Foucault, M., 1975-1976/1997/2003, *Society Must Be Defended: Lectures at the College de France 1975-1976*, Ed. Bertrani, M., and Fontana, A., Trans. Macey, D.,Picador, New York.
Foucault, M., 1988, *Technologies of the Self: a Seminar with Michel Foucault*, Ed. Martin, L. H., Gutman, H., and Hutton, P. H., Univ. Massachusetts, Amherst, USA.
Freud, S., 1917/1940-1952, Trauer und Melancholie,*Gesammelte Werke*, p. 427, London//Deuil et Mélancholie, in *Métapsychologie*, Trans. Laplanche, J., and Pontails, J. B., Gallimard, Paris.
Freyd, P. J., and Scedrov, A., 1990, *Categories, Allegories*, North Holland, Amsterdam.
Gimsing, J., and Iversen, I., 2001 (Eds), *The Tunnel*, Øresund Technical Publications, Øresundsbro Konsortiet, Copenhagen.
Goleman, D., Boyatzis, R. and Mckee, A., 2002, *The New Leaders: Transforming the Art of Leadership into the Science of Results,* Harvard Business School/Little, Brown, London.
Granger,G.-G., 1994, Sur l'idée de concept mathématique 'naturel', in Granger, G.-G., (Ed), *Formes, Opérations, Objects*, Vrin, Paris, pp. 157-182.
Haller, R., 1996, *Meinong und die Gegenstandstheorie – Meinong and the Theory of Objects*, Rodopi, Amsterdam.
Halliday, S., 2001, *Underground to Everywhere: London's Underground Railway in the Life of the Capital*, Sutton, London.

BOOK REFERENCES

Hart, A., 2003, Life and architecture on Mount Athos, *Temanos Academy Review*, pp 11-40.

Hegel, G. W. F.,1807, *Phänomenolgie des Geistes*, Goebhardt, Bamberg and Würzburg / 1970, with an afterword of Lukács, G., Ulstein, Frankfurt am Main, Berlin and Vienna. // *Hegel's Phenomenology of the Spirit*, Trans. Miller, A. V., with a text analysis and foreword by Findlay, J. N. (no less!), Oxford Univ., Oxford.

Heidegger, M., 1927, *Sein und Zeit*, Niemeyer, Tübingen//1962, *Being and Time*, Trans. Macquarrie, J., and Robinson, E., Blackwell, London.

Heidegger, M., 1967, *Der europäische Nihilismus*, Neske, Pfullingen

Heidegger, M., 1963, *Die Technik und Die Kehre*, Niemyer, Tübingen (Tenth edition: Cotta, 2002) // 1977, *The Question Concerning Technology and Other Essays*, Transl. Lovitt, W., Harper, New York.

Hobbes, T., 1651/1968, *Leviathan*, Penguin, Harmondsworth, UK.

Hoopes, J., 2003, *False Prophets: The Gurus who Created Modern Management and Why their Ideas are Bad for Business Today*, Perseus, New York.

Hume, D., 1739, 1740, *A Treatise on Human Nature* / 2000, Ed. Norton, D. F. and Norton, M. J., Oxford Univ., Oxford.

Hume, D., 1748, *An Enquiry concerning Human Understanding* / 1999, Ed. Beauchamp, T. L., Oxford Univ. Oxford.

Husserl, E., 1900,1901/1913, *Logische Untersuchungen*, Niemeyer, Halle//1970, *Logical Investigations*, Trans. Findlay, J. N., Routledge, London.

Husserl, E., 1945, *Erfahrung und Urteil: Untersuchung zur Geneologie der Logik*, Claessen and Govaerts, Hamburg//1973, *Experience and Judgement: Investigations in a Geneology of Logic*, trans. Churchill, J.S., and Ameriks, K., Routledge, London.

Illich, I., 1993, *In the Vineyard of the Text: a Commentary to Hugh's Didascalicon*, Univ. Chicago, Chicago, Ill.

Isacson, T., 2002, Article in *Dagens Industri*, Stockholm, 8 October, p. 23 (in Swedish).

Jaspers, K., 1950, *Einführung in die Philosophie*, Zurich// *Way to Wisdom (sic!)*, Trans. Manheim, R., Yale Univ., Newhaven, USA.

Jaspers, K.,1957, *Die grossen Philosophen*, Piper, Munich // *The Great Philosophers*, Ed. Arendt, H., Trans. Manheim, R., Harcourt Brace, Orlando, Fl., USA.

Jaspers, K., and Bultmann, R., 1954, *Die Frage der Entmythologisierung*, Piper, Munich.

Jonoski, A., 2002, *Hydroinformatics as Sociotechnology: Promoting Individual Stakeholder Participation by Using Network-Distributed Decision Support Systems*, Swets and Zeitlinger, Lisse; UNESCO-IHE Water Institute, Delft.

Jung, C. G., 1944/1952, *Psychologie und Alchemie*, Rascher, Zurich//*Psychology and Alchemy*, Routledge, London.

Kakabadse, A. and N., 1999, *Essence of Leadership*, Int. Thomson, London.

Kant, I., 1781/1787, *Kritik der reinen Vernunft*, Hartknoch, Riga / 1968, Suhrkamp, Frankfurt am Main. / 1979, Reklam, Leipzig // 1855, *Critique of Pure Reason*, Trans. Meiklejohn, J. M. D., reprinted 1934, Dent, London / 1929 and revised 1933, *Immanual Kant's Critique of Pure Reason*, Trans. Kemp Smith, N., Macmillan, Basingstoke, UK.

Kant, I., 1787, *Kritik der praktischen Vernunft*/ 1838-1842, Collected Works, Vol 8, Ed. Rosenkranz, K., and Schubert, F., Voss, Leipzig // 1909, *Critique of Practical Reason and Other Works on the Theory of Ethics*, Trans. Abbott, T. K., Longman, London / 1996, republished by Prometheus, New York..

Kierkegaard, S. Aa., 1843/1976, *Frygt og Bæven*, Gyldendal, Copenhagen, reprinted from Danish Fifth Edition of the Collected Works , Gyldendal, Copenhagen// 1983, *Fear and Trembling*, Ed. and Trans. Hong, H. V. and Hong, E. H.., Princeton Univ., Princeton. NJ / 1985, *Fear and Trembling*, Ed. and Trans. Hannay, A., Penguin, Harmondsworth.

Kierkegaard, S. Aa.,1844/1851 second edition/ *Begrebet Angest*, reprinted from the Danish Fifth Edition of the Collected Works, Introduction and Notes: Sørensen, V., Gyldendal, Copenhagen // *The Concept of Anxiety*, Trans. Thomte, R., and Anderson, B., Princeton Univ., Princeton, NJ.

Kierkegaard, S. Aa., 1847/1920, Den Ethiske og den Ethisk-Religieuse Meddedelelses Dialektik, *Journal Papers VIII 2 B*, pp. 86-88., Gyldendal, Copenhagen//La Dialectique de la Communication Éthique et Éthico-Religieuse, Trans. Jacquet-Tisseau, E.-M., *Oevres Complètes, Vol. 14*, pp.359-383.

Kierkegaard, S. Aa., 1849/1921-1930, *Sygdommen til Døden*, Samlede Værke (Collected Works) Volume IX, pp.129-272 in the Danish Second Edition, Gyldendal, Copenhagen // 1980, *The Sickness unto Death*,

(Ed. and Trans. Hong, H.V., and Hong, E.H.), Princeton Univ., Princeton, NJ /1989, *The Sickness unto Death* (Ed.and Trans. Hannay, A.) Penguin, Harmondsworth, UK.
Klinkenberg, J.-M., 1996, *Précis du Sémiotique Général*, de Boeck et Larcier/ Seuil, Paris.
Koch, C. H., 1992, *Kierkegard og 'Det Interessante'*, Reitzels, Copenhagen (in Danish).
Lafond, R, 1992, (Ed.) *Moralistes du XVIIe Siècle*, Laffont, Paris.
Lambotte, M.-C., 1999, *Esthétique de la Mélancolie*, Aubier, Paris.
Larsen, J., 2003, *À la Recherche du Temps Perdu : The Times of J. Gust Richert and Thereafter*, Zentech Belgium, Brussels.
Latour, B., 1987, *Science in Action: How to Follow Scientists and Engineers Through Society*, Harvard Univ., Cambridge, Mass.
Latour, B., 1993, *We Have Never Been Modern*, Harvester, London.
Law, J., (Ed), 1996, *Power, Action and Belief, a New Sociology of Knowledge*, Routledge, London.
Law, J., (Ed), 1991, *A Sociology of Monsters: Essays on Power, Technology and Domination*, Routledge, London.
Lévinas, E., 1982, *Éthique et Infini*, Fayard, Paris.
Lévinas, E., 1996, *Basic Philosophical Writings*, Ed. Peperzak, A. T., Indiana Univ., Bloomington, USA.
Liddell Hart, B. H., 1930/1934, *History of the First World War*, Faber, London / 1972, Pan, London.
Liddell Hart, B. H.,1970/1983, *History of the Second World War*, Pan, London.
Locke, J., 1690/1706, *An Essay Concerning Human Understanding* / Abridged edition, 1947 and 1990, Dent, London
Locke, J., 1702, *Discourse of Miracles*: see Flew, 1967.
Lyotard, J.-F, 1979/2002, *La Condition Postmoderne: Rapport sur la Savoir*, Minuit, Paris.
Lyotard, J.-F. et al, 2002, in *Lyotard : Philosophy, Politics and the Sublime*, Ed. Silverman, H.J.,Routledge, London.
Machiavelli, N., 1516 $^{t/-}$/ 1929, *Tutte le Operestoriche e Letterarie di Niccolò Machievelli*, . Ed. Mazzoni, G., and Casella, M., Barbèra, Florence // 1970, *The Prince*, Trans. Bull, G., Prelude by Mussolini, B., Folio, London..
Malebranche, N., 1684/1707, *Traité de Morale*, Plaignard, Lyon/ 1958-1965, Vol. 11 of the *Oeuvres Complètes*, Ed. Robinet, A., / 1995, Presented with notes by Osier, J.-P., Flammarion, Paris.
Marin, L., 1997, *Pascal et Port-Royal*, Collège International de Philosophie, Presses Universitaires de France, Paris.
Meinong, A., 1913, *Abhandlungen zur Erkentnistheorie und Gegenstandstheorie*, Barth, Leipzig.
Merleau-Ponty, M., 1945, *Phénoménologie de la Perception*, Gallimard, Paris//1962, *Phenomenology of Perception*, Routledge, London.
Miller, M. C., 2003, *The Bush Dyslexicon*, Bantam, London and New York.
Milne, J., 2004, *The Ground of Being: Foundations of Christian Mysticism*, Temenos Academy, London.
Mintzberg, H., 2004, *Managers not MBAs*, Financial Times and Prentice Hall, London.
Mitscherlich, A. and M., 1967, *Die Unfähigkeit zu Trauern: Grundlagen kollektiven Verhaltens*, Piper, Munich.
Monod, J., 1970, *Le Hasard et la Nécessité*, Seuil, Paris.
Moore, J., and Sonsino, S., *2003, Leadership Unplugged: The New Renaissance of Value Propositions*, Macmillan, London.
Moritz, M., 1984, *The Little Kingdom: The Private Story of Apple Computer*, Morrow, New York.
.Newton, I. S., 1686/1713/1725-26, *Philosophiæ Naturalis Principia Mathematica*, Streater, London// 1934, *Sir Isaac Newton's Mathematical Principles of Natural Philosophy and his System of the World*, Trans. Cajori, F., Ed. Crawford, R. T., Univ. California, Berkeley.
Nguyên Khăc Viên, 2004, *Vietnam: Une Longue Histoire*, Thê Giói, Hanoi.
Nielsen, K., 1967, Problems of ethics, in *The Encyclopedia of Philosophy*, Ed. Edwards, P., Macmillan, London and New York, Vol. 3, pp.117-134.
Norris, C., 1993, *The Truth about Postmodernism*, Blackwell, Oxford.
Oehlenschlaeger, A, 1805/ 1854, *Aladdin, eller Den Forunderlige Lampe*, Hoest, Copenhagen. (in Danish).
Papadimitriou, C. H., 1994, *Computational Complexity*, Addison-Wesley, Reading, Mass.
Pascal, B., 1670, Édition de Port-Royal / 1967, *Œuvres Complètes*, Ed. Lafuma, L., Seuil, Paris.
Quine, W van O., 1960, *Word and Object*, Wiley, New York.
Read, H., 1968, *The Cult of Sincerity*, Faber and Faber, London.
Roy, A., 1999, *The Cost of Living*, Flamingo/Harper Collins, London.

Ruelle, D, 1993, *Chance and Chaos*, Penguin, London.
Sartre, J.-P., 1943, *L'Être et le Néant*, Gallimard, Paris // *Being and Nothingness*, Trans. Barnes, H. E., Methuen, London.
Shiva, V., 2002, *Annadana* – gift of food, in Cadman, D., and Carey, J. (Eds), *A Sacred Trust: Ecology and Spiritual Vision*, Temenos Academy and the Prince's Foundation, 17, pp. 33-43.
Schleiemacher, F. E. D., 1821-22/1831, *Der Christliche Glaube* (Second Edition) // 1924/1976, *The Christian Faith*, Ed. Mackintosh, H. R., and Stewart, J. S., Clark, Edinburgh.
Schopenhauer, A., 1813, Über die vierfache Wurzel des Satzes vom zureichended Grunde, / 1960, *Sämtliche Werke*, Vol. 3, Cotta-Insel, Stuttgart and Frankfurt am Main // 1974, *On the Four-Fold Root of the Principle of Sufficient Reason*, Trans. Payne, E. F. J., Open Court, La Salle, USA.
Schopenhauer, A., 1818/1844/1859, *Die Welt als Wille und Vorstellung* / 1960, *Sämtliche Werke*, Vol. 1 and 2, Cotta-Insel, Stuttgart and Frankfurt am Main //1959/1966, *The World as Will and Representation*, Trans. Payne, E. F. J., Dover, New York.
Stiglitz, J., 2002, *Globalisation and its Discontents*, Allen Lane/Penguin, London.
Thorkilsen, M., and Dynesen, C., 2001, An owner's view of hydroinformatics: its role in realising the bridge and tunnel connection between Denmark and Sweden, *J. Hydroinformatics*, 3.2, pp. 105-136.
Tinbergen, J., 1976, *Naar een Rechtvaardiger Internationale Orde: Een Rapport aan de Club van Rome*, Elsevier, Amsterdam/Brussels. (In Dutch)
Troisfontaines, R., 1953/1968, *De L'Existance à L'Être : La Philosophie de Gabriel Marcel*, Nauwelaerts, Louvain.
Wahl, J., 1959, *Les Philosophies de L'Existence*, Armand Colin, Paris // 1969, *The Philosophies of Existence*, Trans. Lory, F. M., Routledge, London.
Winston, M., 2002, *On Chomsky*, Wadsworth, Belmont, Cal., USA.
Wittgenstein, L., 1922/1933, *Tractatus Logico-Philosophicus*, Routledge, London.
Wittgenstein, L.,1969/1974, *Philosophical Grammar*, Blackwell, Oxford. // 1973, *Philosophische Grammatik*, Suhrkamp, Frankfurt am Main.

Appendix 1

The gender issue in hydroinformatics, or Orpheus in the Underworld

First published in the Journal of Hydroinformatics, 02, 2, 2000, and reproduced by permission of the International Water Association Press, but now modified.

ABSTRACT

Hydroinformatics is a sociotechnical endeavour, which is to say that it deals with social processes that cannot proceed without the provision of appropriate technologies and technologies that cannot succeed without the introduction of appropriate social arrangements. In particular, the introduction of decision-support systems for very large numbers of persons in so-called 'third-world' societies, such as farmers, aquaculturalists and medical help providers, must be prepared by studies of the social and the technical aspects inseparably. Such decision-support systems have typically to provide *advice* on water-related issues to a very wide variety of individuals, families and other social groups, so that the advice that is provided must be the most appropriate to the specific individual, family or other social group to which it is given. This kind of 'personalised' or 'customised' service is identified as being essential to what is introduced here as a 'knowledge-intensive agriculture'. The need to customise knowledge in such a context in turn necessitates that each such individual, family or other kind of social group must be accurately characterised by an 'end-user profile' in such a way that the advice that is given may be appropriate. The construction of these end-user profiles is itself a time-consuming task that calls for special skills and it is essential to the integrated sociotechnical design of widely-distributed advice-serving systems (called *mass-customised advice-serving systems*) that this task is identified and characterised correctly. Entirely symmetrically, once advice has been provided, this must be communicated to the end-user, and the way in which this can best be done in turn requires a careful investigation into the skills that it requires and the training which it may necessitate. Now observations in related problem areas in 'third-world' societies, and specifically in the closely related areas of microbanking and mobile telephony, have shown that many tasks of this kind appear to be particularly well suited to women, rather than to men. The question then comes to be posed of whether and to what extent the provision of advice for knowledge-intensive agricultures should involve women and the ways in which they can best be involved. It is through such developments as these that a more general problem comes to be posed of whether a whole range of sociotechnical systems in hydroinformatics may be operated on the whole more effectively by women and others again on the whole more effectively by men, and designed and analysed accordingly. In certain cases in practice this may come down to designing and analysing some parts of a total system mainly for use by women and other parts again mainly for use by men. Although these issues arise first and are for the most part discussed here only within one field of applications, to mass-customised advice-serving systems, it is suggested that they can be collected together to provide what we can describe in general terms as *the gender issue in hydroinformatics*. It is accordingly anticipated that differences in gender may have much wider implications and applications in hydroinformatics as a whole than are exemplified here. It is at the same time accepted that 'gender issues' are not concerned with sharp divisions between male and female persons, but are much more diffuse and may be strongly subject to many non-genetic, and especially social, influences Thus, we are speaking here more of a bias towards the employment of female persons and not of any sharp demarcation. In the same vein, although this bias may be strong in some societies, such as many of those in Asia, it may be less pronounced in other societies, such as in Europe or North America. Once again, we have to investigate why this may be the case and how we may be able to recognise its presence in any particular class of applications.

THE ROLE OF WOMEN IN A KNOWLEDGE-INTENSIVE AGRICULTURE

By a knowledge-intensive agriculture we understand combinations of agricultural techniques and technologies that can only be realised and justified by a flow of the most relevant and best available knowledge based on as much data as can be made available on past, present and future meteorological, soil moisture and other relevant conditions. We suppose in fact that in many, if not most, situations, a knowledge-intensive agriculture may become inherently unstable unless supported by this flow of knowledge. Evidently this form of agriculture necessitates the establishment of sociotechnical arrangements for the supply and distribution of the appropriate knowledge, but the effectiveness of this knowledge in turn depends upon its right application and thus upon the accurate definition of the individuals, families and social groups who translate this knowledge into agricultural and related activities. Such knowledge must be adapted or 'personalised' or 'customised' or 'tailored' to each of its specific end users. This condition, however, necessitates that accurate and reliable end-user 'profiles' are established, in principle for each and every end user of the knowledge-supply and distribution system. In such an advice-serving system there are accordingly two different knowledge flows. The one, which is the first in chronological order, is composed of knowledge about the end user that is collected by interview, observation, social interaction and other ways of gathering information about the end user. This knowledge is collected at the 'field' or 'village' level, or at the 'outer periphery' of the system, almost invariably in narrative forms, and is only formulated at all into more scientific representations at an inner periphery, where it is matched with the encapsulated knowledge of economists, agronomists, aquaculturalists, soil physicists and all other such repositories of relevant knowledge, and combined together further with all available relevant data. On this basis, knowledge can be provided to the end-user, most commonly in the form of advice, and this second knowledge flow proceeds back to the outer periphery, to be distributed there to the end-users individually. Knowledge structures of this kind, incorporating also their 'knowledge centre', have been described extensively elsewhere (e.g. Abbott and Jonoski 1998; Jonoski and Abbott 1998; Thein and Abbott 1998).

Any system of this kind is a sociotechnical system, which is to say that its technical components cannot function at all effectively unless proper social, including institutional, arrangements are also introduced, while its social objectives cannot be realised without the provision of appropriate technical equipment. In the case of advice-serving systems suitable for supporting knowledge-intensive agriculture in so-called 'third-world' societies, a network of persons has to be introduced at the outer periphery who are able to assemble user profiles, transmit these to the inner periphery and take and transmit the advice that the inner periphery provides to the individual end users. We shall suppose here that the principal technical equipment available at the outer periphery for information transmission to and from the inner periphery is the mobile telephone. This mobile telephone is in turn supposed to have the capacity in bandwidth and other parameters promised by current ongoing developments in so-called 'third generation' telecommunication technologies generally and thus, in particular, to provide combined voice, text and graphics capabilities.

It is supposed further that a 'full-scale' advice-serving system of this kind will service something in the order of 1,000,000 end users. Estimates of the time requirements of its various functions then suggest that some 5,000 persons will need to be employed in knowledge gathering (called 'elicitation') and advice distributing activities within the outer periphery in a steady state mode of operation. The vital question is then posed of the nature of these persons: what qualifications should they possess, what specific talents or abilities should they demonstrate and what kind of training are they likely to require? These and many other questions then however tend to devolve upon one more basic question again, which is whether these persons should be for the most part women, or whether they should rather be for the most part men.

Now consideration of related activities in the provision of micro-banking services and mobile-telephone services in several 'third-world' societies appears to show that there is a definite bias towards the employment of women for this kind of work. By way of an example, women constitute the largest proportion of persons working within the *Grameen Bank* in Bangladesh, which is the world's largest microbanking institution, with some 2,400,000 lenders (92% of them women and a correspondingly large number of women shareholders). Similar proportions of women are engaged by *Grameen Telecom*, and hence *Grameen Phone*, with the longer term aim of providing mobile telephone services in 68,000 villages in Bangladesh, with a potential clientele of more than 100,000,000 persons. Organisations of this kind are not only closely related structurally to those that are at the focus of current developments in distributed decision support, but they are themselves potential partners and providers in such initiatives.

Appendix 1

EXAMPLES OF ADVICE-SERVING SYSTEMS
BASED UPON END-USER PROFILING

There are very many examples in other areas of activity of elementary applications of user-profiling for providing customised advice. Indeed, many products currently on the market may appear at first sight to provide the kind of service which is intended here, although few, if any, in fact do this. Among these simple systems the following are typical.

`http://www.infospace.com`

This is an example of an Internet content provider which offers possibilities for 'personalised content' through its so-called *MyInfoSpace* service and Personal Desktop Portal. After creating an account, the user can define his or her user profile for personalised content, which content can vary from stock quotes to news items and from specific readings to links. On subsequent visits to the site a customised web page is set up for that particular user. It is a general information service and more recently several other companies have come to offer similar possibilities. In fact the word 'My' has become a code word for this approach, and many of the largest Internet content providers use it for labelling their personalisation features (*My Yahoo*, *My Netscape*, *My Excite*, *My Lycos*, etc.).

`http://www.amazon.com`

One of the most prominent features of this well known Internet bookstore is its interactive recommendation service. Here the user profile is created by tracking the user's buying history and comparing this with results from online questionnaires. This information is summarised in a database of the user's likes and dislikes, which is then used to provide advice in the form of recommendations for future purchases.

`http://www.datek.com`

This is an example of a site dedicated to online trading on the stock market. It is one of the most prominent sites for managing a personal stock portfolio and for online trading. The whole service is then necessarily organised as a personalised one so that it is a mass-customised advice-serving system.

`http://www.personalwealth.com`

This site is similar to the previous one, but with possibilities for obtaining personal advice and recommendations on asset allocation or specific stock recommendations by building a 'Personal wealth financial plan'. The last two sites are only examples of an increasing number and range of such services. Indeed, in the field of personal financial investment the provision of 'personalised advice' over Internet has grown exponentially in recent months.

`http://www.dietitians.ca/english/profile/nut-index.html`

The entrance page to this site is http://www.dietitians.ca. This link provides a simple example of building an end-user's 'nutrition profile' on the basis of which personal advice can be provided for appropriate choices of type and quantity of food. This last example typifies the diversity of services which are moving towards 'personalisation' or 'customisation'.

Returning to the examples so far encountered, we observe that they all appear to be profiled entirely upon the basis of information provided by the end-user personally, without the intervention of a knowledgeable, but independent, observer. In the present case it appears unlikely that the individual end user can build an own profile, but this profile must be constructed in co-operation with a knowledgeable – and critical! - person employed at the outer periphery. Entirely symmetrically, the advice that is provided by the system can better be presented at least partially through an intermediary, which again is a person, and in principle this can be the same person employed within the outer periphery. An issue concerning gender thus arises in systems of the kind that are of concern here which does not normally arise in the simpler systems so far employed so widely in other areas.

Once the relevance of this issue is accepted, even if only within the above narrower context, several questions immediately present themselves. At the most superficial level it seems natural to ask 'why' there should be such differences and, correspondingly, 'where' these differences manifest themselves. There is of course an immense literature that takes this approach in the mass market of 'gender literature', most of it of a popular and superficial nature. Since however hydroinformatics is a postmodern technology, or even 'metatechnology', we clearly cannot follow this approach, but only ask 'how?' within our current societies as these pass into postmodern conditions. The question of 'why?' can then only follow from this by an extrapolation back into certain postmodern, and thereby premodern, precedents (Abbott 1999a,b).

ORPHEUS IN THE UNDERWORLD
Among the most significant postmodern and therewith premodern precedents for such studies are the myths of earlier ages, that is to say from times where myths were more carefully selective and refined than they are today. As Barth (1938–1955) pointed out in his monumental *Kirkchliche Dogmatik*, our own times produce myths in great profusion and variety and at an entirely unprecedented rate, but these are altogether more confused and ephemeral than their predecessors in, for example, the times of ancient Greece. Among the Greek myths, moreover, there is one that stands supreme among those that treat of man's attempt to recover the 'essence of woman' as his muse and how he tried to bring this essence back from Hades itself to what we should nowadays call 'the surface of consciousness'. It is made clear in the myth that this could only be achieved even at that time through the application of music and poetry, so that the perpetuation of the myth and the analysis of the processes whereby it is perpetuated in our own times can only proceed through the analysis of acts of communication at their most exalted and most authentic levels. Entirely consentaneously, the modern representations of this myth have necessarily taken the form of opera, and, of the many major essays in this combination of media, that of Offenbach, *Orphée aux Enfers* or *Orpheus in the Underworld*, being the most ironic and the least conformist, seems to be the most appropriate in this place. For surely nothing could be more redolent of Hades, irony and non-conformity in the minds of most current practitioners of hydraulics, hydrology and water resources than an attempt to bring even some fragmentary parts of the 'essence of woman' back to 'the surface of consciousness'! At the same time, the survival of the Orphic myth through such informationally expensive means as opera demonstrates that this myth has remained and continues to remain intensely relevant to the human condition even in the so-called 'modern' era.

The explicit lesson of the original myth must also however still be taken to heart, for Orpheus did not in fact succeed in his quest, and this because he could not resist a backward glance at that which he aimed to recover. Similarly, within our present context, to ask 'why?' is always, to some extent, to look backwards. Similarly again, with reference to Hades, 'Why? is the question of the devil' is a common figure of speech in several European languages. Thus in this place also we can only proceed by looking steadfastly forward, not allowing a single backward glance at our objective until we have truly brought it to 'the surface of consciousness', that is, until we are fully conscious of its essence. We must think steadfastly about the 'how?' and defer all our thinking about the 'why?' until we have completed our basic analysis.

(This kind of procedure, of deliberately setting limits upon and otherwise constraining one's own thinking while investigating a subject, although familiar to those working in phenomenological studies, such as through the Husserlian *epoche*, and in some of the social sciences besides, may be quite unfamiliar to those working in the physical sciences. Some brief explanations may therefore be in order. Our starting point must then be that of all schools of phenomenology, which accept Brentano's way of distinguishing between life forms on Earth and all other forms: that the former have *intentions*, while the latter do not. Thus, to take two frequently cited examples, 'every cell has the intention of becoming two cells' and 'every larva of a particular kind has the intention of becoming a butterfly'. The resulting *intentional objects* engage in *intentional acts* correspondingly. Within our still current biological cosmology these processes are rationalized in terms of a minimisation of entropy production by the accumulation of negentropy in biological structures — membranes, endocrine systems, etc. — and indeed this rationalisation has long since been taken to the level of ecosystems by authors such as Margelef (1968). Since however in modern information theory negentropy has an exact correspondence to a measure of information, and it is information which can change the behaviour of an object, thus becoming 'knowledge', it follows that the acquisition of knowledge may of itself change the behaviour of an organism, whether this be a cell or a human society. It is this feature that sets apart the study of the physical sciences even from the biological sciences, and much more again from the study of several of the social sciences and, albeit in quite another way again, from theological science. In the case of the physical sciences, in particular, our further knowledge and understanding of an object cannot possibly change the behaviour of that object—the melting point of sulphur, for example, is entirely independent of the extent of our knowledge of this melting point—whereas in the case of our own societies and our own selves this is certainly not the case.)

IMPLECTIVE ASPECTS OF ACTS OF EXPLANATION AND ACTS OF UNDERSTANDING

The starting point here is the elaboration of the profiles of the end users, with a special emphasis on the 'how?' of this process. These profiles have to be constructed from all knowledge about the nature and situation of the end user as may influence that user's or users' needs for advice and ability to make use of such advice. This knowledge has to be assembled and collated, by hypothesis already primarily and specifically by a woman or women, from a variety of sources, such as by direct observations, interpretations of speech acts and from acts of exemplification. What all of these 'inputs' have in common is that they convey *meanings* that are relevant to the situation and intentions, and thus to the needs, of the end user of the knowledge that is to be subsequently provided in the form of advice. Thus these inputs all *express* something to this same effect: they are thus *expressions* of the situation of the user or the users and herewith expressions of the corresponding needs of the user or users for advice.

The immediate end point in his process is the return flow and assimilation of knowledge in the form of advice to the end user. Once again, and quite symmetrically, we have to do with the conveying of meaning to the end user, so that this advice expresses something to this end user. Thus the advice also is composed of expressions of intentional acts that are desirable on the part of the end user. In the now-classical theory of objects and values, as originally established by Meinong between 1880 and 1920 (but taken much further since that time) expressions are properly so called because they do express something about the outer world of the expressing (and consequently expressive) agent. Each expresses something that is not itself a belief or a judgement — which are essentially private, subjective and mental — but a state of affairs which is essentially public, objective and tangible. At the same time, of course, the expression has a meaning which is mental and in that way private. In the words of Simons (1996, p. 173): 'In the matter of meaning, it is the relation of presentation that wears the trousers, because it gets us from the private and the mental to the public and objective.'

In the language of the theory of semiotics that is so vital to hydroinformatics, the expression is the sign function that maps (or has the potential to map) a mental content from the transmitting agent into a mental content — 'meaning' — within the mind of the receiving subject. In the event that the expression adopts the sign vehicle of a speech act, the structure of relationships within which the expression functions with a meaning is shown in Figure 1 (adapted from Simons 1996, p. 174).

Appendix 1

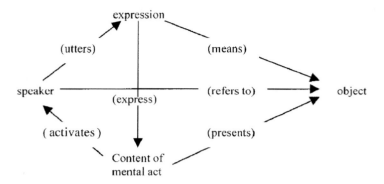

Figure 1 | The system of relationships involved in a speaker's uttering a single expression that acquires a meaning (adapted from Simons, 1996)

The term 'object' is used here in the now-standard, Meinongian, sense as any thing at all, whether it exists or not or whether it can enter the mind of a person or not, which can become the subject of true predication. An object then becomes a phenomenon whenever it is regarded from a particular point of view. Figure 1 uses the sign vehicle of a directed graph, being composed exclusively of nodes and arrows, where both nodes and arrows are themselves again objects.

The node objects in the graph are seen to be described by (unbracketed) nouns and the arrow objects by (bracketed) verbs, so that the arrows represent actions on things. Thus, as one instance, the mental content activates the organs of the speaker that provide the sound of the utterance, or, as one step in Figure 1:

$$\text{content of the mental act} \xrightarrow{\text{(activates)}} \text{speaker} \qquad (1)$$

In the event that we treat any such directed graphical representation as Figure 1 as a definition of a category as this is employed in a standard mathematical sense (Abbott and Dibike 1998a, b), so every process such as that shown in Figure 1 corresponds to a mapping, m (in this case achieved by mental activation) from a source, s (in this case, the content of the mental act) to a target, t (in this case a speaker) or:

$$s \xrightarrow{m} t \quad \text{or} \quad m: s \longrightarrow t \qquad (2)$$

Since the objects in Figure 1 are not in point of fact mathematical objects, Figure 1 cannot define a category in the standard mathematical sense. However, to the extent that all the objects in Figure 1 are imbued by the *intentions* of the speech act, so that they can be regarded as mental acts involving *intentional objects*, whereby they in turn constitute *intentional acts*, so any structure such as that shown in Figure 1 can be described using the physical symbol system (of notation and of operations) of category theory. We may thus still describe Figure 1 as *a phenomenological definition* of an elementary speech act. As is usual in technology, and indeed in much of science as well, we here use a few fragments of the language of mathematics without actually doing any 'real' mathematics at all in the sense of a 'real' mathematician. From the point of view of most (but by no means all!) professional mathematicians, we are really dealing, at most, with 'pseudo-categories', employed only as metaphors.

Now it is an everyday experience in any speech act that a meaning is rarely conveyed by one and only one expression. It is much more usual for the mental content to activate the speaker to provide several utterances that in turn provide several expressions. In relation to the final target object of transmitted meaning, each expression is then in one or more ways *incomplete*: it may be 'partly true' relative to the target meaning but it does not encompass the whole target meaning. The corresponding object is thus an *incomplete object*. To the extent that the objects which participate in a sequence of speech acts complement one another in such a way that the incomplete target object at any stage j in this process, O_j, may be supposed to incorporate in principle *all* the properties of the incomplete target objects at stages, $j-1, j-2$, etc., so $O_j = O_j (O_{j-1}, O_{j-2}, \ldots O_1)$. In more technical terms, the incomplete object at stage j will have all the *nuclear properties* of the incomplete objects at stages $j-1, j-2$, etc. Now, 'when all the nuclear properties of one object are included among those of another, Meinong says the former is *implexively contained* or *implected* in the latter' (Simons 1996, p. 177). Thus in the case of a sequence of speech acts, the earlier stages in the sequence of final target objects, as these appear at $j-1, j-2$, etc., are implected in the final target object at stage j. The category that corresponds to this augmented speech act is shown in Figure 2 (adapted from Simons 1996, p. 179).

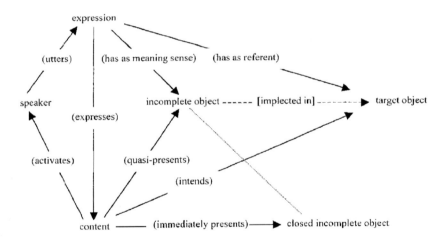

Figure 2 | Objects involved in the more complex category of implected meanings of expressions as implected objects (adapted from Simons, 1996).

Returning now to the immediate practical problem of accumulating meaning from a sequence of speech acts, commonly augmented by other intentionally expressive acts, we see that this can be posed as a problem of sequentially implecting incomplete objects into what is commonly called a 'closed-incomplete object'. However, the term 'closed', when used in this connection, requires some explanation. For Findley (1963/1995, p. 157) a closed object is one that 'not only *has* no further properties but is *incapable* of having any' since the thinker of the object has no further possible interest in any other properties.

Appendix 1

(Since this denotation may at first sound altogether too informal and perfunctory to engineers and others who have been brought up with such entities as 'closed sets', 'linear closures' and 'closed linear closures', a simple example may be in order. Consider accordingly the system composed of the operators '+' and '×', together with '=', and the variables '0' and '1' with all the usual meanings of arithmetic with the single exception that '1 + 1 = 1'. This exceedingly simple system is clearly closed in the mathematical sense, but also in the above sense as well. At the same time, it happens to have a wide range of applications: see Abbott et al. (1993).)

Clearly, the implection process will usually be interspersed by other speech acts on the part of the interlocutor, such as acts of questioning, referring and other such means for facilitating and accelerating the overall process. This in turn extends the category shown in Figure 2, effectively superimposing another layer over it. This does not, however, change the first suggestion to result from this investigation, namely that we might pose the issue of gender in our advice-serving applications as one of identifying a greater or lesser propensity of women to perform certain implexive processes under certain social conditions and cultural contexts. In order to continue along this line of investigation we may then briefly consider the origins of the word 'implexive' with its corresponding meanings and associated concepts.

Within the present context the origin may be sought in Meinong's technical term '*implektieren*'. For Meinong, incomplete objects (*unvollständige Gegenstände*) have implexive being (*das implexive Sein*) by virtue of being implected in (more) complete objects. In his influential work on *Meinong's Theory of Objects and Values*, Findlay (1963/1995) translated Meinong's '*implektiert*' as 'embedded'. As Jacquette explained (1996, p. 233): 'The German word itself derives from the Latin *implecto*, meaning to plait, weave or twist into, entangle in, involve, entwine or enfold . . . An earlier source is the Greek word '$εμπλεχων$'. Clearly, then, we have to enquire into the 'how?' of any observed female predilection for 'plaiting, weaving, twisting into, entangling, involving, entwining and enfolding' within a given social situation and cultural context. In order to do this at all adequately, however, we must move further out again, into a Meinongian theory of *values*. We must do this because the 'how?' of the objective processes must now be related to the 'how?' of their driving forces, and these forces are essentially provided by gradients in values and valuations.

IMPLECTED VALUES
It is well known historically that Meinong initially developed his theory of objects (*Gegenstandstheorie*) and his theory of values (*Werttheorie*) separately, only realising their natural contiguity towards the end of his life. Now this late realisation of Meinong can be represented in the language of category theory in the first place in the form of two *functors*, both of which map directed graphs connecting objects into completely isomorphic directed graphs connecting values. The one functor maps categories of objects into categories of *intrinsic values* while the other functor maps (the same) categories of objects into categories of *social values*. Thus the categories of intrinsic values and social values are themselves isomorphic too. By the intrinsic values of an object we mean, in the usual way, the emotional value to the individual of that object, while by the social value we mean the value, and indeed often the money value, that society places upon that object. It is a matter of common experience that many objects with the highest intrinsic value to an individual may have little social value, and indeed little or no money value at all, and vice versa. In many cases, in fact, and as exemplified by intensely personal possessions, intrinsic values may be inversely proportional to social values, while in other cases, such as are exemplified by certain works of art, they may be strongly positively correlated. Both intrinsic and social values can of course vary considerably in time.

In the specific case of speech acts, as utterances, the social value is the predominant one when the utterance is intended performatively, such has become almost the rule in politics and journalism. In this case the value is measured in exchange value and not in truth value: it is primarily a question of how many more votes will the speaker get by saying this or how much more advertising revenue or political influence the newspaper or television channel will acquire through such an utterance. As Herbert Marcuse observed of language in the USA as a whole: "Exchange value, not truth value, counts". In constative utterances, on the other hand, the speaker is attempting to communicate facts, as statements concerning a certain state of affairs, and it is here that truth value really does count.

Let us first consider the functor that maps the category of implected speech acts of Figure 2 into the corresponding category of intrinsic values. This is schematised in Figure 3.

We observe at once that there may be many modes of implexion that may apply to both the objects and the two broad classes of values to which they are most immediately connected. In Meinongian theory these values are also themselves objects, albeit normally of a higher 'order' than the objects to which they apply a valuation. We may have a simple linear recursive process which we may call a *serial implexion*, in which:

$$O_j = O_j(O_{j-1}(O_{j-2}(\ldots(O_1)))) \tag{3}$$

or we may have any number of more complex (but less constraining) structures, such as may be exemplified by:

$$O_j = O_j(O_{j-1}(O_{j-2}(\ldots(O_k))), O_{k-1}(O_{k-2}(\ldots(O_1)))) \tag{4},$$

where we implicitly introduce a set composed of O_m, $m = 1, \ldots, k, \ldots, j$, which may be objects in the original sense of Figures 1 and 2 or objects in the sense of values.

Now the objects that are values must be connected to the objects in the original sense of Figures 1 and 2 by mappings, as exemplified for intrinsic values in Figure 3, and to these mappings Meinong gave the name of *value feelings*. But now the mappings are themselves functions of the completeness of the objects in the original sense, both in terms of the existence of the objects themselves or in terms of the existence of certain of their properties. In particular, as one object is implected into another, we should expect that the strength of the value-feeling mapping should, on average, increase. Of course, as Findlay (1963/1995, pp. 268–269) explained:

> 'The existence relevant to valuation is an existence for thought and belief, which may or may not be a real existence at all: it is, in terms of Meinongian psychology, an existence mediated by a *judgement*. Value-feelings are therefore as much judgement feelings as they are existence feelings. And with its connection with judgements, and with the existence presented by judgement, valuation achieves something of the objectivity of the latter'.

We may suppose at once that, on some average, the quantities $(V_i(O_j) - V_i(O_k))$, $k = j - 1$, $j - 2, \ldots, 1$) where $V_i(O_m)$ is the intrinsic value of O_m, are positive. We might even suppose that the gradient set up in intrinsic values through the implexive process provides the force that drives the implected elicitation processes that provide the user profile in its appropriate fullness and corresponding completeness (see Abbott and Warren 1974; Abbott et al. 1977).

Appendix 1

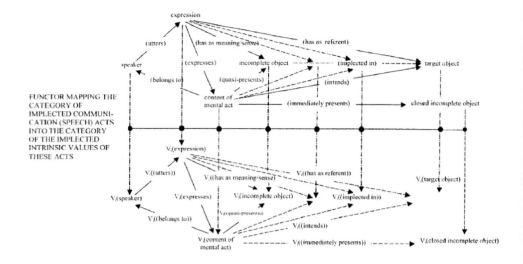

Figure 3 | The functor mapping the category of original implective speech acts into the category of implected intrinsic values. The influence of the incompleteness of the original objects on the value-feelings can be represented by the dual of this functor, with further arrows to represent the structure of the influence, as exemplified in equations (1) and (2). (Only the functor mappings for the original intentional objects are shown and not those for the connecting intentional acts.)

VEDIC INTERLUDE

The knowledge elicitation processes that concern us here have to be repeated at intervals and most commonly when marked changes occur in the profile of the end user. These changes may then be of a fortunate nature, such as through the accedence of new family members to production or the acquisition of new equipment, or it may be of an unfortunate nature, such as the death or illness of family members or their animals, or through the loss or damage of equipment, such as by flooding. The interrogator must then be, among other things, one who can adapt to the new circumstances in the most appropriate manner. Thus the gradient in intrinsic values may well change when making up a new user profile, as compared with the gradient experienced when constructing the previous user profile. The relation between the expression and the content of the incomplete target object, essentially its 'meaning content', may change accordingly.

Now the theory of mappings from expressions (such as sentences) into meanings has been studied on the Indian subcontinent from time immemorial. The central element in most of these studies, and one that dates back way beyond the precipitation of the Greek myths, back to the period of the Vedic legends, is called the *sphoṭa*. The *sphoṭa* is the principle of the mind which is mobilised and functions when an expression is experienced and becomes meaning.

Now the Vedic seers did not all agree upon the nature of the *sphoṭa* and indeed they commonly divided into three camps concerning its origins and nature. Although fairly presenting the alternative views, Sastri (1980) unequivocally came down upon the side of one of these camps, the side of the grammarians, saying of them that:

> 'They adumbrate a theory strikingly original to claim that both word and meaning are indivisible units. The indivisible unit of expression is called *sphoṭa* and the indivisible unit of meaning is called *sphoṭa* or *pratibha*. The grammarians do not believe that a word is divisible into letters or a sentence is divisible into words. Likewise, they do not believe that the meaning of a sentence is the sum-total of the meaning of the words which are ordinarily described as its parts.'

Thus the succession of speech acts of the kind categorised in Figure 3, as this comes to define a succession of 'less and less incomplete' objects, cannot be regarded as the simple sum of its separate acts. The user profile, for example, constitutes an indivisible whole, as an object of higher order than its parts. But then, beyond this again, this user profile must be offered up to the judgement engine of the system as an indivisible union, which is again so much more than its parts (see, just as an example, not as it stands applicable here, Huang et al. 1999). The ghost of the *sphoṭa* must thus enter the digital machine just as much as it enters the mind of the human agent.

We have to do here with a sociotechnical system, and so one in which the human-social elements are bound up indivisibly with the technical elements. However, the theory of the *sphoṭa* as well adumbrates how the specifically female sides of the human-social elements come into relation with the '*sphoṭa*: expression→meaning' mapping and thus how they enter into the present discussion. In order to trace how this happens, one may recall that the Sanskrit *brahman* refers to the expanded consciousness of the individual self, so that the process of attainment of *brahman* corresponds to the journey of this self through a sequence of 'less and less incomplete' objects, with each implected in the next. This process culminates in our case with the target of the closed incomplete object, while in the infinitely more exalted context of Veda it synchronises with the manifestation of *vak* in the individual being, this being experienced as 'a flash of spiritual illumination where expression and thought remain completely identified beyond any [experience of] recognition' (Sastri 1980, p. xi). However, in Vedic lore, *vak* is female, as one who 'does not reveal herself to all and sundry but chooses to bestow her favour on a few who are considered fit for the vision.'

This theory of the *sphoṭa* advances its female elements in other ways as well, of which the following appears to be of the most immediate relevance here (Sastri 1980, p. xi):

> 'The sky [*vyoman*], to our knowledge, possesses maximum pervasion. It is why the *Upanishads* often describe *brahman* as the sky. In this context let us turn our attention to the oft-quoted line of the *Kena-Upanishad* where it is stated that Indra came across a female figure in that sky. She is described as *Uma*. . . . The two words *uma* and *vyoman* bear affinity of meaning and are close to each other. The word *uma*, . . . to protect, is used frequently as an adjective in [the *Rig Veda*]. . . . The word *vyoman*, the sky, is derived from *vi-oman*, meaning "unrestricted favour and protection". A study of the aforesaid forms may enable us to posit that the two words *uma* and *vyoman* may be linked together, *uma* signifying one who grants favour and protects. And if the locus of the female so described is to be the sky or *brahman* we may be warranted in drawing an identification between [1] *uma*, [2] the power of the sky and [3] *brahman*. It may be noted here that the realisation of the power is possible only when she is pleased to extend the favour.'

Thus the power of pervasiveness of insight, which is then coupled inseparably with protection and thus with sympathy and compassion in this experience, can be released only when 'she is pleased to extend the favour.' This pleasure, which is of course universal in its nature, is in our present, much more prosaic, case to be provided by creating 'positive gradients in intrinsic values' for this, essentially female, agent.

We should observe that we are no longer dealing here with a relation between women and a process, but with a process that is itself feminine. In the language of modernity this implies that the human abilities that are mobilized in this kind of communication process are an integral and so inseparable part of the specifically feminine genetic material. It seems reasonable to suppose that this genotypical identification manifests itself more explicitly, on average, among phenotypical women than it does, on average, among phenotypical men.

It should then however be further observed with Findlay that (1973/1995, p. 273):

'Meinong devised an interesting symbolism to express relations of formal sociality. Thus the formula:

$Je\{Ja[Je(x) : -VFe] : -VFa\} : +VFe$

expresses the fact that the judgement of the Ego to the effect that the Alter's (the other person's) judgement to the effect that the Ego is judging and disliking something, leads the Alter to dislike the Ego's state of dislike, is something agreeable to the Ego—in other words, I am helped in my grief over some blow by the commiseration of others, and this, though empirically illustrated, represents a formal theorem. Meinong shows that sympathy has a 'logic', more complex, but quite as rich in *a priori* consequences, as the logic representing more objective relations.'

We should then remark in passing that Meinong's further development of this algebra subsequently developed into a deontic logic (which we may regard here as essentially a logic of obligation) that underlies, among other applications, most current systems used in studies in legal-science (*Rechtswissenschaft*: see Hilpinen (1971) and McNamara and Prakken (1998)).

OBJECTS AS CONSEQUENCES OF INTRINSIC VALUES

In Figure 3 we projected the directed graph of intentional objects and their associated intentional acts into the entirely congruent directed graph of intrinsic values and their relations. In these *schemata*, the intrinsic values and their inter-relations were determined by the objects and their inter-relations. At an earlier time in the process so represented, however, the objects must themselves have been constructed at least partly on the basis of the intrinsic values of the object-creating subject, so that we can infer the existence, prior to the situation shown in Figure 3, of another functor again mapping the category of intrinsic values into the category of objects, so that this functor can be denoted simply by reversing the directions of the functor arrows in Figure 3. In the case of the implection process, however, these two functors may operate alternately, and even synchronously, in time. As Findlay expressed this matter (1963/1965, p. 306): 'Obviously the rich specificity of my encounter with objects is, in different ways, a richness in the objects *and* a richness in me.' One consequence of this is that the sequences of implected objects and their congruent sequences of implected values must usually be considered together in any such processes. We shall not however follow up this aspect here.

SOCIAL VALUES

The above indicators suggest that one way forward towards a better understanding of the gender issue in this area may proceed through the study of the structure of relations between objects in acts of communication and the corresponding structure of relations between intrinsic values. On the other hand, the very socio-economic viability of a service of the kind that we are considering here necessitates that attention be given as well to the social, including monetary, values that are also associated with the gender issue in the processes of knowledge elicitation and provision. Now already when we considered intrinsic values, which are in their essence personal, we were obliged to ground our discussion in certain 'depth psychological', and even specifically Jungian, interpretations of processes of implection and their associated implected values. As we now however proceed into the social sphere, which is essentially collective, we are obliged to ground our investigation at a greater depth again, which is situated at the level of myth, legend and saga. At the same time, if we try to do this within the context of the modern era, which as Barth (1938 1955/1960) explained is more prone to mythologisation than any other period in history, so we must open up a veritable Pandora's box of largely empty imaginings and baseless fantasies. If we are not to be led into complete confusion in this process we must adopt the postmodern position, which is then necessarily also a premodern position, of following the rule of Orpheus, of seeking our ground at the deepest level of experience, which is at the level of the most long-established and consequently most durable of myths, legends and sagas.

Appendix 1

We see that we have to do here with the tetradic allegorical structure schematized within the 'frame' or 'brackets' of the gender issue in Figure 4.

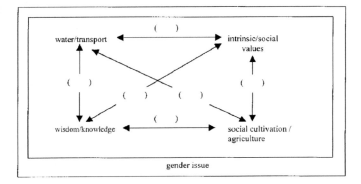

Figure 4 | The tetradic allegorical structure related to social values within the context or 'frame' of the gender issue.

Since we have to do with allegorical mappings between intentional objects, these mappings may be bi-directional, or 'reversible'. There are then six such apparently 'reversible' intentional acts that have to be characterised within the frame of the gender issue. In effect, however, there are really two categories present here, which are dual relative to one another and obtained from one another notationally by reversing the directions of the respective arrows. By analogy with categories composed of mathematical objects, we observe that a category that is a dual of another, original, category commonly resides in an entirely other place in the conceptual and semantic field than does this first, original, category.

Starting with the 'knowledge→water' allegorical mapping processes, we may recall that for the Greeks, as for the early Christians, alchemists and adherents of many other movements, the fount of wisdom, as the arbiter and prime mover of knowledge, was the female figure of Sophia. The conduit of her wisdom, as that which carried knowledge, was provided by the god Mercury. The allegory was realised through depicting Sophia as a fount or other such source of water, commonly as a mountain spring, and Mercury as the channel, or provider of the channel, along which this water flowed. This is only one, even if probably the most prominent one, of many mappings between wisdom/knowledge and water/transport, and of course it can proceed in both directions independently.

(We should observe in passing that for the alchemists, in particular, Mercury was not only the allegorical channel along which water/knowledge was conveyed, but evolved as a god in a drop of this self-same water/knowledge. Thus the process of the evolution of Mercury as a mythical element, as a process occurring in some kind of experiential time, was itself also a mythical element, and, yet again, the very time of this process was of a mythical nature too (see, for example, Ogawa 1978). The time of the myth is thus not chronological time, and indeed in theology (as in Barth 1938–1955/1960) it is common in this way to separate legend and sagas, which are partially ordered in chronological time, from histories, which are totally ordered in chronological time, and myths, which are not ordered at all in chronological time (see also Rowell 1978; Turner 1978).

It was through the actions of the androgynous figure of Mercury that the metaphors mapping both water/ transport and wisdom/knowledge into soil cultivation/ agriculture were also realised. Mercury then took on certain aspect of a more masculine Siva, from whose unplaited hair the waters of the world were produced in his world-creation dance, and who was thus simultaneously the great destroyer and the great creator through the actions induced by the flow of this water. In the work of soil cultivation/agriculture, the nature of both water/transport and wisdom/knowledge was, in self-similarity, both to destroy and to create. It has always been understood since Hellenistic times, however, that Mercury remained only the instrument of Sophia in this dual approach to soil-cultivation/agriculture from both its water and its knowledge sides. The metaphorical relation between the twin notions of the provision of water and all that it contains and the provision of wisdom and all that it sustains in relation to soil-cultivation/agriculture has thus long been understood as appertaining to an underlying female principle.

Let us now recall further, from Jung, that in the later-Dionysian ceremonies the figure of Orpheus was raised to a demi-god who brought harmony into a pristine nature. Thus, in the words of Fiere-David (taken from Jung 1964/1966/1993, p. 121):

> 'Orpheus taught, while he sung and played upon his harp, and his singing was so powerful that it governed the whole world; while he sung along with his harp, the birds flew to him and the fishes left the water and flopped towards him. The wind and the sea were still and the rivers flowed upstream towards him. It rained and hailed no more. Trees and even stones followed Orpheus. The tiger and the lion lay down by the sheep and the wolves by the hart and the hind. What does this mean? It certainly means that, through a godly insight into nature, . . . the events of nature could be ordered from the inside outwards in an harmonious way . . .'

And yet it was just this same Orpheus who descended to Hades in search of his *anima*, 'his' Eurydice!

We are now in a position to move onto the characterisations of the mappings that provide the last apex of Figure 4, which connect all of soil-cultivation/agriculture, wisdom/knowledge and water/transport to intrinsic/ social values. Since our principal concern at this point is with social values, we must seek our metaphorical tokens at least to some extent at a lesser depth within the collective unconscious, and thus from a later period than those so far employed at this metaphorical level. We are here beginning to move away from the level of the myth and are now of necessity ascending, to move into the level of the legend, and at some point further again into the level of the saga. Seeking the most durable of such metaphorical structures we must again seek instances where musical forms of expressions have been used to carry over the respective tokens into our 'modern' era, as reinforcement. Our natural and indeed almost inevitable choice is then *Der Ring des Nibelungen*, the *Ring of the Nibelungs*, both in its original form, as *Das Nibelungenlied,* and in the form of the opera cyclus of the same name written and composed by Richard Wagner (Heusler 1987). In Donington's (1963) Jungian in-depth analysis of Wagner's work, the entire opera begins (pp. 35, 36) with:

> 'The primordial chaos at the world's beginning [being] regularly depicted as a waste of waters from which the first self-generated gods appeared. . . . Before very long we are going to be shown another regular feature of creation myths: the coming of light into the darkness of the waters.'

However, instead of continuing like any regular creation myth into the formation of life, which also serves in this case as a metaphor for the formation of consciousness, and so of 'intention', the *Ring* takes quite another turn, depicting gold glittering under the waters of the Rhine. This, however, also has many mythical precedents (p. 53):

> 'We learn from the Prose Edda that gold "gave forth light and illuminated the hall like fire" for the sea-giant Aegir beneath the waters, and incidentally that Aegir had a daughter . . . called Ran, who seems to have been a mermaid; in consequence of which "gold is new called" among other poetic synonyms "Fire of Waters or Rivers". There is a comparable reference to gold giving off light like fire under the water in [the Anglo-Saxon language foundation myth of] Beowulf's fight with the Mother Monster; indeed this poetic synonym by which "gold" is paraphrased as "fire of waters" or

Appendix 1

> "of rivers" or "of the sea" is widespread throughout the Icelandic Sagas, and is certainly no accident . . .'

In the *Ring of the Nibelungs*, the opening of the first act shows us the gold shining like fire from below the water of the Rhine, as the pleasure and the sport of the Rhine Maidens, for whom it has exclusively an intrinsic value, but then an immensely important one. This gold is stolen however by 'man', who turns it into a social value, and thereby ultimately destroys not only himself but also his gods, as the repositories of his highest values. Only with this destruction at the end of the *Ring* cyclus does the gold revert to the Rhine Maidens again, to retake its original role of imparting intrinsic value. Thus value, as symbolized by gold, is in its origins intrinsic value, and only in a secondary and essentially other social context does it become social value. (Let us observe at this point that, since we are here rising up to the level of Germanic legend and Skaldic saga, we can already descry certain partial orderings in the sign vehicles — the linguistics tokens — themselves. These orderings also caught the special attention of Manin in his celebrated *Course in Mathematical Logic* (1977, p. 56), as follows:

> 'It has become very popular in modern linguistics to attempt to find a suitable description of natural language by means of [introducing] generating rules. . . . There has been at least one poetic system in which generating rules occupied an important place. One of the basic elements of skaldic (ancient Icelandic) poetry consisted of special formulas called *kennings*. A kenning is an expression which can replace a single word. For example,
>
> "fire of war" is a kenning for "gold"
>
> "sky of sand" and "field of seals" are kennings for "sea"
>
> A *simple kenning* is a kenning no part of which is a kenning. The examples above are all simple kennings. They play the role of axioms; obviously only very great poets have the right to create new simple kennings'

Manin observed further in this respect that:

> 'Even the most casual attempt at writing poetry reveals the psychological reality of prohibitions in versification. But it is much less obvious that there is a set of generating rules which also has a psychological reality'

It is through such generating rules, as one among many other ordering devices of linguistics, that the legend and the saga come to express their psychological realities and thus cast their own light upon such issues as those of gender that confront us here.)

While apologising for so many quotations at this stage, we can best continue at once to the next mapping, from wisdom/knowledge to intrinsic/social value. We then meet the same kind of metaphorically equivalent mappings as we saw earlier, but now with water/transport equivalent to wisdom/knowledge in relation to intrinsic and social value. Thus, reverting to Donington (1963 p. 53):

> 'The general reference to such images is to a stirring in the deep unconscious as some light of consciousness is lit; their particular piquancy arises from the familiar incompatibility of fire and water in ordinary outside circumstances, where fire burns but water quenches and candles do not stay alight in the depths of the sea. We have in this paradox a typical symbol of the reconciliation of opposites, by which is meant not suppressing one side of an unwanted conflict into unconsciousness, but somehow learning to live with both sides.'

Within the context of the gender issue this 'reconciliation of opposites' arising from the employment of wisdom/knowledge can be construed as a reconciliation between the intrinsic values associated with objects arranged within a given structure and the social values associated with these same objects arranged in the same structure. We shall return to this in conclusion.

Appendix 1

For the third and last of the mappings in this last quadrant of Figure 4, from soil-conservation/agriculture to intrinsic/social values, and in the opposite direction again, we can return once more to the principle of the Orphic myth, with its reliance on and search for the essential female principle. In this case we have to do more with Bacchus as the god of cultivation (commonly symbolised by the cultivation of the vine). For Bacchus, the sought-after female element was personalized by Ariadne, who had been abandoned by her faithless betrothed on the island of Naxos, but remained always faithful to her vows and maintained her natural purity. These virtues indicate once again the functional components of 'the female principle' that provide the mapping from soil cultivation/agriculture to social values and it was essentially for her possession of these virtues that Bacchus raised her up to the status of a goddess. Similarly, the perpetuation of the myth in operatic form in the Strauss–Hoffmansthal *Ariadne auf Naxos* clearly indicates its continuing relevance in our own times, while Hoffmansthal himself explained the relations of the virtues so prescribed to the female side of the process of procreation itself. We may in this place also therefore characterise those aspects of 'the female principle' that are necessary to realise the corresponding mapping.

With these functional elements of mappings introduced, even if only so summarily, the reader can fill in the bracketed intentional acts in Figure 4. The full structure of the implected expressions, meanings and understandings between the end user of the advice-serving system and their intermediaries within the outer periphery, together with the corresponding congruent structures of implected intrinsic values and implected social values, can then be portrayed as shown in Figure 5.

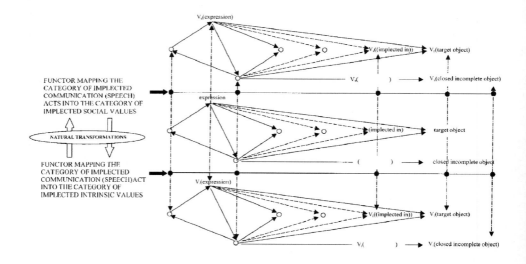

Figure 5 | The category of objects, intrinsic values and social values for knowledge elicitation and provision, their functors and the 'natural transformations' that map these functors, the one into the other.

CONCLUSIONS

With all of these constructions now in place we can hope to have reached a position where we can safely turn back to confront the question of 'why?' that we posed at the beginning. In the first place our question is simply: why should there be a bias towards women in a sociotechnical system of this kind? After this we can examine the consequences of the answer that we obtain to the design and analysis of systems of this kind.

1. The procedure that has been followed here for investigating the special relevance of women within sociotechnical systems in hydroinformatics, and specifically within widely distributed, mass-customised advice-serving systems, has been that of identifying the special propensities of women towards the objects that enter most naturally into these systems. Since these propensities are grounded for the most part below the level of consciousness, at the (Husserlian) level of the pre-predictive and the pre-linguistic, their phenomenology is not generally accessible to a direct modern-scientific (predicative and conventional-linguistic) analysis. Instead it has been necessary to analyse certain arcane repositories of knowledge in this area, such as are encountered in their most concentrated form in the most durable of the ancient myths, legends and sagas. Everything in this case functions in terms of the most potent symbols and their symbolisation processes. As Donington expressed this matter (1963 p. 21):

> 'A symbol invariably arises from the heart upward. This is because a symbol is not an intellectual counter at all. Thoughts are intellectual counters; symbols are emotional counters, compounded at once of feeling and intuition. Not only do symbols represent inner realities; they are inner realities.'

This is to say that the primary role of women in the hydroinformatics systems considered here is not in the first place an intellectual one (even though the intellect of the woman is important here too!) but it is *primarily* one of feeling and intuition. The basic reason for preferring women over men on average within certain key parts of the hydroinformatics systems exemplified here is the natural consonance which they demonstrate, quite intrinsically, with the main tasks which they have to perform. Expressing this in more popular terms, what is most necessary here is a well-grounded and properly directed sympathy and understanding, and this must have precedence over intellectual ability even though it cannot replace it. It would not be difficult to find intellectually brilliant persons—we all know at least one!—who would be complete disasters in this kind of work.

2. The question of what in fact constitutes 'a well-grounded and properly directed' sympathy and understanding within a given social context may be answered by seeking *indicators* of such inclinations and propensities within that context. As exemplified in the text, a natural propensity of women towards an implexive construction of end-user profiles might be expected in a society where women are inclined 'to plait, weave or twist in to, entangle in, involve, entwine or enfold'. More generally, each of the mappings examined here indicates the specific female traits that lend certain functions more to the attention of the female element.

3. This predominance of the 'emotional' and 'intuitive' aspects in this kind of work corresponds to the location of the forces that drive the work process to the level of intrinsic values in the first place, and to the level of social values only in the second place. However, one of the essential attributes of women within these activities is an ability to balance between the often apparently conflicting requirements of intrinsic and social values, as exemplified in the kennings for the repository of values, or gold itself, as ' "the fire of waters" or "of rivers", or "of the sea" ', and the related female element subsequently identified. Beyond this again, as explained at several places in the text, women in many societies have an innate wisdom that makes it possible for them to reconcile apparently conflicting interests, often in unusual but productive ways. Although much is commonly made of conflicts between intrinsic and social values, the main point that is made here is that there is nothing essential about these conflicts. The *Ring* itself exemplifies how 'the love of gold' in man and gods drives out love and consequently destroys man and gods alike, but it opens and closes with a natural love that is identified with the intrinsic value of gold and which remains implicitly present, because musically recalled, throughout Wagner's work. In the words of Donington (1963 p. 52):

> 'Inwardly, "gold" may certainly operate as a "poison of love" . . . but on a symbolic level, gold has other association of a very positive, not to say archetypal importance, as

innumerable myths reveal; and these deeper associations are subliminally but effectively at work on us in [the *Ring*]'.

4. This ability to balance the intrinsic values and the social values of structures of objects can be given a representation in the model of category theory which we have used to notate this paper. On the one hand we have a functor that maps a category of the objects that are of central concern into a category of intrinsic values, and on the other hand we have a functor that maps this same category of objects into a category of social values. The intrinsic congruence of these functors when a well-grounded and properly directed sympathy and understanding is associated with them leads to the notion that any one of these functor could map into the other through a *natural transformation*. Indeed, although the use of this term in mathematics has now become so specialised as to be apparently very far removed from the present application, the origins of the term and the use of the word 'natural' itself, as something irreducible to further analysis, does not seem to be so far removed from our present situation. It is this natural-transformation feature that is especially exemplified in Figure 5.

5. Taking these last two points further, towards so to say their *natural conclusion*, we may say that although a man may excel in developing the intrinsic values of objects as such and a man may excel in developing the extrinsic or social values of objects as such but very rarely both simultaneously, a woman can better maintain a *natural balance* between developing the intrinsic and the extrinsic values of objects. It is not sufficient however only to arrive at this conclusion, but to understand how it is reached. As countless poets, theologians, mystics, phenomenologists and others have emphasised time and time again, the road that is followed when travelling to a destination is just as important as arriving at the destination itself. What we have seen when traversing the route followed here is that this conclusion is reached at the level of a *natural transformation*, and it is precisely this that makes the balance of values in woman a *natural balance* and our conclusion a *natural conclusion*, where the word 'natural' means 'as something given by The Creation'. In a remarkable essay *Sur l'idée de concept mathématique 'naturel'* // 'On the idea of the mathematical concept of 'natural'', the French mathematician Gilles-Gaston Granger (1994, pp. 157,158) explained this significance as follows:

> 'Mathematicians, who do not usually show much repugnance about using metaphors, have not made much use of the word 'natural'. In more recent times, in French, one could at most make a case for the expression 'fundamental transformation' in Category Theory. The word seems then to refer to a univocal determination of a correspondence that is transposed from one universe of mathematical objects to another; but in this sense it is generally the adjective 'canonical' that is utilised... It is however a more ancient, traditional usage of this adjective 'natural' that serves as the starting point for our commentary; [It is used in the sense that] one speaks of 'natural numbers'...
>
> The first characteristic that appears to justify at least provisionally the introduction of the concepts of 'natural' is that these are immediately *present* before any mathematical elaboration, at one and the same time as tools and objects of thought at the centre of our spontaneous [mathematical] activity...
>
> And this that we call their 'presence' signifies the fact that they have to be shown and employed in an *experience*, which we shall try to show does not demand anything of the senses but must be recognised as an *intellectual intuition* [as an *intellectual experience*].'

Thus, in effect, we have reached a conclusion that cannot be reduced further: it is as we say 'irreducible', as a natural conclusion. We see here also why, like Orpheus, we could not once look backwards during the development of this paper.

6. Hydroinformatics proceeds for the most part through creative business, which is business activity that attempts to maintain a balance between the creation of intrinsic values and the creation of extrinsic or social values. There is abroad today the stupid notion that the only purpose of business is 'to make money' as the most superficial of all social values. Since it is the intention of mass-customised advice-serving systems that they should create both intrinsic and extrinsic or social value in a balanced way, the participation of women in these constructs is essential.

7. The archetypal traits and propensities identified and reified in this paper thus indicate the necessity to involve women directly, closely and extensively in many, and probably most, knowledge-intensive agricultures and indeed in many other sociotechnical systems now being prepared in the field of hydroinformatics. The gradients in intrinsic value provide the one motivating force while the gradients in social values form another, and these two forces have the capacity to reinforce one another, and thus to provide a synergy between the two object-value systems. The consequences of this for the generation of a more commodious life and for the alleviation of poverty in rural areas are potentially momentous. In the words of Muhammad Yunus, the founder of the *Grameen Bank* and now the godfather of the *Grameen* family of companies (Yunus 1997):

> 'It is the responsibility of any civilised society to ensure human dignity to each and every member of the society, and to make sure that each and every member gets the best opportunity to reveal his or her creativity. Poverty is not created by the poor. It is created by the institutions we have built and the policies that we pursue. We cannot solve the problem of poverty with the same concepts and tools which created it in the first place. To create a poverty-free world we need a new conceptualisation, a new analytical framework, which takes ensuring human dignity to every human being as its central task. We can achieve what we want to achieve. The essential condition, however, is that we must have a burning desire to achieve it. If we believe in a poverty free world, we can create it. To begin with, instead of basking in the glory of our wisdom, let us severely question it. It is about time that we did that.'

ACKNOWLEDGEMENTS
The author thanks A. Jonoski, now Lecturer at the UNESCO Institute for Water Education in Delft, The Netherlands, for his extensive and wide-ranging searches of the World Wide Web for examples of advice-serving systems. This paper was based upon discussions of the gender issue with Dr K. N. N. Thein, now Senior Advisor, UNEP Dams and Development Project, Nairobi, Kenya. Although these discussions covered several cultural contexts, the paper was written entirely by the present author and so necessarily from a predominantly Eurocentric point of view. Dr Thein and the author apologise for this Eurocentricity.

REFERENCES
Abbott, M.B., 1999a, Forchheimer and Schoklitsch, a postmodern retrospection, In *Memorial Symposium P. Forchheimer and A. Schoklitsch, Proc. 28th IAHR congress*, Graz (ed. Graf, W.H.)
Abbott, M.B., 1999b, Introducing Hydroinformatics, *Journal of Hydroinformatics*, 1, 1, pp 3-20.
Abbott, M.B. and Dibike, Y.B., 1998a, On the representation of processes in the post-symbolic era, in Babovic and Larsen, (eds.), pp.1177-1184., Balkema Rotterdam.
Abbott, M.B. and Dibike, Y.B., 1998b, The symbolic representation of hydroinformatics processes using elements of category theory, in Babovic and Larsen, (eds.), 1998, pp.1185-1192, Balkema Rotterdam.
Abbott, M.B., Hodgins, D.O., Dinsmore, A.F., and Donovan, M., 1977, A transit model for the city of Miami, *Journal of Environmental Management*, Given by Internet, pp. 229-242.
Abbott, M.B. and Jonoski, A., 1998, Promoting collaborative decision-making through electronic networking, in Babovic and Larsen, (eds.), pp. 911-918, Balkema Rotterdam.
Abbott, M.B., de Nordwall, J. and Swets, B., 1993, On applications of artificial intelligence to control and safety problems of nuclear power plants, *Civil Engineering Systems* 1, 1, pp. 69-82.
Abbott, M.B., and Warren, R.I., 1974, A dynamic population model, *Journal of Environmental Management*, Given by Internet.
Babovic, V., and Larsen, C.L. (eds), 1998, *Hydroinformatics 98*, Balkema, Rotterdam.
Barth, K, 1938-1955 / 1960, *Kirchliche Dogmatik*, Evangelischer, Zollikon-Zurich // *Church Dogmatics*, transl. Bromiley, G.W., and Ehrlich, R.J., Clark, Edinburgh, in 13 volumes.
Donington, R., 1963, *Wagners 'Ring' and its Symbols*, Faber, London.

Findlay, J.N., 1963/1995, *Meinong's Theory of Objects and Values*, 2nd ed., Oxford Univ., Oxford / Gregg Revivals, Ashgate, Aldershot, UK and Springfield, USA.

Fraser, J.T., Lawrence, N., and Park, D., 1978, *The Study of Time III*, Springer, New York.

Granger, G.-G.,1994, Sur l'idée de concept mathématique 'naturel', in Granger, G.-G. (Ed.), Formes, Opérations, Objets, Vrin. Paris.

Haller, R. (ed.), 1996, *Meinong und die Gegenstandstheorie: Meinong and the Theory of Objects*, Rodopi, Amsterdam and Atlanta, USA.

Heusler, A.,ed., 1987, *Das Nibelungenlied, Mittelhochdeutsch und Neuhochdeutsch*, trans. Simrock, K, Vollmer, Wiesbaden.

Hilpinen R. (ed.), 1971, *Deontic Logic: Introductory and Systematic Readings*, Reidel, Dordrecht, Holland.

Huang, Y., Solomatine, D.P., Velickov, S. and Abbott, M.B., 1999, Distributed environmental impact assessment using Internet, *Journal of Hydroinformatics*, 1, 1, pp 59-70.

Jacquette, D., 1996, Meinong's concept of implexive being and non-being, in *Meinong und die Gegenstandstheoretie: Meinong and the Theory of Objects*, (Haller R.), pp 233-271. Rodopi, Amsterdam and Atlanta, USA.

Jonoski, A, and Abbott, M.B., 1998, Network distributed decision-support systems as multi-agent constructs, in *Hydroinformatics '98*, (eds. Babovic and Larsen), pp 1219-1226. Balkema, Rotterdam.

Jung, C.S., 1964, *Man and his Symbols*, Aldus, London.

Margalef, R., 1968, *Perspectives in Ecological Theory*, Chicago University Press, Chicago.

McNamara P. and Prakken H. (ed.), 1998, *Norms, Logics and Information Systems. New studies in Deontic Logic and Computer Science*, Artificial Intelligence and Applications Series, IOS, Amsterdam.

Ogawa, H., 1978, The concept of time in the Mithraic mysteries. In *The Study of Time III* (eds. Fraser *et al*) pp. 683-701, Springer, New York.

Rowell, L., 1978, Time and sacrifice – the sacrifice of time and the ritual of modernity; in Fraser *et al*, In *The Study of Time III* (eds. Fraser *et al*) pp. 578-613, Springer, New York.

Sastri, C., 1980, *A Study in the Dialectics of the Sphota*, Banarsidass, New Delhi.

Simons, P., 1996, Meinong's theory of sense and reference, in *Meinong und die Gegenstandstheoretie: Meinong and the Theory of Objects*, (Haller R.), pp 171-186. Rodopi, Amsterdam and Atlanta, USA.

Thein, K.N.N., and Abbott, M.B., 1998, Intranet-based management of water resources for a new Burma, in *Hydroinformatics '98*, (eds. Babovic and Larsen), pp 957-963. Balkema, Rotterdam.

Turner, F.,1978, Poiesis: time and artistic discourse, In *The Study of Time III* (eds. Fraser *et al*) pp. 614-653. Springer, New York.

Yunus, M., 1993/1997, *Raising the Productivity of the Poor: Grameen Bank Experience in Managing New Technologies*, reprinted by Grameen Bank, Dhaka.

Yunus, M., 1997, *Towards Creating a Poverty-Free World*, reprinted by Grameen Bank, Dhaka.

Appendix 2

On Definitions

First published in the Journal of Hydroinformatics, Issue 04. 2. 2002, and reproduced by permission of the International Water Association Press, but now modified. Some repetition of quotations used in the main body of this book has been unavoidable in the present case.

CONTENTS
Summary
1. Introduction
2. The origin and purpose of the definition
3. Objects and contents: expressions, meanings and definitions
4. Dictionaries and encyclopædias
5. The defining subject: the self and its selfhood
6. The definability of reality and truth, of space and time
7. The fourfold means of communication, beginning with signs and symbols
8. Continuing to indicators
9. Concluding with icons
10. The general typology of tokens
11. Models
12. Knowledge
13. Information in relation to education and training
14. Understanding as a product of predicative judgement
15. Judgements
16. Judgement engines, fact engines and advice-serving systems
17. Science, technology and society: scientific, technological and societal discourses
18. *Gerede*
Acknowledgements
References

SUMMARY
Originating from a concern about the use of terms in hydroinformatics, this paper takes up the question of the nature of a definition and its consequences in such a technical, and increasingly sociotechnical field. It is explained that the way things are defined is not so simple and so obvious as might at first appear, but is in fact an essentially ideological matter, having consequences not only within an individual discipline, but also for the applications of that discipline within a wider context. A mode of definition that satisfies the needs and expectations of a subject of this kind is then advanced.

The notion of a defining self is introduced in order to explain how the mode of definition attains to a greater influence in social and ecological applications. This influence is exerted through communication, which is necessarily realised through the use of tokens. The four classes of tokens necessary for all processes of communication are introduced, delineated and defined.

The way in which such broad concepts as 'reality' and 'truth' are defined is then seen to influence the definition of a model in the widest sense. Further definitions that are of central concern in such a sociotechnical discipline are developed accordingly. The paper concludes with a description of a phenomenon known only by its German name, as *Gerede*, that is at the root of much current confusion of terms in hydroinformatics, as in so many other places, and how its malign influences can be opposed.

INTRODUCTION
Although most of us may think out of hand that we know what a definition is and how it is used, reference to any philosophical encyclopædia will no doubt persuade us that the way in which we define things is neither simple nor straightforward. The question concerning 'right definitions' has puzzled many of the greatest thinkers in every age, while in the last century it emerged clearly as an *ideological* question. The way in which one 'defines a definition' was seen to mark a division in ways of looking at the world as a whole, and especially at the position of mankind within this world (Abelson, 1967). This division has caused an understandable confusion in the minds of those who have been exposed to it. The resulting confusion has in turn had the gravest consequences, both for humanity alone, and most clearly so in the first half of the twentieth century, and for humanity and its natural environment inseparably in the second half of that century and into the present century again. Hydroinformatics is intensely concerned with the second of these consequences. Thus a paper on definitions used in a sociotechnical discipline like hydroinformatics is not the relatively simple, technical matter that it might at first appear to be, but carries deeper issues along with it. As will be explained, this question concerning definitions carries with it also the future of this and many other subjects and is thus of vital importance.

THE ORIGIN AND PURPOSE OF THE DEFINITION
Every department of thought that we call a discipline is, simultaneously, a discipline of language. A discipline of thought is essential to the formation of a discipline of language and a discipline of language is essential to the maintenance of a discipline of thought. Any and every subject of enquiry becomes and remains a discipline just so long as it introduces and maintains a disciplined language.

But what do we mean by a disciplined language? Most languages such as are realised in everyday discourse, are of course not particularly disciplined at all, and indeed they have no need to be so. Most everyday discourse is intelligible enough for most everyday purposes. Following Heidegger (1927/67), we speak of a *discourse of average intelligibility*. However, as soon as this mode of discourse has to treat a matter that is not so everyday, conforming less to the average experience, then it encounters several difficulties. Thus (*ibid.*, 1927/1962, p. 212):

> "In the language which is spoken when one expresses oneself there lies an average intelligibility; and in accordance with this intelligibility the discourse which is communicated can be understood to a considerable extent, even if the hearer does bring himself into such a kind of Being [or state of awareness] of what the discourse is about as to have a primordial understanding of it. We do not so much understand the entities which are talked about; we are already listening only to what is said-in-the-talk as such. What is said-in-the-talk gets understood, but what the talk is [really] about is understood only approximately and superficially."

It is then in the nature of this most common kind of discourse that it uses words and expressions in a loose and largely undifferentiated way. Words such as 'sign', 'symbol', 'icon', 'model', 'calibration', 'validation' and so on are frequently used with little regard to their precise meanings. Although, once again, this may be of little real consequence in casual conversation, it can lead to great confusion when matters of some substance, such as are not everyday and average, must none the less be discussed. This confusion in turn leads to apparently endless discussions which seem to have no definite outcomes at all — or may even lead to outcomes that were never intended.

This confusion and the apparently endless and fruitless discussion which accompanies it was well known to the ancients, and in particular to the ancient Greeks and Romans from whom our so-called 'Western' culture is derived, and whose labours have provided the primary languages of modern science and technology. The ancients observed that the confusion was founded upon an undisciplined use of language, and that the root of this undisciplined mode of communicating was the use of imprecise terms. They accordingly set out to *put an end to* such modes of unproductive discourse by making the meanings of words and expressions more precise. These were then ways to 'bring to an end', the Latin *definire*, from which we have the French *définir* (decomposing to *de finir*, such as in *Je lui ai demandé de finir: I have asked him to finish*), so that the English verb *to finish* has the same root. By making the basic materials of discourse, and in the first place words, more *definite*, the ancients already forged an instrument, called a *definition*, which would put an end to otherwise uncontrolled and uncontrollable proliferations of discourse, with all their negative consequences.

The word definition is thus itself defined by what it *achieves* in the world of discourse. But how does it achieve this and can it then also be defined by *how* it achieves its purpose?

OBJECTS AND CONTENTS: EXPRESSIONS, MEANINGS AND DEFINITIONS

An object is anything to which a mental process can be directed (Findlay, 1963/1995, p. 67). The mental process directs itself to objects, but it is not itself an object in that it contains other elements which we do not and indeed usually cannot call into our minds during the mental process itself. These other elements are subsumed collectively under the rubric of *content*. Thus (Findlay, 1963/1995, p. 30):

> "The relation between content and object shows a curious reciprocity; objects cannot enter the mind but are made accessible by means of contents; contents, though they are in the mind, are difficult to approach directly, and so are generally grasped by means of objects."

Accordingly, what are normally called the attributes of objects, such as their colour, for example, are not themselves objects even as they may function as content, but they can none the less be *objectified*. Thus, to continue this last example, the colour 'blue' can be objectified as 'the colour which I can project in my mind when I think of the word "blue"', which is then indisputably an object. An object constructed in this way is commonly called, following the foundational studies of Alexius von Meinong, a *pseudo-object*, and is said to be constructed by a process of *objectification*.

Among all the objects that enter into mental processes there are some which function in a very specific way within their embedding content, in that our awareness of one object causes our minds to pass over to the awareness of another object. Any object which can be given up in place of another object in this way, so that it can take the place of another object in our minds, is called a *token*. The object that is so represented is then said to be *betokened*. In everyday speech, tokens are often referred to simply as 'signs', but this usage is too imprecise to be employed here, signs in the strict sense—to be identified shortly—being but one species of tokens. Despite this, we shall retain the most familiar word, *semiotics*, commonly understood as *the study of signs*, for the study of tokens generally.

Among the most common of tokens are *words*. In their function as tokens, "words serve a double function: they *express* our inner experiences and they *mean* or refer to the objects of those experiences" (Findlay, 1963/1995, p. 61). Findlay explained further (*ibid*):

> "The tendency to confuse the expressive and the significant function of words goes back to the more fundamental confusion of the content and object of mental states.... But if content and object are clearly distinguished, and it is realised that no physical object is ever a constituent of any mental state, then it is plain that the sense in which a word is a sign of a mental process in the user of the word, and the sense in which it is a sign of something he is thinking of, are totally different."

We shall follow a standard practice in the theory of semiotics (*e.g.*, Eco, 1976; Klinkenberg, 1996) by denoting the fact that an object is functioning as a token for another object by enclosing that betokening object between virgules: / /. We denote the description of the object that comes into our mind, as the *meaning* of the token, by enclosing this description of meaning within guillemets:

<< >>. We then define the definition of an object x as that function of the mind, $def(x)$, that maps the token that calls x to mind into the signification of x, which is then the *meaning* of the token:

$def(x)$: token for $x \rightarrow$ betokened meaning

This corresponds to the formula of Locke (1690/e.g. 1976, p. 208): "words, in their primary or immediate signification, stand for nothing but the *ideas* in the mind of him that uses them". Thus, for example, if we take the word-token /pen/ and, as a one and only meaning of this token, <<a device for writing with ink>>, we have:

$def(pen)$: /pen/ $\rightarrow$ <<a device for writing with ink>>

Clearly one and the same word-token may produce different ideas depending upon the ideas in the mind of the user of the word, which we may describe as *the context within which the word is used*.

We may anticipate our later development of this theme already by emphasising that the central element in any definition is the function $def(x)$. We then reflect this central position in our notation by writing the token that initiates the operation of the function by $\Box\, def(x)$ and the meaning that $def(x)$ produces by $def(x)\Box$. Thus, for any x:

$$def(x) : \Box def(x) \mapsto def(x)\Box \tag{1}$$

where we shall explain the introduction of a barred arrow shortly.

There are three immediate and important consequences of this definition. In the first place we see that definitions are defined only for the case of objects and not for the case of contents (see, already, Locke, *loc cit*, pp. 205-206 and, more critically, Hume, 1748/1999, *e.g.* pp. 96-100; see further Bolzano, 1837/1963, pp. 42-61). Any element of content can only be defined to the extent that it can be 'made objective', or 'objectified' or 'becomes a pseudo-object' so that it can be represented by a token. As a further example of this property, we now see that a definition must itself also be an object, even though it will most usually be a very different kind of object than that which it defines. We can clearly regard a definition as a form of judgement, and in this case a judgement of the meaning of something that is initially experienced and identified as a token. We experience the definition as 'being the case' or as a 'fact' in relation to the token-like object which addresses it. Then (Findlay, 1963/1995, pp. 67, 69):

> "Meinong proposes to use the word 'objective' for those entities which can be judged or assumed, and which are in some cases facts. He sets them against objects in the narrower sense, which can be given to us by mere ideas (*Vorstellungen*), and which are never the case. We may use the word 'object' to translate Meinong's *Gegenstand* .... For Meinong's word *Objekt*, which applies only to objects in the narrower sense, i.e. to those which are not objectives, we use the word 'objecta'. Objects therefore divide into the two classes of objectives and objecta."

> "... Normally an objective is judged (*geurteilt*) or assumed (*angenommen*); while the objects involved in it are judged about (*beurteilt*) or assumptions are made about them (they are *beannahmt*) . Now it is perfectly possible for an objective to play the part of an objectum in the sense that we no longer judge or assume it, but make judgements *about* it. To do this has the additional advantage of proving, with the greatest possible clearness, that objectives belong wholly and solely to the realm of objects, and are utterly indifferent to the [contingent] workings of our minds."

In effect, we can say that only objects can be defined because we extend the world of objects so extensively, following Meinong. We observe, as a second consequence, that we speak of the 'definition of an object' when we might appear to mean, strictly speaking, 'the definition of the token used to represent the object'. Thus, it might appear as though, strictly speaking, we should use $def(\Box def(x))$. There is, however, a very fundamental reason for the usage adopted here, which is that in the event that our tokens are words in a technological or, even more, sociotechnical discipline, one and the same word may have several, and even quite disparate, meanings, but each such meaning then corresponds to the particular object which we have in mind when we use the word. Thus, within its linguistic context, *the representation of the object x is commonly not a word but a word that is set within a specific denoting context.* The denotation in this case clearly follows the object, which we have in mind. In real-world dictionaries this is indicated by repeating the word that is defined while following each such repetition immediately with an indication of the specific context that is intended, before the corresponding definition is given. As explained later here, this would appear not to be necessary in the case of an ideal scientific language, but even in that case we can motivate it by the simplest of mathematical examples, of mapping the set of positive integers I^+ into itself or a subset of itself by functions of the form $f: x \mapsto x^n$, where x is an element of I^+ and n is an element of I^+. Then the number 2, for example, maps into the number 4 if n=2, into 8 if n=3, and so on depending upon the function-object that we have in mind during the process. Once again, we shall explain the significance of the barred arrow in such a case shortly. In a similar vein, if we consider the special case that $\Box def(x)$ is a word, different words in different languages will commonly refer to one and the same object. Thus, we may speak of 'the definition of a river' rather than 'the definition of the word /river/', on the understanding that 'river' can be replaced by *fleuve, Flüsse*, or any number of other words in other languages. This usage marks our present approach as quite resolutely *essentialist*, in that we suppose that definitions convey information which may provide meanings. This contrasts with the *prescriptive* approach as represented by modern formalism, where the definition is *restricted* to the token and does not refer to the object which is in the mind and which it thereby betokens (Abelson, 1967). As we shall see later, it is this difference that corresponds to the profound ideological difference in the view of the relation between mankind and its languages that we have mentioned above.

The third consequence follows from the first when we observe that already within any one 'natural' language (English, French, German, etc.), there will be 'overlaps' between some of the $\Box def(x)$'s and between some of their $def(x)\Box$'s, so that these collections will not normally be 'crisp' sets in the classical (Cantorian) sense. It is only necessary that x is an object that can be designated: the collection of x's does not necessarily have to have a structure. However, because the basic notions of classical set theory will most likely be the most familiar to readers, we shall often simply use the term 'set', when describing the collections of objects with which we are here concerned. We shall denote the set of x's by $\{x\}$, the set of $\Box def(x)$'s by $\{\Box def(x)\}$, the set of $def(x)\Box$'s by $\{def(x)\ \Box\}$, but we shall continue to describe the function that connects these in the same way for every x by $def(x)$.

With this notation, then, we can define a more general function $def(x)$ that maps a set $\{\Box def(x)\}$ into a set $\{def(x)\Box\ \}$. This notational movement from the anonymous instance to the more general 'domain→codomain' transformation case mimics that employed in mathematics generally, where, to return to our previous example, the mappings 1→1, 2→4, 3→9, etc., provides the anonymous instance $x \mapsto x^2$ which maps the set of positive integers, I^+, into a proper subset of itself. We observe here that we have already earlier introduced a barred arrow, $\mapsto$, in the anonymous case, but a straight arrow in the definite, including the 'domain→codomain', case.

We then recall from the teaching of elementary mathematics that we can visualise any function f that performs this kind of mapping in terms of the shooting of an arrow from some kind of *source* to some kind of *target*. This metaphor then serves to emphasise that it is the set of arrows that indicates both the set of sources and the set of targets. It is in order to emphasise this dependency in that branch of mathematics that is used to describe mappings of the kind exemplified here by definitions, that is, in *Category Theory*, that some authors use the notation

$\Box f$ to represent the source *set* of the mapping realised by the function f, and $f\Box$ to represent the target *set* of the mapping realised by f. Then $\Box f$ and $f\Box$ constitute unary operations on f. Since the $f\Box$ of one function f may act upon the $\Box g$ of another function g to provide a composite function, $f\,g$, we introduce further a binary partial operation to accommodate this. Then *Category Theory* is defined by these operations and by the axioms:

$f\,g$ is defined if and only if $f\Box = \Box g$,
$(\Box f)\Box = \Box f$ and $\Box(f\Box) = f\Box$,
$(\Box f)f = f$ and $f(f\Box) = f$,   2)
$\Box(f\,g) = \Box(f(\Box g))$ and $(f\,g)\Box = ((f\Box)g)\Box$,
$f(g\,h) = (f\,g)h$.

The ordinary equality sign, as exemplified above, is used only in the symmetric sense, that if either side is defined then so is the other, and they are equal. In the event that the asymmetric sense of equality may arise—so that we can only assert that if the left side is defined then so is the right side and that these are equal—another notation is required, but we shall make no use of this here.

Freyd and Scedrov (1990) then explain that:

> "A theory such as this, built on an ordered list of partial operations, the domain of definition of each given by equations in the previous, and with all other axioms equational, is called an *essentially algebraic theory*."

We should observe further that in many disciplines, including much of the literature on Category Theory, the terms /morphism/, /domain/ and /codomain/ are used instead of /arrow/, /source/, and /target/ when the source and target are sets.

(For our own part we may observe [following E.Rossinger, private communication] that Category Theory, together with the Allegory Theory that we shall do no more than mention here, is not regarded as a part of mathematics by some mathematical purists, and especially by the Bourbakist school. This is primarily because the objects which these theories address are not restricted to mathematical objects, but can equally well be non-mathematical objects, as already exemplified. It is precisely this feature, however, that makes these theories so applicable to studies of the kind that predominate in hydroinformatics, and especially on its sociotechnical side: see also Abbott, 2000).

The fourth consequence of our definition is that it necessarily leads us into the study of self-referencing systems. This was obvious already as soon as we spoke of a 'definition of a definition', which could clearly be extended indefinitely. Now we observe further levels of self referencing in that every list of definitions introduces tokens that have in turn to be defined. Such 'circles' of representations and meanings have been called, since the nineteenth century writings and teachings of Wilhelm Dilthey (*e.g.* 1976), *hermeneutic circles*.

DICTIONARIES AND ENCYCLOPÆDIAS

According to the differing nature of their self-referencing properties, or hermeneutic circles, we have two names for defining those functions, $def(x)$, which, when taken together with their source sets and their target sets, provide the categories of definitions. Taking their cues from linguistics, the one of these is called a *dictionary*, and the other is called an *encyclopædia*.

A mapping of the form $def(x)$ is said to provide an *ideal dictionary* if and only if every element of the target set $\{def(x)\Box\}$ is composed exclusively of sequences of elements of the source set $\{\Box def(x)\}$. Thus, an ideal dictionary is a *closed and completely self-referencing system*. For his part, Foucault (1966//1970/1989) spoke in a similar case of a "language that only ever speaks about itself".

Appendix 2

We have already introduced a notational device for distinguishing between the function that takes the domain into the codomain, for which we use a straight arrow and the function that takes a particular input datum to its corresponding output datum, for which we use a barred arrow. This distinction is often required because the domain and the codomain are determined by their relation, as source and target, of the function. Thus in Category Theory a function is not only a rule, but it is a rule that must be taken together with its domain and codomain. This condition corresponds to the need to maintain *a very strong form of typing*. Thus the function *def*(x) has to be taken together with the {□*def*(x)} and the {*def*(x)□} upon which it operates: very obviously, for example, the category defined by *def*(x) operating on words in the English language is not the same as the category defined by *def*(x) operating on words in the French language even as the nature of the act of definition remains the same. If, however, we do keep to the example of any one particular natural language as this functions within the greater part of a society at a particular time, we see that:
1. *Every word, when understood as the representation of a specific object, and so situated within a specific context, has one and only one definition.* Of course, the one word may still have several *connotatively* different meanings even when associated with one and the same object, but then each element of the target set is composed of all of these connotative meanings, as in real-world dictionaries.
2. *Two or more words may nonetheless share the same definition.* Thus, in British politics, 'Conservative' and 'Tory' nowadays have identical definitions, regardless of their different historical origins. In more general terms, two distinct elements in the source set {□*def*(x)} may map into one and the same element in the target set {*def*(x) □}.
3. *There are some meanings for which we can find no words at all within the language concerned.* This is to say that, in this linguistic example at least, we may have words in other languages that do express these otherwise inexpressible meanings, as will be illustrated later in this paper. We may also, of course, have all manner of life experiences that possess great meaning to us, but for which we can find no words at all.

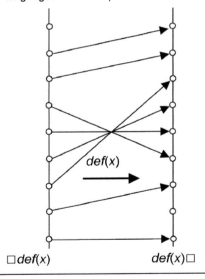

Figure 1. Mappings from tokens to the meanings associated with these tokens

It follows that the function *def*(x) as defined in (1) is injective, but, not being surjective, it is not bijective. This situation is schematised in Fig. 1. The categorical nature of all definitions is then presaged in the structure of all dictionaries.

An *ideal encyclopædia* is one that does not possess this totally self-referencing property at all, so that it effectively already presupposes—and in fact is also presupposed by—the existence of a dictionary. It presupposes much more again, however, for whereas we might characterise the ideal dictionary as a *completely closed system*, as something that is ideally invariant in time, an ideal encyclopædia is an *always incomplete system*, taking as its themes matters of interest occurring in the world outside itself, a world which is forever changing. As we shall intimate later, these two ideal cases correspond to two distinct *models* of description of meaning, the one proceeding through the definition of objects in terms of definitions of other objects and the other proceeding through statements of beliefs about and relations between objects.

Of course, real dictionaries and real encyclopædia still differ quite considerably from their ideal counterparts. Most prosaically, both of these real forms are provided with total-ordering functions $\hat{O}(\{\Box def(x)\})$, providing sets $\{def(x_i), i=1,2,...., ii)\}$, where, recursively, $\hat{O} = \hat{O}(\{\Box def(x)\})$. More basically, in semiotics, the difference between these real forms is commonly expressed in terms of differences between *analytic propositions*, these being propositions that are always true simply by virtue of the meanings of their component terms, and *synthetic propositions*, understood as propositions that can only be judged as true or false on the basis of conditions outside of themselves (Klinkenberg, 1995, pp. 108-110; much more definitively, see Kant, 1787/1924/1971, pp. 58-66//1929, pp. 48-55). Thus, the distinction here goes back to the Meinongian one between words as signs of mental processes and words as referents in events occurring outside the thinking subject, as already introduced above. Whereas the first is of dominant interest within disciplines like linguistics, the second is of a much greater interest in sociotechnical subjects like hydroinformatics which have to do with information of and communications about 'the real world'. In semiotics, as just observed, these two forms of defining systems are said to constitute two different *models*—but then 'model' is a word that still has to be defined here in its full generality. Despite their differences at the level of models, however, we still have to insist that real encyclopædia can only be built upon the foundations provided by real dictionaries, so that definitions are as important in hydroinformatics as they are in any other discipline. We should observe, if only passing, that whereas the dictionary model of meaning can be formalised within Category Theory, the encyclopædia model of meaning, having to do with so many other kinds of *relations between objects*, cannot generally be so constituted. The encyclopædia model has instead to be constituted as some kind of allegory, so that its formal representation falls, at best, under the subject matter of *Allegory Theory*.

THE DEFINING SUBJECT: THE SELF AND ITS SELFHOOD

We have defined definitions in terms of 'functions of the mind', but we have now increasingly to enquire into whose mind this is. In a world in which nature is being subjected to so much destruction and desolation, and where an ever greater number of humans are being reduced to destitution, this question comes to be posed ever more urgently. As hydroinformatics as a whole, regardless of its different approaches, attempts to reduce and even reverse this tendency to increasing desolation and destitution through its application of advanced information and communication technologies to the worlds of the waters, so it must inevitably pose this question. Hydroinformaticians are themselves proxies for their fellow humans and for the creations of nature, and in this position they must relate their own selves and their own selfhood to the selves and selfhoods of others through that substance, water, that is common to all life on Earth. Whether it is through the ways of a data mining for knowledge discovery that is directed to 'listening to nature' so as to 'understand what nature is trying to tell us', or whether it is through its ecological associations, in which hydroinformaticians participate in alleviating and restoring the lives of their fellow creatures, or whether it is in the direct sociotechnical direction, in which hydroinformaticians strive to provide the means for their fellow humans (directly) and other creatures (indirectly) to participate in the decisions that so influence their lives, questions concerning the 'self' and 'selfhood' are constantly and increasingly posed. We may conceive that these 'other selves' create objects in their minds and associate these objects through their own content, and these processes cannot be indifferent to us. How are we then to *define* 'self' and 'selfhood' in this general context? There are obviously very many approaches to this question, and correspondingly a considerable literature has been devoted to it. Since the self cannot 'it-self' be an object, it can only be objectified for the purpose of expressing its meaning by the application of metaphor and allegory, and many such devices can be found in the literature for this purpose (*e.g.* Hermans, 1996). However, most current approaches to expressing the meaning of 'self' and 'selfhood' follow one or the other of two encyclopædic models, the one corresponding to a *computer metaphor* and the other to a *narrative metaphor*. The first, being associated with agents, agenthood and agent communication languages, will probably be the most familiar to hydroinformaticians. The second, which is however closer to our present theme,

Appendix 2

is more associated with the humanities and is often traced back to the work of Henry James (1890/1902) on the psychology of the self. In particular, James' characterisation of the 'self-as-knower' with both a 'sense of personal identity' and a 'sense of sameness' remains apposite to our present theme despite its logical-empiricist origins (see also the collection of essays in James, 1957). In a very different vein, however, it also relates back to the now classical definition originally given by Hegel (albeit with two obvious Biblical allusions) in the *Phänomenologie des Geistes* (1807//1952). This is in turn best known, nowadays, as the starting point for one of Kierkegaard's three great explorations of an already rapidly advancing nihilism as this was experienced at the level of the individuated self. Kierkegaard's (1849/1920-31//1989) formula becomes, in one of the better translations into English:

> "The self is a relation that relates itself to itself, or is the relation relating itself to itself in the relation; the self is not the relation but is the relation relating itself to itself."

Thus, in the notation of Category Theory, the definition of the self, s, as denoted by $def(s)$, is:

$$def(s) = s{:}s \to s, \qquad (3)$$

so that $\Box s = s$ and $s\Box = s$. In popular terms, then, the self might be described as 'the ultimate *self*-referencing system' in that, so to say, 'it defines itself'. We observe here already the premonition on the part of Kierkegaard (who in fact had an excellent mathematical education) of the necessity of what we nowadays call 'strong typing', in that the self is not defined exclusively in terms of its functionality, but inclusively with the sets upon which it acts and the sets that are the result of its action. The self is then that unique entity for which all three are one and the same. Formulæ similar to that of Kierkegaard have taken a prominent place in the works of several later authors (*e.g.*, Sartre, 1943//1958). Among these authors, however, it is probably Sartre who has most popularised the concept of the *other* as something that is defined by the *self* in the image of this self, and which in this process simultaneously defines another, and higher, state of the self. This self then relates the other to itself in the same manner as relates its own self, and thereby it is said to attain to a higher state of *selfhood*. To the extent that a self creates objects within the same value system as it applies to its own self, so it transcends its view of its world in terms of objects, as items of *primary reflection*, and instead attains, if only by degrees, to states of *secondary reflection*. We then speak of the resulting self as a *subject*, being one who views the others as subjects too. This then applies not only to fellow humans, but to all other creatures. Thus, when Gabriel Marcel said (see Troisfontain, 1968, part 3, p. 8) that "to be a subject is not a fact or a point of departure, but a conquest and a purpose of life", he was regarding the subject in just his way.

Thus, when the other is experienced in this way, it is said also to have attained to *selfhood* in the mind of the self, and this is then, entirely symmetrically, the necessary condition for the individual experiencing the other, his-*self* or her-*self* also to attain to *selfhood*. It is only within this relation that any kind of authentic interaction can take place at all between the self and the other.

The self is of course not a single whole, but is divided within itself. Sartre gave the example of the person who says 'I am ashamed of myself' to illustrate this, although this 'I-me' distinction is also found in James (*e.g.* 1890/1902) and is there more psychological than existential. The inner division goes very much deeper, as identified and analysed by Kierkegaard, both within the inner and the outer worlds of the self, but we only need some notion of these concepts to proceed further.* These notions are already fundamental to the entire 'ecological' and 'green' movements,

---

* If we may be permitted to proceed to a deeper level for a moment, we may observe, following Jung (1944//1953) that the self, being self-referencing to the point of defining itself, can only objectify itself in terms of mutually contradictory statements. Thus, from the *Īśā Upaniṣad*, verse 4, in the more poetic and accessible, but less academic, translation of Purohit and Yeats: "The Self is

as these function at both their individual and social levels, and so they are fundamental to hydroinformatics. They also motivate aid programmes of all types and descriptions. For more current and mainly psychologistic views on self and selfhood, reference may be made to the extensive bibliography of Hermans (1996).

THE DEFINABILITY OF REALITY AND TRUTH, OF SPACE AND TIME.

If we keep to the computer metaphor of self and selfhood, we can similarly describe each part of the division within the self as an *agent* which may attain to *agenthood* as it interacts with other agents within the self and the other while recognising these other agents as 'equal partners'.

Continuing with the metaphor of computing, this development of the agents to agenthood is associated with the development of *competencies* on the part of these agents. In studies of agent-orientated systems, the notions of agent and agency are thus inseparable from those of competence (Shoham, 1997). In our present essentialist view, then, each self has an *inner world*, which it normally experiences as something inseparable from its Being and is contained entirely within itself, and an *outer world* which it normally experiences as being entirely outside itself. The outer world includes the others with whom the self may conduct a discourse in their status as subjects, and other, and usually less animate, objects with which the self does not normally conduct a discourse. Then, roughly following Augustine (398//e.g. 1961):

> Reality is the name that the self gives to the interface between its inner and its outer worlds
> and a truth is the self's intimation of the oneness of these two worlds.

Thus, reality is only defined through the name of a something that may very well not be 'objectified', or 'made objective', or indeed may conceivable not even 'exist' at all. Entirely consentaneously, truth is defined in terms of an intimation that can only be 'objectified' or 'made objective' by well-chosen and illustrative descriptions of the special feelings of pleasure and satisfaction that it evokes within the self, which can again only be described and characterised in terms of its associated objects through the devices of a finely-tuned *rhetoric*. We refer to Augustine (398//e.g. 1961, and specifically sections IV.15; X.23; XI.3-7 and XII.25-32; see also Chisholm, 1966 and 1982, and Findlay, 1961) for the paradigmatic explanation of the processes of objectification in these cases. It is remarkable that the experience of truth so beautifully delineated by Augustine is reaffirmed even in the logical-positivistic writings of Henry James (*e.g.* 1976). The relation of this essentialist and experiential definition of truth to the experience of 'mathematical truth' is very well described in popular form by Huntley (1970).

Reverting now to the observation of the inner division of the self, as is commonly identified with various agencies, and thus agents, we see that there may be any number of realities and truths even within any one self and certainly over a considerable number and range of perceptions of the others. In everyday discussion we speak, using visual metaphors, of a multitude of 'points of view' or 'perspectives', and then essentially upon objects. Then:

> An object that is seen from a particular point of view or
> within a certain perspective is called a phenomenon.

The study of the ways in which the inner world of the individual self influences its view of its outer world, and how this in turn influences its own inner world again, is the subject of *phenomenology*. We can of course only speak about *a* truth: *the* truth, the Platonic *noumenon*, remains forever closed to us in this view.

We experience reality as extending over space and proceeding in time, while we usually experience truth as coming to presence in space and time. Now so long as we are treating of reality and truth in a purely modern-scientific manner, so that space is totally orderable, perfectly

---

one. Unmoving, it moves faster than the mind. The senses lag, but Self runs ahead. Unmoving, it outruns pursuit. Out of Self comes the breath that is the life of all things."

measurable, additive within a dimension and multiplicative over dimensions, and time is also totally orderable, perfectly measurable and additive, we feel no need to enquire further into the definitions of space and time. However, as soon as hydroinformatics moves out into its sociotechnical dimensions, these idealities of modern science become inadequate and we are obliged to consider our definitions of space and time much more carefully and generally. We then recall from Kant (ibid, p42//p71) that "Space is ... the subjective condition of sensibility under which alone outer intuition is possible for us". This space is then not even a component of content, but 'only' the necessary condition for the operations of content in its dealings with our outer world. How then is this to be objectified for the purpose of defining space? The solution of this problem was long sought, and was largely found, through the introduction of processes of *measurement*: space became definable just to the extent that it could be measured. Entirely consentaneously, *geometry*, as the first pure science, began with this means of definition through its ideal objectification of space. However, the *arithmetic* theories of measure – and even such a deviant theory as that of Whitehead (.e g. 1920) - demonstrate that 'an exact measurement' would necessitate an infinite thermodynamic entropy production, i.e. it would consume an infinite quantity of negentropy or 'free energy' (Kolmogorov and Fomin, 1961; Brillouin, 1956). An 'exact definition' is thus unrealisable. Apart from this, however, the hydroinformatician has, it seems, little to learn about the definition of space.

The situation regarding time, however, is of a much greater concern to the hydroinformatician, as well as to many others (see, for example, Wittgenstein, 1958, p26). For Kant (ibid, p46 // p74,75) "Time is a necessary representation that underlies all intuitions. ... Time is ... given *a priori*. In it alone is actuality of appearance possible at all. Appearances may, one and all, vanish: but time (as the condition of their possibility) cannot itself be removed." Thus the device of objectifying time by introducing measures of it directly, in imitation of space, is not possible: a further step in abstraction is required. This step, which appears to have dated back at least to Pharaonic Egypt, was to employ space as a source of metaphors for time. These metaphors were sought, and largely found, in the ever-changing positions of the sun, the moon, the planets and the stars relative to an observer on Earth, whereby measurements of distance could be used to provide measurements of time. By these means time could be objectified and thereby defined. This metaphor so impressed the ancient Greeks (who were very sensitive to such conceptual movements) that they could not ascribe it to any human agency, but only to that of a god, who they then called *Cronos*, and who was himself correspondingly the fruit of the union between the goddess of the Earth (*Gæa*) and the god of the Heavens (*Uranus*). Time which is measured and thus defined in this way is accordingly called *chronological time*. We employ the word *clock* generally for any device, artefactual or natural, that realises this correspondence between time and measurable representations in space. This time is clearly something quite other than time as it is experienced in our everyday affairs, which instead provides a wide variety of *experiential*, or *subjective*, times. Thus although the hydroinformatician working in a purely modern-scientific domain need be concerned only with chronological time, when working in the sociotechnical domain, which includes the ecological domain and in the domain, of the natural environment generally, he or she must take account of the times of human and other creatures' experiences, which are for much the greater part experiential, or 'subjective', times. Thus the hydroinformatician working with natural organisms and their habitats can for the most part only use chronological time for reference when reporting results, working otherwise with the experiential times of the organisms and their habitats. For example, the blossoming of certain plants may occur in April in one year and in February in another year, depending on the sequences of weather conditions which they experience. Only when the sequence of experiences is strongly influenced by the movement of the heavenly bodies, as occurs for example in tidal processes, or, more weakly and, over a longer span, with the intensity of solar radiation, do experiential and chronological times come into some kind of correspondence. (See, especially, Cloudsley-Thompson, 1978, and Palmer, 1978, and, more generally again, the whole work edited by Fraser *et al*, 1978.)

Appendix 2

THE FOURFOLD MEANS OF COMMUNICATION STARTING WITH SIGNS AND SYMBOLS

Communication is a process that the self conceives as proceeding backwards and forwards between its own inner world and the inner worlds of the other(s). This proceeds essentially through processes of *betokening*, in which either an object is given up in place of another object by the self to the other and is accepted as such by the other, or the other gives up an object in place of another object to the self and is accepted as such by the self. It is usual to distinguish four classes of betokening processes, and thereby four classes of tokens. We shall first distinguish the two of these which are of the most immediate relevance to our present theme. These are, from the point of view of the self:

1. Signs (in the strict sense).

A sign (in the strict sense) is a token that, when given up to the other *is replaced* by that which it evokes (and in this case *signifies*) in the mind of the other. Thus, to use a familiar metaphor, the sign is that object which introduces the entirely other object which it evokes (and in this case signifies) onto the stage of consciousness, and then, having done its job, steps back into the wings of the stage, leaving the stage entirely to the signified object. Its category thus has as the simplest form of sign function:

Sign function: betokening object $\to$ *betokened object* (4)

2. Symbols.

A symbol is a token that, when given up to the other, *replaces* that which it evokes (and in this case *symbolises*) in the mind of the other. In this case then, to continue with the previous metaphor, the symbol is that which, after introducing that which it evokes (and in this case symbolises) onto the stage of consciousness of the other, sends this, now symbolised object into the wings and takes over the role of this object itself. Thus, the symbol function proceeds in the opposite sense to the sign function. Its category takes the form:

Symbol function : betokened object $\to$ *betokening object* (5)

In Category Theory, the category obtained by reversing the direction of the arrows in a given category, as exemplified by (4) and (5), but then so that what was the target set in the one becomes the source set in the other, and *vice versa*, is said to be the *dual* of that given category. Thus, the *sign function* and the *symbolisation function* are seen to provide dual categories when the domain and the codomain of the one become, respectively, the codomain and domain of the other.

It may be useful to give two simple examples that will be familiar to most hydroinformaticians and indeed to engineers and scientists generally. The simplest of all partial differential equations is that which describes a continuous rectilinear translation or advection of any measure f with a velocity u along a direction x in time t. We represent this process by:

$$\frac{\partial f}{\partial t} + u \frac{\partial f}{\partial x} = 0 \qquad (6)$$

We can read this as a sign, in which case we are led to think about the physical process of advection occurring in space and time that is so signified. We can, however, equally well regard it as symbolising the process of advection, so that we can operate with this equation without ever thinking about what it 'means', the equation having now taken over the stage from all our thoughts of worldly processes. Thus, to make of this a second example, if $f = u$, interpreted as the momentum per unit mass that is being advected under these conditions, we could write (6) in a conservation form as:

$$\frac{\partial u}{\partial t} + \frac{\partial (u^2/2)}{\partial x} = 0 \qquad (7)$$

and then differentiate (7) to obtain the original form of (6):

$$\frac{\partial u}{\partial t} + u\frac{\partial u}{\partial x} = 0 \qquad (8)$$

In this operation of differentiation that produces (8) we do not care at all what f, t, x and u signify—they could signify anything at all for all that we care during this process—for we are only concerned with them as symbols that are adaptable to mathematical manipulation. They have completely taken over the stage in our attention. A more detailed discussion of the historical background and the social consequences of this symbolisation process in technology is provided by Abbott (1999). There it is seen to have provided a paradigm, called the *symbolic paradigm* in science and technology that has extended over a period in history that is called the *symbolic era*. Hydroinformatics is nowadays marked by a more general reaction to the ideology of that era. This reaction is identified at the technical level with *sub-symbolic processes*, as exemplified by artificial neural networks, many evolutionary algorithms, classification systems as exemplified by applications of support vector machines and the many other developments of this kind that so occupy the pages of the *Journal of Hydroinformatics*. Similarly, the engineer, and to a considerable extent the scientist too, nowadays work in socially-orientated applications for the most part with signs through the user interfaces of tools that encapsulate all the operations of symbolic processes, so that we may now speak of a *post-symbolic era* (Abbott et al, 2001).

Now it is commonly observed in Category Theory that the dual of a given category may describe a process that is very far removed conceptually from the process described by the given category. The category of signs and the category of symbols with interchanging domains and codomains are no exceptions in this respect. They obviously provide very different means to communicate, corresponding to very different intentions on the parts of the communicating agents, both from the side of the self and from the side of the other. The directed-graphical representation of the category of the communicating sign is then usually perceived as a tetradic structure as shown in Fig. 2:

We see that the arrow f in Fig. 2 corresponds to the composition f of the mappings f_1, f_2 and f_3, so that $f = f_1 f_2 f_3$, i.e. $f(\Box f) = f_3(f_2(f_1(\Box f_1))$ so that $\Box f = \Box f_1$.

Appendix 2

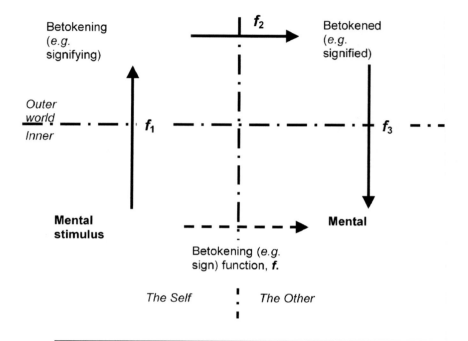

Figure 2. The tetradic structure of a betokening function, such as a sign function (adapted from Klinkenberg, 1996, p. 93)

Communication through the use of symbols in the mathematical sense nowadays proceeds for the most part in two directions, the one being between our own selves and the 'machine-other' and the second being between the productions of this 'machine-other' — which we may interpret as communications from the 'machine-other' — and our own *understanding* of how this device is actually functioning. The first is concerned with the representation of processes in symbolic forms suited to our own understanding and means of mental manipulation, as just exemplified above, and the translation of these into statements like numerical schemes, that are better adapted to the ways of working of our machines, as 'the others', and the programming of these latter forms into a working code. The most common aids to symbolic manipulation, or 'methods', are then those of elementary algebra and calculus, Taylor series and Fourier series, occasionally augmented by Fourier Transforms. The second direction of symbol-enabled communication is concerned with the self's own understanding of how its machine-other is functioning *in reality* on the basis of the productions of this machine. We then use much of the same methods, albeit in other ways. This process has been described further by Abbott (1993: see also Abbott and Basco, 1989).

We can provide categories for these two complementary processes by adapting the triadic structure used by some semioticians to represent the action of the token generally to represent the action of the symbol. In the first of the above cases this provides the category:

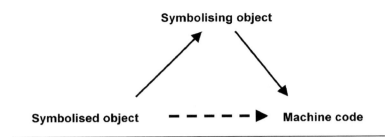

Figure 3. The encapsulation of knowledge in information

while in the second case it provides the category:

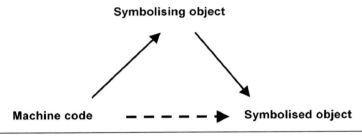

Figure 4. The interpretation of information as knowledge

In the first case, 'that which is significant', or 'has meaning' for the designer of the knowledge encapsulating device, is transformed into a machine-compatible code, which we may conceive, at least in metaphorical terms, as 'having meaning', and therefore 'being significant' to the machine. In the second case, certain outputs of the machine, and usually outputs from carefully chosen 'test rigs', are analysed by the designer in order to understand 'what the machine is really doing' under the instructions of his or her code (see Abbott and Minns, 1998, pp. 463-517). These two processes are again seen to produce categories that can be construed as dual. Once yet again, in this respect, we observe that they are markedly different processes and it is correspondingly often observed that a person with a high level of competence in the one may display a lesser competence in the other.

Of course, these processes are those followed by the 'tool builder': the user of the tool, the 'tool user', proceeds along a different path again when translating the output of the tool into actionable knowledge (Abbott, 1993).

It might at first appear as though the choice of which token should serve as a sign or as a symbol is quite arbitrary: it may appear as though anything at all may serve as a sign or as a symbol for almost anything at all to someone or the other. However, the classes of symbols must in fact differ from the classes of signs in ways that will facilitate their specific way of functioning as just described above. This can perhaps best be seen by first considering how symbols can most easily present themselves when 'taking over the stage' from that which they symbolise. This presentation must be such as to enhance their acceptability and thus their legitimacy as symbols rather than signs, for it is clear that whoever or whatever introduces itself onto the stage and then proceeds to take possession of the stage, as a symbol has to do, must exhibit some trait or traits of similarity to that which it symbolises. There must then be traits that are recognised by the audience of users, who are therefore more inclined to accept the legitimacy of the symbol, *qua* symbol. Referring back to the use of symbols in mathematics, and thence in science and technology, it is instructive to follow the origins of their selections. Taking first the example of the velocity, this was originally symbolised in its entirety, subsuming both its magnitude and its direction, by the first letter in /velocity/, or, more historically correctly, /*velocité*/ as v. The advantages of using orthogonal coordinate systems in mechanics led, before the introduction of tensor and vector notations, to the need to use three different letters, which gave rise to the use of u, v and w as the velocities along the x, y and z coordinate directions, the letters u, v and w then also being neatly sandwiched between x and the symbol long accepted for time, t. The symbol x in turn had much longer historical precedents as <<the unknown>>, being an entity which itself of course had to remain unknown only until it could be determined. But such digressions into the archaeology of scholastic thought must necessarily be truncated at this juncture. It is only necessary to understand that if science and technology had not been formulated primarily in French at the time when this usage came into practice, but instead had been formulated in another language, such as German, the notation would have been different. It is in this sense that the choice of symbols, as of signs also, is essentially arbitrary.

Similarly, but in less specialised contexts, /black/ for <<mourning>>, or /a weighing scale/ for <<justice>> all constitute symbols in that they take one or the other aspect of that which they symbolise, and use this to replace the symbolised object. It is by these means that these symbols attain to recognition as symbols, and thus their legitimacy as symbols, by those whose acceptance they require (see Klinkenberg, 1996, p. 189 and 193). Thus, the symbols are tokens possessing some socially accepted identifying element. In the theory of semiotics this process is described in terms of a *partitioning* of the symbolised object and a selection of one of the parts so as to provide a *correspondence* with one of the parts provided by a partitioning of the object that the symbol has to replace in the minds of its audience. The semiotician then speaks of a 'corresponding partition' (*découpage correspondant*) that applies in the case of the symbols. Which parts are chosen in this process still remains arbitrary, however, and there is no intrinsic motivation to adopt any one particular correspondence over another.

In the case of the sign, no such device is necessary, since the sign, as a signifying object that has now done its job, hands over the stage to the signified object, which is legitimate in its own right. Thus, the sign, having fulfilled its purpose, is legitimised by what it has already done, while the signified object is legitimised simply by virtue of its presence in consciousness. For example, if u signifies a fluid velocity, this fluid velocity itself stands in no need of any legitimising feature. The semiotician in this case speaks of a 'non-corresponding partition' (*découpage non correspondant*). Otherwise, however, signs can in principle be chosen just as arbitrarily as symbols.

CONTINUING TO INDICATORS
An indicator is a token that is chosen by virtue of its resemblance to a particular attribute of the object which it betokens, so that it is determined by a process of correspondence with an element in the partition of the betokened object. By virtue of the legitimacy thus attained, the indicator can take over the stage from the object which it indicates, so that it functions in this sense in the manner of a symbol. However, unlike the symbol, the choice of the particular element that constitutes an indicator is now highly motivated, or even determined, by this resemblance. Thus, an indicator resembles a symbol in the sense that it is defined by a corresponding partition of the betokened object and can thereby replace the betokened object in our thoughts, but it differs from a symbol in that it is defined in a quite highly motivated, rather than in a relatively arbitrary, way. The examples of /smoke/ for <<fire>> and /green/ for <<environmental protection>> are examples of indicators. More pertinent to our present interests is the example of the indication of a velocity vector in a graphical user interface. This may be indicated by an arrow or a blob with a

line element, but there are scarcely any other alternatives that are sufficiently motivated to provide the required indication.

As established in the definitive work on the origins of logical thought by Husserl (1900/1901//1970) and as subsequently developed by Husserl and several other phenomenologists, indicators are described and analysed at a much great depths than can possibly be followed here, but then taking on more of the nature as well as the name of *indicative signs*. Although 'indicators' and 'indicative signs' are not, strictly speaking, synonymous, and despite the corresponding risk of confusion on the semiotics side of our subject, it will be more advantageous in the present context to use the term 'indicative signs' instead of 'indicators' (see, for example, Husserl, 1938/1948//1973, pp. 235 *et seq.*). Signs in the strict sense, which are not 'indicators' or 'indicative signs' but have an expressive power, are then called *expressive signs*.

CONCLUDING WITH ICONS

Icons resemble signs in that they point towards and thereby introduce a something else, which they therefore signify; correspondingly they are generated through non-corresponding partitions. However, unlike signs in general, which are tokens that can be chosen in a relatively arbitrary way, icons are tokens the choice of which is more or less strongly motivated by the nature of their respective signified objects.

Klinkenberg (*loc cit*, p. 193) gives the examples of a photocopy, the reflection in a mirror and an architectural plan, among others. Icons have a special significance in hydroinformatics when they are used to symbolise selfhood. A video clip of a flock of birds alighting upon an open stretch of clear blue water (preferably accentuated by framing this event within glittering ice-flows or lush vegetation!) provides an example of an icon that directs our minds towards the "primal purity of nature in all its naturalness", whereby the birds in particular became imbued with an own selfhood, and thereby enter into another and higher value system in our estimation. The video clip is strongly motivated, but it does not constitute a 'mere' indicator—the frame of ice-flows or vegetation serves that purpose—but it points towards a something that is much deeper and more profound. In terms of its semiosis, the partition at the level expressed by <<the visual image of the alighting birds>> proceeds independently of any partition of the intrinsic value of the life-world of these creatures in the fullness of their selfhood. This example illustrates what are generally called the *technologies of persuasion*, such as are necessary adjuncts to any activities of the hydroinformatician working in the social sphere (see Thorkilsen and Dynesen, 2001).

THE GENERAL TYPOLOGY OF TOKENS

We have concentrated here on a division of tokens according to their different functions, but we have also tried to sketch the way to a more architectonic typology in terms of the differences in motivations and correspondences of partitions of these tokens relative to those objects which they betoken. Concentrating more on this latter aspect, (Klinkenberg *loc cit*, p. 189) provides the following table:

	Motivated	Arbitrary
Corresponding partitions	Indices or indicative signs	Symbols
Non-corresponding partitions	Icons	Signs in the strict sense

Table 1

When we discussed the dictionary and the necessary incompleteness of dictionaries within the confines of linguistics, we observed that there were some meanings which could be expressed by tokens—that in this case were words—and others that could not. The question naturally arises, and has been discussed in one way or the other for centuries, as to whether a more general process of semiosis would allow for *every* meaning to be represented. Would it ever be possible to construct even so much as a model of an ideal dictionary that would provide bijective mappings between the representation of objects and the represented meanings of these representations? Already in hydroinformatics practice we observe the use of images, that are nowadays usually coloured and are becoming increasingly dynamic, to induce meanings into the minds of those who should be persuaded of certain ways of proceeding rather than other ways of proceeding in the worlds of the waters. More recently, this process has started to move further again, to providing means for the others to express themselves on matters of water and the environment, with a similarly extended arsenal of semiotic devices at their command (*e.g.*, Jonoski, 2002). We shall return to this issue in a moment when we consider the use of words from different languages in a single text, and again when we speak further of the technologies of persuasion.

We may distinguish two major streams of thought that have developed concerning the matter of the completeness of the set of betokening-to-betokened functions over the last century. The one, already identified here by the name of logical positivism, as associated with authors ranging from Mach to Carnap, proposed a project whereby every meaning within a specific—and most commonly mathematical—language should be expressible, with the implicit corollary that every question that was posed within this language should be decidable through the construction of a suitable algorithm, called a *decision procedure* (see, for example, Carnap, 1934//1937, and, by way of retrospection, 1954). From this point of view, language is a completely human construct, and thereby totally subject to the workings of human reasons. The other, opposing, stream of thought, as initiated in the nineteenth century by Kierkegaard, Schopenhauer and Nietzsche, and represented in more recent times in 'the West' by the phenomenologists and existentialists on the more philosophical side and several socially-engaged churchmen on the theological side, castigated this project and opposed it at every turn (see, for example, John Paul II, 1999). From their perspective, mankind is just as much a product of language as language is a product of mankind. As Wittgenstein expressed this matter, not only is the ritual of the myth a form of language, but every language of a society implicitly contains all the myths of the society as residues of the primal truths learnt over eons of time that are automatically passed on to those who learn and further employ the language: "Our language is an embodiment of ancient myths... A whole mythology is deposited in our language" (see Rhees, 1982).

We may then define a *natural language* of a social group as the sum of the means necessary to express the myths of the group, understood as the repositories of the most profound truths of the group. The spontaneity of the emergence of the so-called 'Green', 'Ecological' and 'Environmental' movements, such as may be directed to the welfare of all manner of creatures as well as to our fellow human beings, cannot be understood in any other way than this. *The language of hydroinformatics as it proceeds further into its sociotechnical dimensions (which again include its ecological and general-environmental dimensions) thus itself becomes increasingly a natural language.* It follows that although it may make use of scientific languages as means for accessing its scientific 'assets', as exemplified here by the use of fragments of Category Theory and Object Theory, it cannot remain constrained to scientific language as it goes about its work in the real world.

The consequences for hydroinformatics of the adoption of the present position are momentous in the extreme, leading for example to a complete reversal of the so far established paradigm of decision-making in society by placing a new emphasis on the use of narrative discourse as the immediate expression of natural language (see, for example, the questionings of Durning, 1999, de Jong, 1999, and Hoppe, 1999, on the side of Policy Analysis; and the consequences drawn by Abbott and Jonoski, 2001, and Jonoski, 2002, on the side of hydroinformatics).

It should be observed, corresponding to this on the side of definitions, that one of the classics of logical-positivistic thought, the *Principia Mathematica* of Whitehead and Russel (1910/1925), defined a definition in a quite different way than that employed here. Thus (*ibid*, vol. 1, p.11) "A definition is a declaration that a certain newly-introduced symbol or combination of symbols is to mean the same as a certain combination of symbols of which the meaning is already known". The approach that is followed in this case is thus again purely prescriptive, and continues in the same vein over all aspects of definitions (*ibid*, vol. 1, pp. 11-26).

The programme of logical positivism, extending even to the requirement of 'exact definitions' and 'infallible proofs' in mathematics, has been rejected by many, if not most, practising mathematicians. An unparalleled exposition of this dispute in its mathematical context is provided by Lakatos (1976/1979).

MODELS

We may now define a model in the very general terms that our subject requires as follows:

A model M of an object x, denoted by M(x), is that which provides a set of indicative signs (i_1, i_2, ..., i_j, ..., i_{jj}) all of which have x as their referent and which can be operated upon by a function of the mind, mod(x), to provide an expressive sign e, = e(x), that expresses a truth about the object x.

Thus, more formally:

M = M(x) if and only if M(x) provides (i_1, i_2, ..., i_j, ..., i_{jj}) such that:

$$mod(x) : (i_1, i_2, \ldots, i_j, \ldots i_{jj}) \to e \qquad (9)$$

where that which is expressed by e = e(x) is true of x.

Put another way again, only when $M(x)$ provides a set of indicative signs that constitute the domain $\{\Box mod(x)\}$ of some $mod(x)$ does it constitute a model for x. It is easily seen that this definition applies to all conventional applications of /model/, such as /an artist's model/, a /model-year of a particular motor car/, a /physical model/, a /numerical model/, or even, when properly formulated, a /data model/. It also, however, casts such less obvious objects as /geographies/, /histories/, /legends/, /sagas/, /myths/ and many others as models when the mappings also impose particular kinds of spatial differentiations (such as by the use of different colourings), or total or partial ordering in experiential and chronological times, upon the indicative signs (Abbott, 1992). To return to our more mundane earlier examples, a collection of velocity vectors on a monitor screen may express in the mind of the viewer the existence of isolated circulations, or trains of eddies, or local tidal races or other features of a flow in a physical prototype. If the expression $e=e(x)$ truly expresses such a meaning, so that $mod(x)$ can provide a 'reading of a meaning' into the set of indicative signs (such that the presence of this meaning in the inner world of the modeller coincides with the outer-world experience of the modeller, whereby this modeller has an intimation of the oneness of these two experiences) then the device that provides the set of indicative signs constitutes a model. The structure induced by the function $mod(x)$ is shown in Fig. 5.

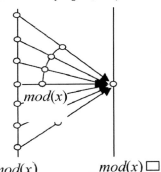

Figure 5. The category generated by *mod(x)*

In the event that a device provides a set of indicative signs appertaining to an object x for which no function $mod(x)$ exists, then this set is said to constitute *data* for x. The construction and operation of devices for evolving functions $mod(x)$ from data for x is already an important part of hydroinformatics, called *data mining for knowledge discovery*. (See Babovic and Keizer, 2000.)

It is seen that, since the codomain contains one and only one element for any one $mod(x)$, the system composed of the function $mod(x)$ with the indicative signs as domain and the expression sign as codomain must again constitute a category. We may of course only refer to *a* model of x, because, in principle, there may be any number of individual models of x corresponding to different choices of the domain and codomain of $mod(x)$ in the category.

We observe that this definition of a model may appear to differ from the popular one. Most persons would suppose that a model already exists if it simply provides a set of indicative signs, but all existing dictionary usages insist that, however and whatever indicative signs are provided, that which provides them does not constitute a model unless these indicative signs can be associated in the mind to provide meaning. Thus:

'No capacity to induce meaning: no model'

Accordingly, to continue our earlier example, it is only if the observer of a field of velocity vectors is able to distinguish such relevant features as circulations, eddies, vortex streets and tidal races that a model exists. Further to this again, all existing usages insist that the meaning provided by the expressive sign must in this physical case be true relative to the observed state of the outside world. Thus, we have further:

'No capacity to induce truth: no model'

In the practice of *numerical modelling*, it is unusual for the truth of the expressive statement to impress itself on the mind of the modeller on the basis of the indicative signs that are first produced by the machine. Usually the code is run repeatedly under different sets of assumptions in such a way that, on average, the expressive sign increases its veracity during the sequence of runs. Each model-object is then a consequence of a preceding model-object and in turn provides a precedent for a succeeding model-object again. Following Meinong, we then speak again of a sequence of *implected* objects (see, more definitively, Abbott, 2000). A more common term nowadays is that of 'nested objects', but these are really quite different entities: 'nested' has the connotation of the one object being *contained* within the successor-object, while 'implected' has the connotation of the one object being *woven into the very fibre* of the successor-object. When an intimation of truth is attained—by whatever means—that is adequate for supporting the intentions of the modeller, this implection process is ended, at which point the sequence of implected objects is said to be *closed*.

The process of implection carried out on the objects employed to provide the indicative signs whereby the modeller arrives at his or her truth is the process that is called *calibration*. The model that is provided by the closure of this process of implection is said to be *validated*. If, for example, the sequential inundation of a land area is observed in a model to take 6 hours and it is known from experience that it should take 60 hours, then again no model exists—even though in that case the model might still signify that we should be looking askance at the infiltration rates into the soil and indeed of the entire modelling of the subsurface flows. In this case the model has not been calibrated and thus cannot have been validated either.

It follows further that a device, such as an artificial neural network, that has been trained to transform, for example, rainfall recordings into runoff records with a good agreement with observations, does not as it stands constitute a model, since no meaning can be adduced from it for the observed behaviour. Of course, such a device may be very valuable in practice and its predictions may be accurate, and so true, but it is not a model in terms of the centuries-long established definition. At another extreme, we observe that the curve of a graph can sometimes be construed as a model when it provides an expressive sign.

We observe further that models of different classes may have to be connected together through compositions of their mapping functions in order to provide expressive signs and thus to function as models at all. Thus, for example, a numerical-hydraulic 'model' may provide a water depth of one meter at a certain place, but the true significance of this—what it really expresses to the human-other—only emerges when this place is identified within a geographical context. It is essentially because of this feature that so much effort has been expended on providing seamless interfaces between numerical-hydraulic models and geographical information systems (GISs). The numerical hydraulic model is in this case still a model, but then only because it provides an expressive sign through the agency of the artefactual GIS-other.

KNOWLEDGE

Hydroinformatics is nowadays very taken up with knowledge, seeing in the provision and exchange of knowledge means to improve the state of the world through improvements in the employment of its waters (Abbott and Jonoski, 2001). The case of the model, and with this the modelling process encapsulated in the function $mod(x)$ in (9) above, illustrates a process of a taking up of objects into consciousness within a medium of content, and the application of transformations, or mappings, upon these objects together with the products of these transformations or mappings. Such processes must then necessarily alter the inner world of the self in which they occur, and then, further, they may alter the outer world of that self by the actions of the self upon the others that follow from this self's own inner world modifications. The impressions again of these outer world changes upon the inner world of the self complete a cycle of development that, ideally at least, should repeat itself in the general development of selfhood. Of course, this ideal process remains always incomplete in practice.

The changes that occur in the inner world of the self through this implection process and which change the way in which the self behaves relative to its outer world are naturally associated with the notion that the self changes its 'inner state' by acquiring something. This something that causes these observable changes is, as a first approximation, that which we call 'knowledge'. Since the 'acquisition of knowledge' is essential to the self in its striving towards selfhood, 'knowledge' is then necessarily existential, that is, it is inseparable from the Being of the self.

Theology, of course, expands upon this again, by extending the notion of knowledge to comprehend the direct intimation of reality and truth outside of the direct conscious experiences of the self. This is still necessarily realised by an outside agency, and in this perspective by virtue of *grace*, such as is inseparable from a state of the inner world of the self which is called *faith*. The relations are then expressed in the formula of Anselm, of *Credo ut intelligum*, or "Faith precedes knowledge". Several existential and phenomenological philosophers have extended this formula outside of its theological origins and into the sphere of the secular. We may then broaden the definition of knowledge so as to comprehend all such positions as follows (Barth, 1938-1950/1961, p. 188):

> "*By the knowledge of an object by men we understand confirmation of their acquaintance with its reality in respect of its existence and its nature. ... Their acquaintance with it, instead of being a contingent and outward determination of their own existence, now becomes a necessary and inward determination. Knowing, they are affected by the object known. They no longer exist without it but with it... ...Whatever else and however else they may think of it, they must begin by thinking of the truth of its reality. ...Its truth has come home to them, has become their own. And in the process they themselves have become the truth's. This event, this confirmation, in contrast to mere cognizance, we call knowledge. Cognizance becomes knowledge when man becomes a responsible witness to its content.*"

We observe that as soon as we regard our fellow creatures as subjects we commonly project our own experiences of knowledge acquisition and employment on to these creatures also. We then suppose that such functions as $def(x)$ and $mod(x)$ are not confined to humans alone, but are shared with many other, and possibly all, our fellow creatures, albeit using very different semiotics to those that we employ and which have been introduced here.

Appendix 2

INFORMATION IN RELATION TO EDUCATION AND TRAINING

Information in the present sense can only have the form of tokens that are presented to the self into which knowledge is to be induced. Information can then only be transformed into knowledge to the extent that the vehicles for mapping betokening objects into betokened objects—and specifically the sign functions, symbol functions, indicator functions and icon functions—are already present as knowledge within the self. Thus, the acquisition of knowledge through the provision of information presupposes the presence of another knowledge again that will implement this acquisition. In hydroinformatics, as in several other disciplines besides, we refer to such an enabling knowledge as a *knowledge frame* (Abbott, 1993). It is this knowledge frame which contains the various functions that provide meaning to the tokens that are presented to the self within any such *learning* context or situation, and all transformations from information in the form of tokens to the corresponding knowledge must occur within the one or the other such frame. We also often say that the new knowledge *comes to presence* within its corresponding knowledge frame. This process is clearly also recursive: all new knowledge that comes to presence may provide, and indeed will commonly provide, enhancements of existing knowledge frames, and even new knowledge frames again. When regarded as objects, the knowledge frames are again always incomplete objects, but, to the extent that knowledge is accumulated, the previous such incomplete objects become implected in the succeeding, so to say, 'less incomplete', object.

These objects also always remain incomplete in the real world, but each successive object absorbs and subsumes its predecessor as more and more knowledge is assimilated. When the acquisition of knowledge in this way is associated in its turn with an agent of the self, its manifestation is the development of an increased outer world competence. We observe, still following Meinong's terminology, that the process of implection may stop when a certain desired or acceptable level of competence is attained, in which case the set of implected objects is once yet again said to be *closed*. When this process is confined to one or only a few agents, we speak of *training*. In the case that this development extends over more, and even many, agents, so that the set of implected objects remains *open*, we speak instead of *education*. Thus, in its primitive sense, /training/ applies to a development of one aspect or agency of the self towards selfhood, which can be completed in time, while /education/ is associated with a movement of the self as such towards its selfhood, a condition which is hardly ever completed in time. Education is then essentially a drawing out of the inherent capacities of the self. In either event, *information is that which has the capacity to augment the knowledge of the self and thus induce the development of the self towards its selfhood*. For the genesis of these now well-rehearsed formulations in the era of Enlightenment, see Hume (1739/2000, *e.g.*, pp. 286-290).

The requirement of Enlightenment and indeed of the entire modern movement of which Enlightenment was one part, that everything in the world should be ordered, numbered and computed, or even more, as Spinoza expressed the matter most succinctly, that "the whole world should be reduced to a tautology", has led to the discipline of *information theory*, as celebrated in the works of such as Szilard, Shannon and Brillouin. Although the definitions of /information/ given by these authors obviously has its own relevance, they are, on the one hand, so well known and, on the other hand, so specialised, that we shall not discuss them here. (See, at its broadest range, Brillouin, 1956).

Clearly, information in its functioning is itself a function of content, so that its definition necessitates objectification, which in this case is easily available in the sense that the Latin *informare* derives from the infinitives *to shape, to form* an idea of, or *to de-scribe*. As it is assimilated into knowledge, information is that which shapes objects, forming them within the matrix of content so as to provide circum-scribing descriptions as elements of thought. Thus, the processes just introduced correspond to those which we commonly identify with *communication* between the self and the other and *vice versa*. Communication presuppose the existence of channels and tokens that are shared between the self and the other and, being so shared, they are held in common by both: 'speaking together' always implies the presence of a common language. (See, further to this, Heidegger, 1939/1971).

The process that proceeds in the opposite direction to that of 'information→knowledge' is that whereby knowledge becomes represented in tokens, whereby 'knowledge→information'. The knowledge concerned in this latter case is then said to be *encapsulated* in the respective tokens, as already introduced above.

Corresponding to the division of the self and the formation of its various agents with their different agencies or *faculties*, knowledge has long been divided into different parts, commonly called *disciplines*. Each one presupposes a particular configuration of the inner world of the self, so that each constitutes 'a world in itself', so to say. The collection of all such actual and real worlds is then said to constitute a *universe*. Thus, an institution directed to the development of selfhood irrespective of the geographical origins of the individual selves was originally intended to accommodate all these worlds as *faculties*, so as to constitute a *university*.

UNDERSTANDING AS A PRODUCT OF PREDICATIVE JUDGEMENT
Clearly, understanding is something else, and mostly something more than knowledge, just as to understand someone is something else and usually something more than simply knowing them.

In the case of understanding, which we conceive as situated, so to say, 'on the other side of knowledge' from that of information, the mode of objectification is apparent simply from the meaning of the decomposition of the words used to represent it. For example, we may have metaphoric objectifications in terms of standing—*for-staa* in Danish, *under-stand* in English, *ver-stehen* in German—and in terms of taking or taking hold of something—*com[me]-prendre* in French and *be-grijpen* in Dutch. In its relation to knowledge, understanding clearly occurs when knowledge becomes the subject of predication. Thus, from the time of the Englightenment, with Hume (1739-40/1999, *e.g.* p. 15), understanding was conceived as the faculty of factual reasoning or reasoning from experience, where reason was in turn understood as the faculty of immediate intuition and demonstration. In the more general terms employed here, we may regard understanding as *that process occurring within the self which changes the knowledge of the self in the direction of advancing its selfhood without the acquisition of further information from outside the self*. Of course, information by its very nature can initiate, and promote this process, and this function of information is of the greatest relevance to hydroinformaticians when they wish to induce understanding, but the process of understanding is different in kind to the processes of communication, of 'information→knowledge'. *Understanding arises only when knowledge works upon itself in the direction of advancing the self in the direction of its fulfilment in selfhood.*

JUDGEMENTS
It is only through the faculty of understanding that anything like a token can have 'meaning', so that /meaning/ in the sense of a definition presupposes the presence of this faculty. Since the times and works of Husserl (as exemplified here by 1938/1948//1973) it has been usual to identify the transformation 'knowledge→understanding' with the process of making judgements, which are then necessarily predicative judgements. Husserl, as usual, is unsurpassed in his description of the process involved in terms of objects and their objectification (*op. cit.* p.62):

> "*Objectification* is thus always an *active achievement of the ego*, an active believing cognisance of that of which we are aware, this something being *one* and continuously the *same* through the continuous extension of consciousness in its duration. It is that which is identified in distinct acts which form a synthesis; in this synthesis we are aware of it as the same, as that which can always be recognized, or also as that which is freely repeatable in recollections or freely producible in perceptions (when we go there and take one more look). It is precisely this identity, as the correlate of an identification to be carried out in an open, boundless, and free repetition, which constitutes the *pregnant concept of an object*. Just as every other praxis has its practical goal, the that-about-

Appendix 2

> which of the act, so the existing object is, as existing, the goal of the doxical, the act of cognition, the act which explicates the existent in its modes of being, which are here called determinations. To be sure, it is really only on the higher level that the *confirmation* [*Feststellung*] of the existent, of its how and what, which constitutes the objectifying function of the judgment, becomes a confirmation to which we can return again and again and, as such, a permanent possession of knowledge. This is the level of the act of predicative judgment, the sedimentation of which is found in the declarative statement. As the sedimentation of a store of knowledge, this confirmation is freely available, preservable, and communicable. Only the act of predicative judgment creates this store of knowledge and the objects of knowledge in the pregnant sense of the term, and not the act of judgment typical of merely receptive contemplation, although the latter already creates knowledge which persists as habitual. *Every act of predicative judgment is a step in which a permanent store of knowledge is produced.* It is in itself a complete step in determination ... and the primal cell of thematic determination."

A judgement is thus made on the basis of the information available at the moment of judgement, and often the judgemental act is deferred so as to access as much information as possible in the time available. We often therefore speak of making a judgement on the basis of the available *facts*. These facts are, consentaneously, those which the self considers desirable, or even necessary, in the making of its judgement. The self then makes its judgements based upon its own beliefs about itself and the facts that it has available that it considers (or 'judges to be') relevant, and it does this by taking an *attitude* towards these facts. It is only on the basis of this attitude towards the facts that it proceeds to a judgement. We may then formalise each such process most simply as a string of inferences, as follows:

$$(beliefs, facts) \rightarrow attitudes \rightarrow judgements \rightarrow decisions \rightarrow actions \qquad (10)$$

where both the action and the facts are observables and, of course, the <<action>> may subsume also a total inaction.

We now see that, whereas (10) represents the simplest judgement process about things, including 'the other', as facts, the self's judgement about the underlying beliefs of the other, as an *understanding* of the other, corresponds to the same structure but with the arrows reversed:

$$(beliefs, facts) \leftarrow attitudes \leftarrow judgements \leftarrow decisions \leftarrow actions \qquad (11)$$

where now, however, both the action and the facts are observables. The set of all mappings of the form of (11) covering all judgement-related agencies of the other are then said to constitute a *profile* of the other (Abbott, 2000). We observe that (11) with interchangeability between domains and codomains would appear to behave as the dual of (10). A judgemental process is then said to be *transparent* to the self if the inference strings in both (10) and (11) are simultaneously available and can be called to presence at will within the mind of the self.

(We cannot resist observing, in passing, that the duality of (10) and (11) corresponds to Kierkegaard's celebrated aphorism that "we live our life forward, but we understand it backwards").

JUDGEMENT ENGINES, FACT ENGINES AND ADVICE-SERVING SYSTEMS
A *judgement engine* is a device that takes the profile of the other and the sociotechnical facts relevant to the situation of the other as input and which provides a judgement upon the best course of action of the other as output. A *fact engine* is any device that feeds the judgement engine with the facts that this judgement engine requires. Generally, a judgement engine is served by several fact engines of different kinds, such as, on its scientific-technical side, data networks, numerical models, sub-symbolic models, GIS's, GPS's, cartographic coordinate

transformation systems and devices for interpreting the products of remote sensing devices, such as those of satellites, aerial photography and weather radars.

A system composed of one or more judgement engine(s) that can accommodate a range of profiles of the others involved in a project, and which is fed by facts that are relevant to the project, constitutes an *advice-serving system* if its actions are in the form of items of advice directed towards these others involved in the project. We observe that the judgement engines of advice-serving systems must normally incorporate encapsulated knowledge (Abbott and Jonoski, 2001; Jonoski, 2002).

SCIENCE, TECHNOLOGY AND SOCIETY: SCIENTIFIC, TECHNOLOGICAL AND SOCIETAL DISCOURSES

Among the worlds into which the self may divide itself there are three which are of primary importance to hydroinformatics. These are the worlds of *science, technology* and *society*. Each has its own way of communicating, and so its own way of using tokens, corresponding to a scientific discourse, a technological discourse and a social discourse, which last may itself cover a range of overlapping discourses. There is a tendency from the side of semioticians to identify the divisions themselves with differences in the respective discourses and we cannot be indifferent to this tendency here, but must again try to accommodate it.

Science can be defined rather conventionally as that activity of the Self that is directed to the accumulation of knowledge within all possible worlds, whether real or unreal, so long as this knowledge is true. As introduced in Chapter 1 above, this accumulation is commonly realised through the production of collections of propositions, so that we define a science conventionally as a totality established through an interconnection of true propositions. Each individual science can then be regarded as the body of knowledge that is expressed by, or encapsulated in, this totality. The study of physically unreal worlds that none the less possess 'inner truths' has long and increasingly constituted a part of mathematics, essentially the part commonly called 'pure'—but it has also penetrated deeply into certain parts of the physical sciences over the last century (see Lyotard, 1979, *e.g.* p. 13//1984, *e.g.* p. 73):

There is then a science of the outer world, with disciplines ranging from anthropology to astronomy and from biology to business, and so on through the alphabet, and there is a science of the inner world, ranging over disciplines like the many branches of 'pure' mathematics, a variety of logics, various systems of law, the manifold 'systems' of psychology and many, many other. There is then also a long established division between the scientific studies of society, called the *social sciences*, and of scientific studies of nature, called the *natural sciences*. It has further been usual, since the teachings and writings of Brentano (as developed between 1862/1960 and 1889-1915/1930) to divide the natural sciences into worlds dealing with animate nature, which is characterised by the presence of *intention* in its objects, making of them *intentional objects*, and a world dealing with inanimate objects, which are supposed to have no such intentions. Accordingly, the studies of living beings proceeds through analyses of their intentions, commonly leading to the identification of structures of intentionality, while the studies of the inanimate world do not (nowadays) follow this course at all. The manner in which the natural sciences have passed through a geometric era and a symbolic era over the last millennium and the way in which they are now being taken into a post-symbolic era is described in Abbott (1999).

Technology is that activity of the mind that is directed to creation in all the different worlds within which it applies itself. There is then again a division, but now between a technology of the outer world, as appears to be all too familiar, and a technology of the inner world, as represented by such disciplines as psychiatry and—of primary importance to hydroinformaticians—by what have already been illustrated as the technologies of persuasion. We may then again recall the already so much quoted definition of Heidegger (1963//1977, pp. 12, 13; see also Abbott, 1991, p, 6):

> "Technology is therefore no mere means. Technology is a way of revealing. If we give head to this, then another whole realm of the essence of technology will open itself up to us. It is the realm of revealing, *i.e.* of truth.
>
> This prospect strikes us as strange. Indeed, it should do so, should do so as persistently as possible and with so much urgency that we will finally take seriously the simple question of what the name 'technology' means. The word stems from the Greek. *Technikon* means that which belongs to *technç*. We must observe two things with respect to the meaning of this word. One is that *technç* is the name not only for the activities and skills of the craftsman, but also for the arts of the mind and the fine arts. *Technç* belongs to bringing-forth, to *poiçsis*; it is something poietic [creative, formative, productive, active].
>
> The other point that we should observe with regard to *technç* is even more important. From earliest times until Plato the word *technç* is linked with the word *epistçmç*. Both words are names for knowing in the widest sense. They mean to be entirely at home in something, to understand and be expert in it. Such knowing provides an opening up ...
>
> Technology is a mode of revealing. Technology comes to presence in the realm where revealing and unconcealment take place, where *alçtheia*, truth, happens."

Away and beyond these worlds there are others again, which are those of the study of the human condition, and especially of this condition as it is experienced within its various social settings. These are the worlds of *the humanities*. Among the traditional studies in this latter field are those already mentioned as *rhetoric*. The relations between—and primarily the contrasts between—rhetorical and scientific discourse is well covered by Klinkenberg (1996, pp. 365-376).

As it moves increasingly into paradigms of communication within society, hydroinformatics takes on more and more the form and substance of a *sociotechnology*.

> *Sociotechnologies are worlds where social and technological aspects have become so woven together to provide the very fabric of these worlds that they have become inseparable in thought.*

A useful metaphor for the sociotechnical is that of a beam that spans between two columns, which are those of the social and the technical. This beam is then a quite other kind of structure than are the columns upon which it is supported. As explained in Abbott (1996, 1999), it is this sociotechnical dimension of hydroinformatics that makes of it a *postmodern technology*, with all the consequences—and literature!—that follow from that position.

GEREDE

Gerede is a German word that has within its various accepted meanings one that is not provided by any English word. It can only be expressed in English at all in such more or less derogatory terms as *gossip, chatter and idle talk*, and indeed it is often translated into English in this way. However, *Gerede* has also a more technical, non-derogatory sense, which is also much more profound, and indeed even possessing certain quite sinister connotations. Its now classical characterisation is that of Heidegger (1927, pp. 167-180//1962, pp. 211-224).

Gerede is a form of discourse in which the persons participating suffer a degradation of selfhood so that the quality of the discourse is degraded correspondingly. *Gerede* is that process which causes a group of persons, all of completely reasonable intelligence, to arrive at decisions which many of these persons individually would consider inappropriate when thinking independently. *Gerede* is that process which causes a group of persons of unimpeachable character to decide upon a project that must appear as in some sense dishonest to several of them when they later come to think about it individually. *Gerede*, however, has in itself nothing whatsoever to do with stupidity or dishonesty, but belongs to a category all of its own. Neither can it be neatly bracketed as some kind of collective trance or hallucination induced by the discoursing, for it has none of the usual attributes of states of trance or hallucination. Neither again does it involve any kind of conspiracy: the nominal 'leading figures' in any such movement are just as surely taken down with the movement when it founders as are any of its other participants. The nominal 'leaders' of such movements may certainly know how to lead them, but, as Carl Jung so succinctly expressed their predicament (1944//1953) "One cannot possess this kind of knowledge without being oneself possessed by it". If one tried to characterise it in simple terms at all, one could only say that it arises when the pleasure of sociability, and especially of social conformity, overcomes the pleasure of truth in those participating in the discourse, but that is surely too superficial also. This discourse is of course by no means restricted to the spoken word, but extends, and indeed persists for the most part, in written form.

Gerede has always been prevalent in processes of collective decision making, but perhaps never more so than at the present time. *Gerede* may take hold of a group of persons that may range from a few individuals to whole groups of nations, leading to the destruction of much that previous generations had accomplished.

The current movements directed to studies of 'ozone layer depletion' and of global warming through the emission of 'greenhouse-promoting gasses' (already a 100 million dollar a year enterprise) provide several excellent examples of *Gerede*. The quite devastating critique of so-called 'development aid' by Easterly (2001) illustrates the malign influences of *Gerede* again, but at much larger scales of expenditure. Of more immediate interest here, however, is the form of *Gerede* which does so much damage to disciplines. Thus, for example (Klemes, 1986):

> "Hydrology, having no solid foundation of its own and moving clumsily along on an assortment of crutches borrowed from different disciplines, has always been an easy victim of this practice. Every mathematical tool has left behind a legacy of misconceptions invariably heralded as scientific breakthroughs. The Fourier analysis, as was pointed out by Yevjevich (in 1968), had seduced the older generation of hydrologists into decomposing hydrologic records into innumerable harmonics in the vain hope that their reconstruction would facilitate prediction of future hydrologic fluctuations (fortunately few computers were available at the time so that the Fourier fever did not become an epidemic); various statistical methods developed for evaluation of differences in repeatable experiments have been misused to create an illusion of a scientific analysis of unrepeatable hydrologic events; linear algebra has served to transform the idea of a unit hydrograph from a crude but useful approximation of a soundly based concept into a pretentious masquerade of spurious rigor now exercised in the modelling of flood events; time series analysis has been used to remake inadequate 20-year stream flow records into 'adequate' 1000-year records, or even more adequate 10,000-year records, and the theory of pattern recognition is now being courted in the vain hope that it will lend scientific legitimacy to the unscientific concept of mindless fitting that dominates contemporary hydrologic modelling. In all these cases, mathematics has been used to redefine a hydrologic problem rather than to solve it."

To this list we can now add the current frequent misuses of sub-symbolic devices in which all manner of 'strong relations' are established between data sets which in physical reality cannot possibly be much related at all. Corresponding as it does to a reduction of selfhood and thus of agenthood, *Gerede* is most commonly identified subsequent to the failures that it produces as *incompetence*.

Among the means developed to combat *Gerede*, probably the best known and the most publicised is that of *deconstruction*. Deconstruction is the process of subverting *Gerede* with its own instruments but used in other, and indeed opposite, ways. Thus (Derrida, 1997, p. 41):

Appendix 2

> "The movements of deconstruction do not destroy structures from the outside. They are not possible and effective, nor can they take accurate aim, except by inhabiting those structures. Inhabiting them *in a certain way*, because one always inhabits, and all the more when one does not suspect it. Operating necessarily from the inside, borrowing all the strategic and economic resources of subversion from the old structure, borrowing them structurally, that is to say without being able to isolate their elements and atoms, the enterprise of deconstruction always in a certain way [also] falls prey to its own work."

The so-called 'velvet revolutions' that occurred in 1989-1991 in Central and Eastern Europe have become the classical examples of deconstruction. It is important to understand here, however, that this approach provides what is in effect *another language* (*ibid*, p. 241; see also Derrida, 1967//1990):

> "But is there a proper place, is there a proper story for this thing [deconstruction]? I think it consists only of transference, and of a thinking through of transference, in all the senses that this word acquires in more than one language, and first of all that of the transference between languages. If I had to risk a single definition of deconstruction, one as brief, elliptical, and economical as a password, I would say simply and without overstatement: *plus d'une langue*—no more of one language."

In the language of postmodernism, *Gerede* is nowadays seen to take a hold upon large numbers of people, so as to form *Grand Narratives*. One of the aims of postmodernism is then to subvert these narratives, such as by deconstructing them.

In its destructive power, *Gerede* has always been closely associated with that which is called in English *nothingness*. This is Kierkegaard's *Intethed*, the *das Nichtige* of Barth and the later Heidegger, and the *le néant* of Sartre and other French existentialists. Nothingness is the abnegation of the self and of selfhood; it is hostile to Being, of the self and of the other, and thus to creation as a whole. For the theologians, nothingness is that which is inimical to God, and thus to His Creation. And then since, in the words of Heidegger, "Language is the house of Being", it is in the first place hostile to and destructive of language.

Among the many traits of nothingness identified and analysed by Barth, a central one is its need to impress with all manner of pseudo-achievements using the most exaggerated and bombastic language. As Kierkegaard expressed this trait, nothingness is always 'going beyond' anything that has come before: it is always proclaiming new 'achievements', it is always seeking for new and ever more exciting 'headlines'. In his usual delightfully ironic manner, Kierkegaard observed how extraordinary were the claimed achievements of his own time in the direction of an enhanced 'spirituality': "After all, Jesus only transformed water into wine, but these geniuses have gone so much further: they have succeeded in transforming wine into water!"

We must refer to the classical exposition of Barth (1938-50//1961, pp. 289-531 of the third part of the third volume of that monumental work) concerning the nature, ambitions and fatal weaknesses of nothingness. That which nothingness fears most and which it does everything that it can to evade is *truth*. And since the foundation of truth in language resides in its definitions, these are among our most powerful weapons against these forces of destruction.

Appendix 2

ACKNOWLEDGEMENTS

The author wishes to thank the many colleagues in the hydroinformatics community who have so much contributed to this work by their encouragement and criticism, even while he takes the sole personal responsibility for the views expressed here.

REFERENCES

Abbott, M.B., 1991, *Hydroinformatics: Information Technology and the Aquatic Environment*, Ashgate, Aldershot, U.K., and Brookfield, USA.

Abbott, M.B., 1992, The theory of the hydrologic model, or: The struggle for the soul of hydrology, in *Advances in Theoretical Hydrology, a Tribute to James Dooge* (ed. O'Kane, J.P.), Elseviers, Amsterdam pp.237-254.

Abbott, M.B., 1996, The sociotechnical dimension of hydroinformatics, in *Hydroinformatics '96* (ed. Müller, A.). Balkema, Rotterdam pp.3-18.

Abbott, M.B., 1999, Forchheimer and Schoklitsch: a postmodern retrospection, in *P. Forchheimer and A. Schoklitsch Memorial Symposium* (ed. W.H. Graf), *Proc. XXVIII IAHR Congress*, Graz, pp.135-154.

Abbott, M.B., 2000, The gender issue in hydroinformatics, or Orpheus in the Underworld, *J. Hydroinformatics*, **2**, 2, pp.87-104.

Abbott, M.B., 2001, The democratisation of decision making processes in the water sector, 1., *J. Hydroinformatics*, **3**, 1, pp.23-34.

Abbott, M.B., Babovic, V.M., and Cunge, J.A., 2001, Towards the hydraulics of the hydroinformatics era, *J. Hyd. Res.*, **39**, 4, pp.339-349.

Abbott, M.B., and Basco, D.R., 1989, *Computational Fluid Dynamics, an Introduction for Engineers*, Longman-Wiley, London and New York.

Abbott, M.B. and Jonoski, A., 2001, The democratisation of decision making processes in the water sector, 2., *J. Hydroinformatics*, **3**, 1, pp.35-48.

Abbott, M.B. and Minns, A.W., 1998, *Computational Hydraulics, second edition*, Ashgate, Aldershot, U.K., and Brookfield, USA.

Abelson, R., 1967, Section on definitions in *The Encyclopædia of Philosophy* (ed. Edwards, P.), Macmillan and Free Press, New York, and Collier Macmillan, London.

Andrews,E.A., Lewis, T.C. and Short, C., 1879, *A Latin Dictionary*, Clarendon, Oxford.

Augustine, 398//e.g. 1961, *Confessions* (transl. Pine-Coffin, R.S.), Penguin, London.

Babovic, V., and Keizer, M., 2000, Genetic programming as a model induction engine, *J Hydroinformatics*, **2**, 2, p35-60.

Barth, K., 1938-1950, *Die Kirkliche Dogmatik*, Evangelische, Zollikon-Zurich//1961, *Church Dogmatics* (transl. Bromiley, G.W., and Torrance, T.F.), Part III, vol. 3, Clark, Edinburgh.

Barr, M. and Wells, C., 1995, *Category Theory for Computing Science*, Prentice Hall, London.

Baudrillard, J., 1973, *Le Miroir de la Production, l'Illusion Critique de la Matérialisme Historique*, Astermans, Paris. //1981, *Mirror of Production* (transl. Poster, M.), Telos, St.Louis, USA.

Bolzano, B., 1837, *Wissenschaftslehre*, Seidel, Sulzbach / *Grundlegung der Logik (Wissenschaftslehre I,II)*, Ed. Kambartel, F., Meiner, Hamburg.

Brentano, F., 1862, *Von der mannigfachen Bedeutung des Seindes nach Aristoteles*, Herder, Freiburg in Breisgau/1960, Olms, Hildesheim.

Brentano, F., 1889-1915/1930, *Wahrheit und Evidenz* (ed. Kraus, O.), Meiner, Leipzig.

Brillouin, L., 1956, *Science and Information Theory*, Academic, New York.

Carnap, R., 1934, *Logische Syntax der Sprache*, Springer, Vienna // 1937, *The Logical Syntax of Language* (transl. Smeaton, A.), Routledge, London.

Carnap, R., 1954, *Einführung in die symbolische Logik mit besonderer Berücksichtigung ihrer Anwendungen*, Springer, Vienna.

Chisholm, R.M., 1966, *Theory of knowledge*, Prentice Hall, Englewood Cliffs.

Chisholm, R.M., 1982, *The Foundations of Knowing*, Harvester, Brighton.

Cloudsley-Thompson, J.I., Biological clocks and their synchronisation, in Fraser *et al*, 1978, pp 189-213.

Derrida, J., 1991, *A Derrida Reader: Between the Blinds* (ed. Kamuf, P.), Harvester, New York.
Derrida, J., 1967, *L'Ecriture et la Différence*, Seuil, Paris//1990, *Writing and Difference* (transl. Bass, A.), Routledge, London.
Dilthey, W., 1976, *W. Dilthey: Selected Writings* (ed., transl. and introd. Rickman, H.P.), Cambridge Univ., Cambridge.
Durning, D., 1999, The transition from traditional to postpositivist policy analysis: a role for Q-methodology, *J. Pol. Anal. and Manag.*, **18**, 3, pp.389-410.
Easterly, W., *The Elusive Quest for Growth: Economists' Adventures and Misadventures in the Tropics*, MIT Press, Cambridge, Mass. See also: >http://www.foreignpolicy.com/issue_novdec_2001/easterly.html<
Eco, U., 1976, *A Theory of Semiotics*, Indiana Univ., Bloomington.
Findlay, J.N., 1961, *Values and Intentions: a Study in Value Theory and Philosophy of Mind*, Macmillan, New York.
Findlay, J.N., 1963, *Meinong's Theory of Objects and Values*, Oxford Univ., Oxford/ 1995, Ashgate, Aldershot, U.K. and Bloomington, USA.
Foucault, M., 1966, *Les Mots et les Choses*, Gallimard, Paris // 1970, *The Order of Things*, Tavistock, London / 1989, Routledge, London.
Fraser, J. T., Laurence, N., and Park, D. (eds), 1978, *The Study of Time, III*, Springer, Heidelberg.
Freyd, P.J. and Scedrov, A., 1990, *Categories, Allegories*, North Holland, Amsterdam.
Hegel, G.W.F., 1807, *System der Wissenschaft, Erster Theil: Phänomenologie des Geistes*, Goebhart, Bamburg and Würzburg/1952, facsimile edition, (ed. Hoffmeister, J.), Olstein, Frankfurt/M.
Heidegger, M., 1927, *Sein und Zeit*, Neimeyer, Tübingen // 1962, *Being and Time* (transl. Macquarrie, J. and Robinson, E.), Blackwell, London.
Heidegger, M., 1939, *Unterwegs zur Sprache*, Neske, Pullingen // 1971, *On the Way to Language*, (transl. anonymous), Harper, New York.
Heidegger, M., 1961/1967, *Der europäische Nihilismus*, Neske, Pfullingen.
Heidegger, M., 1963, *Die Technik,und Die Kehre*, Neske, Pfullingen // included in 1977, *The Question Concerning Technology and Other Essays* (transl. Lovitt, W.), Harper and Row, London.
Hermans, H.J.M., 1996, Voicing the self: from information processing to dialogical interchange, *Psych. Bull.* **199**, 1, pp.31-50.
Hoppe, R., 1999, Policy analysis, science and politics: from 'speaking truth to power' to 'making sense together', *J. Science and Public Policy*, **26**, 3, pp.201-210.
Hume, D., 1739/2000, *A Treatise of Human Nature* (ed. Norton, D.F. and Norton, M.J.), Oxford Univ. Oxford.
Hume, E., 1748/1999, *An Enquiry Concerning Human Understanding* (ed., Beauchamp), Oxford Univ., Oxford.
Huntley, H.E., 1970, *The Divine Proportion; A Study in Mathematical Beauty*, Dover, New York.
Husserl, E., 1900/1901, *Logische Untersuchungen*/1913 Second Edition, Niemeyer, Halle/1970, *Logical Investigations* (transl. Findlay, J.N.), Routledge, London.
Husserl, E., 1938/1948, *Erfahrung und Urteil: Untersuchungen zur Geneologie der Logik*, Claassen and Govaerts, Hamburg // 1973, *Experience and Judgement: Investigations in a Geneology of Logic* (transl. Churchill, J.S. and Ameriks, K.), Routledge, London.
James, H., 1890/1902, *The Principles of Psychology, Vol. 1*, Macmillan, London.
James, H., 1976, *Essays in Radical Empiricism* (collection of articles and correspondence from 1889 to 1909, edited by Bowers, F.), Harvard Univ., Cambridge, Mass., and London.
John Paul II, 1998, *Fides et Ratio*, Libraria Editrice Vaticana // 1998, Veritas, Dublin.
Jonoski, A., 2002, *Hydroinformatics as sociotechnology: Promoting Individual Participation by Using Network Distributed Decision Support Systems*, Balkema, Rotterdam.
Jung, C.G., 1944, *Psychologie und Alchemie*, Rascher, Zurich//1953, *Psychology and Alchemy*, Routledge, London.

Kant, I., 1787/1924/1979, *Kritik der reiner Vernunft*, facsimile reproduction of the 1924 *Kehrbachsche Ausgabe*, Reclam, Leipzig // 1929, *Immanuel Kant's Critique of Pure Reason*, (transl. Kemp Smith, N.), Macmillan, London.

Kierkegaard, S.Aa, 1849, *Sygdommen til Døden*, Reitzel, Copenhagen / 1920-31, *Samlede Værker* (ed. Drachman, A.B., Heiberg, J.L., and Lange, H.O.), Gyldendal, Copenhagen // 1989, The Sickness unto Death (ed. and tranl. Hong, H.V., and Hong, E.H.), Princeton Univ., Princeton, NJ; (see also transl. Hannay, A., Penguin, London).

Kleines, V., 1986, Dilettantism in hydrology; tradition or destiny, *Water Resour. Re.*, **22**, 9, pp.177-188.

Klinkenberg, J.-M., *Précis de Sémiotique Générale*, De Boeck et Larcier / Seuil, Paris.

Kolmogorov, A. N. and Fomin, S.V., 1961, *Elements of the Theory of Functions and Functional Analysis: Measure, Lebesgue Integrals and Hilbert Space*, Academic, New York.

Lakatos, I., 1976, *Proofs and Refutations : The Logic of Mathematical Discovery*/1979, Corrected edition (Eds. Worrall, J., and Zahar, E.), Cambridge Univ., Cambridge.

Law, J. (ed.), 1986, *Power, Action and Belief: A New Sociology of Knowledge*, Routledge, London.

Law, J. (ed.) 1991, *Sociology of Monsters: Essays on Power, Technology and Domination*, Routledge, London.

Lyotard, J.-F., 1979, *La Condition Postmoderne : Rapport sur la Savoir*, Minuit, Paris // 1984, *The Postmodern Condition : a Report on Knowledge*, Manchester Univ., Manchester.

Palmer, J. D., 1978, The living clocks of marine animals, in Frazer *et al*, 1978, pp.216-235.

Purohit Swâmi and Yeats, W.B., 1937, Translation of the *Ten Principal Upanishads*, Faber, London.

Rhees, R., Wittgenstein on language and ritual, in *Wittgenstein and his Times*, (ed McGuiness, B.) Blackwell, Oxford, pp 69-107.

Sartre, J.P., 1943, *L'Être et le Néant : Essai d'Ontologie Phénoménologique*, Gallimard, Paris // *Being and Nothingness, An Essay on Phenomenological Ontology* (transl. Barnes, H.E. and Warnock, M.), Methuen, London.

Shoham, Y., 1997, An overview of agent orientated programming, in *Software Agents* (ed. Bradshaw, J.M.), MIT Press, Boston.

Thorkilsen, M., and Dynesen, C., 2001, An owners view of hydroinformatics: its role in realising the bridge and tunnel connection between Denmark and Sweden, *J. Hydroinformatics*, **3**, 2, pp.105-135.

Troisfontaines, R., 1968, *De l'Existence à l'Être: la Philosophie de Gabriel Marcel*, Nauwelaerts, Louvain and Paris.

Weingart, P., 1999, Scientific expertise and political accountability : paradoxes of science in politics *J. Science and Public Policy*, **26**, 3. pp.151-161.

White, G.L., 1994, Policy Analysis as discourse, *J. Policy Anal. and Manag.*, **13**, 3, pp.506-525.

Whitehead, A.N., and Russell, B., *Principia Mathematica*, 1910/1925, Second edition, Cambridge Univ., Cambridge.

.Wittgenstein, L., 1958, *Preliminary Studies for the Philosophical Investigations: The Blue and Brown Books*, Oxford Univ, Oxford.